iPad
For Seniors

9th Edition

by Jesse Feiler

for
dummies®
A Wiley Brand

iPad® For Seniors For Dummies®, 9th Edition

Published by **John Wiley & Sons, Inc.,** 111 River Street, Hoboken, NJ 07030-5774, www.wiley.com

Copyright © 2017 by John Wiley & Sons, Inc., Hoboken, New Jersey

Media and software compilation copyright © 2017 by John Wiley & Sons, Inc. All rights reserved.

Published simultaneously in Canada

For general information on our other products and services, please contact our Customer Care Department within the U.S. at 877-762-2974, outside the U.S. at 317-572-3993, or fax 317-572-4002. For technical support, please visit https://hub.wiley.com/community/support/dummies.

Wiley publishes in a variety of print and electronic formats and by print-on-demand. Some material included with standard print versions of this book may not be included in e-books or in print-on-demand. If this book refers to media such as a CD or DVD that is not included in the version you purchased, you may download this material at http://booksupport.wiley.com. For more information about Wiley products, visit www.wiley.com.

Library of Congress Control Number: 2016959687

ISBN: 978-1-119-28015-6

ISBN (ePDF): 978-1-119-28017-0; ISBN (ePub): 978-1-119-28016-3

Manufactured in the United States of America

10 9 8 7 6 5 4 3 2 1

Contents at a Glance

Introduction 1

Part 1: You, Your iPad, and the World. 5
CHAPTER 1: Exploring Your iPad 7
CHAPTER 2: Using Your iPad 27
CHAPTER 3: Apple IDs, iCloud, and Security 69
CHAPTER 4: Making Your iPad More Accessible. 81

Part 2: Reaching Out with Your iPad. 103
CHAPTER 5: Talking to Siri. 105
CHAPTER 6: Browsing the Internet with Safari .115
CHAPTER 7: Keeping in Touch with Email .143
CHAPTER 8: Getting Social with Your iPad .163

Part 3: Treating Yourself to Apps and Media 187
CHAPTER 9: Shopping the iTunes Store 189
CHAPTER 10: Working with Apps. 201
CHAPTER 11: Apps for You and Your Home 215

Part 4: Having Fun and Consuming Media. 237
CHAPTER 12: Using Your iPad as an E-Reader. 239
CHAPTER 13: Playing Music on the iPad. 259
CHAPTER 14: Playing with Photos 273
CHAPTER 15: Getting the Most Out of Video Features 303
CHAPTER 16: Playing Games 313
CHAPTER 17: Finding Your Way with Maps .321

Part 5: Managing Your Life and Your iPad. 333
CHAPTER 18: Keeping On Schedule with Calendar and Clock 335
CHAPTER 19: Working with Reminders and Notifications. 359
CHAPTER 20: Managing Contacts 373

CHAPTER 21: Making Notes 387
CHAPTER 22: Getting the News You Need 403

Index 411

Table of Contents

INTRODUCTION 1

    About This Book.. 1

    Foolish Assumptions 1

    Icons Used in This Book 2

    Beyond the Book 3

    Where to Go from Here.................................. 3

PART 1: YOU, YOUR IPAD, AND THE WORLD 5

CHAPTER 1: **Exploring Your iPad**................................... 7

    Discover What's New in iOS 10 and the New iPads............ 8

    Discover iPad Basics 10

    Choose the Right iPad for You 13

    Decide How Much Memory Is Enough 14

    What Else You May Need: Internet and Computer 16

        Use basic Internet access for your iPad 17

        Pair your iPad with a computer 17

    Choose Wi-Fi Only or Wi-Fi + Cellular 18

    Consider iPad Accessories 21

    Explore What's in the Box 22

    Take a First Look at the Gadget 24

CHAPTER 2: **Using Your iPad** 27

    See What You Need to Use the iPad 27

    Turn On the iPad for the First Time....................... 29

    Charge the Battery....................................... 30

    Visit the Screens... 32

        Start from the lock screen............................. 32

        Tour the home screen 33

        Visit Today view...................................... 34

        Check Notification Center 35

    Navigate the Multi-Touch Screen......................... 36

        Experiment with the touchscreen 37

        Try out tapping and swiping 38

Display and Use the Onscreen Keyboard 41
Use the Split Keyboard 45
Flick to Search 47
Update the Operating System 48
Be a Multitasker 49
    Try out multitasking 49
    Explore multitasking gestures 49
Use Slide Over and Split View 52
    Starting with Slide Over 52
    Moving to Split View 55
Discover Control Center 56
Understand Touch ID 59
Lock the iPad, Turn It Off, and Unlock It 60
Explore the Status Bar 60
Take Inventory of Preinstalled Apps 61
    Dock apps 62
    Home-screen apps 62
Examine the iPad Cameras 66

CHAPTER 3: **Apple IDs, iCloud, and Security** 69
Manage Apple ID Accounts 70
    Create an Apple ID 70
    Choose an existing Apple ID for a service 72
Sync to iTunes Wirelessly 73
Use iCloud 75
    Turn on iCloud backup 76
    Make iCloud sync settings 77
    Find a lost or stolen iPad 78

CHAPTER 4: **Making Your iPad More Accessible** 81
Use Magnifier 82
Set Brightness and Night Shift 84
Change the Wallpaper 85
Set Up VoiceOver 87
Use VoiceOver 89
Make Additional Vision Settings 91
Adjust the Volume 93
Set Up Subtitles and Captioning 94
Manage Mono Audio 95

Work with AssistiveTouch 96

Manage Home-Button Speed 98

Focus Learning with Guided Access 99

PART 2: REACHING OUT WITH YOUR IPAD 103

CHAPTER 5: **Talking to Siri** 105

Turn on Siri on Your iPad 105

Work with Siri 109

Ask Siri questions 109

Issue commands 110

Are we there yet? A Siri case study 111

Use Siri with Third-Party Apps 112

Improve Your Communication with Siri 113

CHAPTER 6: **Browsing the Internet with Safari** 115

Connect to the Internet 116

Connect via Cellular 116

Connect via Wi-Fi 117

Explore Safari 118

Navigate Web Pages 120

Use Tabbed Browsing 122

View Browsing History 123

Search the Web 124

Share Items from the Web 125

Add and Use Bookmarks 128

Add a bookmark 128

Visit a bookmarked site 129

Organize bookmarks 130

Save Links and Web Pages to the Safari Reading List 130

Add an item to the Reading List 130

View your Reading List 131

Enjoy Reading with Safari Reader 132

Add Web Clips to the Home Screen 133

Send a Link 134

Print a Web Page 135

Save an Image to Your Photo Library 137

Post Photos from Safari 138

Make Private Browsing and Cookie Settings 139

CHAPTER 7: **Keeping in Touch with Email**. 143

Add an Email Account 144
Set Up a POP3 or IMAP Email Account ("Other"). 147
Open Mail and Read Messages 148
Reply to, Print, or Forward Email 151
Create and Send a New Message 153
Format Email. 154
Search Email 156
Mark Email as Unread or Flag for Follow-Up 157
Create an Event from Email Contents. 159
Delete Email 160
Organize Email 161

CHAPTER 8: **Getting Social with Your iPad** 163

Use Social Media from Your iPad. 164
  Set up your account and password 164
  Use the Share button. 168
Use Messages. 169
  Set up a Messages account. 170
  Send a message 171
  Read messages 173
  Conduct a Messages conversation. 174
  Clear a conversation. 178
  Send an audio message. 179
  Send a photo or video message 180
Use FaceTime 183
  Activate FaceTime. 183
  Make a FaceTime call 183
  Accept and end a FaceTime call 184
  Switch views. 185

PART 3: TREATING YOURSELF TO APPS AND MEDIA. 187

CHAPTER 9: **Shopping the iTunes Store**. 189

Explore the iTunes Store. 189
Find an Item 193
Preview an Item 195
Buy or Get an Item. 196
Rent a Movie 196
Set Up Family Sharing 197

CHAPTER 10: **Working with Apps** 201

Understand App Store Apps 201
Search the App Store 202
Buy or Get Apps from the App Store 204
Organize Apps 207
　　Organize apps on your iPad's home screens 208
　　Organize apps in iTunes for your iPad's home screens 209
　　Organize apps in folders 209
Delete Apps 211
Update Apps 212

CHAPTER 11: **Apps for You and Your Home** 215

Get to Know HomeKit 216
Set Up accessories 217
　　Add an accessory 218
　　Adjust an accessory 223
Work with scenes 225
　　Add a scene 226
　　Combine accessories into scenes 228
　　Adjust a scene 229
Set up a room 231
Use Automations 232

PART 4: HAVING FUN AND CONSUMING MEDIA 237

CHAPTER 12: **Using Your iPad as an E-Reader** 239

What Is an E-Book? 240
Find Books with iBooks 241
Explore Other E-Readers 243
Buy Books 243
　　Get books from the iBooks Store 243
　　Get books from other sources 245
Navigate an E-Book 246
Adjust Brightness 249
Change the Display Settings 250
Search in Your Book 252
Add Bookmarks, Highlights, and Notes 253

View a Bookmark or Note. 255
Check Words in the Dictionary. 257
Adding a PDF. 257

CHAPTER 13: **Playing Music on the iPad** 259
View the Library Contents. 259
Create a Playlist 261
Edit a Playlist. 264
Search Your Music Library 265
Play an Individual Song 266
Play a Playlist 268
Shuffle Music 269
Adjust the Volume 270
Use AirPlay 270

CHAPTER 14: **Playing with Photos** 273
Understand the iPad's Cameras. 274
Review the Camera Controls 274
Take Pictures with the iPad. 277
Import Photos. 281
Import from a digital camera 281
Import from an SD card. 282
Save Photos from the Web. 282
View an Album 283
View Individual Photos 284
Edit Photos 285
Create a New Album 290
Organize Photos in an Existing Album 291
View Photos by Year and Location. 292
Search for Photos. 293
Share Photos with Mail, Twitter, and Facebook. 294
Share Photos with AirDrop. 295
Share Photos with iCloud Photo Sharing 296
Print Photos 298
Run a Slideshow 299
Delete Photos 300

CHAPTER 15: **Getting the Most Out of Video Features** 303
    Capture Your Own Videos with the Built-in Cameras 304
    Play Movies or TV Shows 306
    Turn on Closed Captioning 309
    Go to a Movie Chapter or Episode 310
    Share a Video 310

CHAPTER 16: **Playing Games** 313
    Choose Games for Your iPad 315
    Explore Games in the App Store 316
    Find and Purchase Games 318

CHAPTER 17: **Finding Your Way with Maps** 321
    View Your Current Location 322
    Set Your Map Options and Preferences 323
    Change Views 324
    Zoom In and Out 326
    Find a Location 326
    Get Directions 328
    Share Location Information 331

PART 5: MANAGING YOUR LIFE AND YOUR IPAD 333

CHAPTER 18: **Keeping On Schedule with Calendar and Clock** 335
    View Calendars 336
    Navigate Calendars 339
    Add Calendar Events 340
    Add Events with Siri 342
    Create a Repeating Event 343
    View an Event 344
    Add an Alert 344
    Search for an Event 346
    Subscribe to Calendars 347
      Working with Apple accounts 347
      Working with other acccounts 349
    Create a Family Calendar 350
    Delete an Event 351
    Display Clock 353

Add or Delete a Clock 354

Set an Alarm 355

Use Stopwatch and Timer. 356

CHAPTER 19: **Working with Reminders and Notifications**. 359

Create a Task in Reminders 360

Edit Task Details 361

Schedule a Reminder. 362

Create a List 363

Sync with Other Devices and Calendars. 364

Mark as Complete or Delete a Reminder 366

Set Notifications. 367

View Notification Center 369

Check Out Notification Pages. 370

Go to an App from Notification Center. 370

Get Some Rest with Do Not Disturb 370

CHAPTER 20: **Managing Contacts**. 373

Add a Contact 374

Assign a Photo to a Contact 376

Set Ringtones for Contacts 378

Sync Contacts with iCloud. 380

Search for a Contact 382

Address Email with Contacts 382

Share a Contact 383

View a Contact's Location in Maps. 384

Delete a Contact. 384

CHAPTER 21: **Making Notes** 387

Open a Note 388

Create a Note 389

Create a Note from a Document 390

Copy and Paste Text from a Note 391

Insert a Photo or Video into a Note. 392

Add a Drawing or Sketch. 394

Apply a Text Style to a Note 395

Create a Checklist in Notes. 396

Search for a Note 397

Share a Note 398

Add People 398

Adjust Notes Settings. 399

Delete a Note 400

Moving a Note 401

CHAPTER 22: **Getting the News You Need** 403

Explore News 403

Read Your News. 405

Select Favorites. 406

Set Notifications 407

Explore Channels and Topics 408

Search for News 409

INDEX 411

Introduction

To me, the most amazing aspect of iPad is the date April 10, 2010, the date it first shipped. In less than a decade, we've learned how to use a new device for new activities. I've watched the evolution of iPad from the point of view of a user as well as a developer. I can remember when we were trying to figure out as users and developers what this device was and how to use it. I think we're in pretty good shape now, but there certainly are more adventures coming down the road.

This book helps you get going with the iPad quickly and painlessly so that you can move directly to the fun part.

About This Book

This book is written specifically for mature people like you, folks who may be relatively new to using a tablet device and want to discover the basics of buying an iPad, working with its preinstalled apps, and getting on the Internet. In writing this book, I've tried to consider the types of activities that might interest someone who is 50 years old or older and picking up an iPad for the first time.

There's something else we have to talk about: You're probably not starting from scratch. Most likely, you've used one or more computers over the years. There's a bit of un-learning involved in using the latest technologies. To the extent that you can avoid bringing your past technological experiences with you, you may get more out of your iPad.

Foolish Assumptions

This book is organized by sets of tasks. These tasks start from the beginning, assuming that you've never laid your hands on an iPad, and guide you through basic steps in nontechnical language.

This book was written about the iPad Pro (with a 12.9-inch display), iPad Air 2 (the 9.7-inch model), the iPad mini 2 and 4 (the 7.9-inch model), and the iPad Air 2 (with a 9.7-inch screen). Most material is relevant whether you have an iPad second-generation or later, though I strongly recommend that you update to the latest operating system, iOS 10, which is quick and easy to do (see Chapter 2). iOS 10 is the operating system I based this book on.

This book covers both the Wi-Fi and the iPad Wi-Fi + Cellular features. Examples that involve iTunes are based on version 12.2 of that software. (Specific cellular features depend on the cellular carrier you use but at the moment 3G and 4G LTE are the most common in the U.S.)

Icons Used in This Book

There are four icons used in this book to alert you to special content:

TIP

This icon points out shortcuts and best practices to help you get the most from using your iPad.

TECHNICAL STUFF

Technical Stuff icons indicate paragraphs that cover interesting technical stuff. Feel free to skip this information if you're in a hurry.

REMEMBER

This icon marks a generally interesting and useful fact — something you may want to remember for later use.

WARNING

If you see a Warning icon, pay attention and proceed with caution.

Beyond the Book

Like every *For Dummies* book, this one comes with a free Cheat Sheet that brings together some of the most commonly needed information for people learning to use, in this case, iPad. To get the Cheat Sheet, head for www.dummies.com and enter **iPad For Seniors For Dummies 9th Edition Cheat Sheet** in the Search box.

Where to Go from Here

Dive in and get started! You can work through this book from beginning to end, or simply open a chapter to solve a problem or acquire a specific new skill whenever you need it. The steps in every task quickly get you to where you want to go, without a lot of technical explanation.

Note: At the time I wrote this book, all the information it contained was accurate. Apple may introduce new iPad models and new versions of the iOS and iTunes between book editions. If you've bought a new iPad and its hardware, user interface, or version of iTunes looks a little different, be sure to check out what Apple has to say at www.apple.com/ipad. You'll no doubt find updates on the company's latest releases. Also, if you don't set up iCloud to automatically update your iPad, perform updates to the operating system on a regular basis, as described in Chapter 2.

When a change is very substantial, I may add an update or bonus information that you can download at my website for this book, http:// northcountryconsulting.com or at my app website http:// champlainarts.com.

1

You, Your iPad, and the World

IN THIS PART. . .

Get started with your iPad.

Make your iPad useful.

Share thoughts and info with others.

Make your iPad easier to use.

Chapter **1**

Exploring Your iPad

Hundreds of millions of iPads have been sold, and whether your iPad is a new purchase of your own, a gift, or a device owned by your employer or a volunteer organization you work for, this book will help you get the most out of it.

Your current iPad may be your first iPad, or it may be your second or third. I develop apps and write books about developing apps, so I'm certainly not a typical iPad user, but I have three on my desk (it's a big desk), as well as an original iPad 1 that still works and that I keep around to show people how long-lasting the devices can be.

With the extraordinary integration of devices that Apple has developed using its tools such as AirPlay, AirDrop, and continuity, my data and I move seamlessly among the iPads, my primary iPhone, the iPod touch I use for testing, my Apple TV, and CarPlay in my car. I don't spend too much time searching for the piece of paper where I wrote down something important because I know where the something important is: It's in my iCloud account, and I can get to it from any device.

Whether you're a first-time iPad user, a longtime expert, or anyone else in the vast iPad universe, this book has something for you. You even get some tips on unlearning things you already know that are no longer needed with the latest and greatest iPad.

Discover What's New in iOS 10 and the New iPads

» **Size:** The iPad is available in various sizes, depending on the version of iPad. Here are the three basic sizes, by iPad type:

- *iPad:* The first iPad (the 2010 model) featured a touchscreen that measures 9.7 inches diagonally as do the iPad 2, iPad 3, iPad 4, iPad Air, and iPad Air 2. The iPad itself is slightly larger to accommodate the edges (*bezels,* to be specific). (The formal names of iPad 3 and iPad 4 are iPad 3rd Generation and iPad 4th Generation.) As of this writing iPad 4, iPad Air, and iPad Air 2 are on sale.

- *iPad mini:* Along with the iPad 4 in October 2012, a smaller version, the iPad mini, made its debut with a screen measuring 7.9 inches diagonally. Versions iPad mini 2 and iPad mini 4 are currently on sale. They differ in memory size and processor type.

- *iPad Pro:* In November 2015, the larger iPad Pro appeared, with a screen measuring 12.9 inches diagonally. A 9.7-inch version of the iPad Pro appeared in March 2016.

TECHNICAL STUFF

Dimensions of devices are typically shown in the units of measurement commonly used in a region. This means, for example, that the basic iPad is shown on Apple's U.S. site as being 9.4 inches (240mm) high and 6.6 inches (169.5mm) wide. In metric-system countries, both dimensions are given, but the order is reversed. When it comes to screen sizes, however, the dimensions are given in inches.

» **Screen resolution:** In addition to screen size, screen resolution has evolved so that Apple's *Retina display,* which supports very-high-resolution graphics, now appears across the line. (The name derives from the concept that individual pixels on the screen are so small that at normal viewing distance, they can't be distinguished.) The Retina display has many more pixels to use in display images. Thus, the iPad versions starting with iPad 3 display 2048x1536 pixels in 9.7 inches, but earlier versions displayed only 1024x768 pixels in the same space. That translates to 264 (pixels per inch — ppi) in Retina display versions and 132 ppi in earlier version. The more pixels in the same space the sharper the image. It may also be easier to read. The iPad mini adopted Retina displays with iPad mini 2.

» **Apple Pencil:** With the release of iPad Pro, Apple introduced Apple Pencil, which lets you draw and write on the iPad screen with a familiar pencil-style tool rather than with your finger. The Apple Pencil contains a batter and sophisticated processing powers that make the experience of using it very much like (and sometimes better than) traditional pencils. Third-party pencils and drawing tools exist, but Apple's integration of Apple Pencil is remarkably smooth; the product has taken off quickly among graphic artists, illustrators, and designers. As other people have discovered its usability for marking up documents, it is becoming more and more common in business environments.

For what it's worth, I consider myself "other people" in this context. I couldn't live without my Apple Pencils. It's easy to pair one with an iPad Pro — you just connect it and it draws power for its battery very quickly. That pencil becomes paired with that iPad Pro until you connect it to another one. I use mine with the iPad Pro (the 9.7-inch model) that's on my desk at all times. I scribble things down as I need to. I use the other Apple Pencil with my 12.9-inch iPad Pro for when I'm in meetings. For up to six people, the larger iPad Pro and Apple Pencil are preferable to a whiteboard (at least for me).

From a practical point of view, Apple now has two main iPad lines: models that support Apple Pencil (at the time of this writing, iPad Pro 9.7 and 12.9-inch models) and models that don't (iPad Air 2 and iPad mini 4). When you combine Apple Pencil with an iPad, you get a remarkably powerful combination for many purposes.

Discover iPad Basics

Apple's iPad is a combination of hardware and a software operating system (called *iOS*). The current operating system is iOS 10, though small updates appear all the time, so by the time you're reading this book, you might have 10.2, 10.3, or 10.4.

In addition to the features of previous iPads, the latest iPad models offer

» **Updated body:** Apple has made the iPad Air 2 and the iPad mini 4 a bit thinner than earlier models and made improvements to screen and camera features. The iPad mini 4 has a fully laminated display with antireflective coating, just like the iPad Air 2 and iPad Pro. The iPad Air 2 weighs 0.96 pound; the iPad mini 4 weighs 0.65 pound; and the big brother of them all, iPad Pro, weighs 1.57 pounds, which is impressive given the dimensions of the display.

» **New processor chip:** The 64-bit A8X processor in the iPad Air 2 is faster than the A8 chip in the previous-generation iPad Air. The iPad mini 4 has advanced to an A8 processor. iPad Pro sports the best processor of the bunch, an A9X, which makes it the fastest performer of the trio.

» **Wi-Fi:** Two-antennae, dual-channel Wi-Fi and the use of MIMO (multiple input, multiple output) technology allows for much faster wireless connections. The iPad Air 2 supports the latest Wi-Fi standard, 802.11ac as well as a, b, g, and n; the iPad mini 4 supports 802.a/b/g/n/ac.

» **Faster motion coprocessor:** This coprocessor processes game features such as the gyroscope and accelerometer. The iPad Air 2 and iPad mini 4 have an M8 motion coprocessor. The iPad Pro offers a slightly faster M9 motion coprocessor.

» **New photo and video recording features:** Video recording features added to the iPad mini 4 include the addition of Slo-mo mode for video recording and Burst mode for taking and optimizing a series of pictures. There is more on photos in Chapter 14, and more on video in Chapter 15.

» **Touch ID:** This security feature is now included on all new iPad models. Sensors in the Home button allow you to train the iPad to recognize your fingerprint and grant you access with a finger press. Touch ID also allows you to use the Apple Pay feature to buy items without having to enter your payment information every time.

» **Barometric sensor:** Now on all three iPad models, this sensor makes it possible for your iPad to sense air pressure around you. This feature is especially cool when you're hiking a mountain, where the weather may change as you climb. Perhaps more to the point, the changes in barometric pressure can be sensed on a smaller scale so that elevation can be sensed and measured as you move normally.

» **Apple Pencil:** With iPad Pro, some exciting new hardware features include the ability to use the optional Apple Pencil stylus to interact with the screen.

» **3D Touch:** This feature allows for three levels of pressure on the screen. They can be used for different input meanings. For example, the lightest tap on an object selects it; medium pressure displays a preview (called Peek by Apple); the heaviest pressure opens the item (called Pop).

» **More keyboard options:** The iPad Pro has a full-size onscreen keyboard. Because there's more space on the screen, the top of the keyboard can contain extra commands for use in filling in passwords and more advanced input techniques. There's more on this in Chapter 2.

» **Smart Connector** for Smart Keyboard: Additionally, you can use a Smart Connector to hook up a Smart keyboard, which makes it much easier to get complex work done.

» **Live photos:** Using the 3D Touch feature, you can press a photo on the screen to make it play like a short video. The Camera app captures 1.5 seconds on either side of the moment when you capture the photo, so anything moving in the image you photographed, such as water flowing in a stream, seems to move when you press the still photo. See Chapter 14 for more on photos.

» **News app:** This app is an intelligent news aggregator, which means that it gathers news stories from various sources. It's intelligent because it "learns" to present content similar to other content you've viewed. See Chapter 22 for more about how News works.

» **Notes:** The Notes app gets a facelift with iOS 10, allowing you to use Apple Pencil (and even your finger) for sketching notes as well as using the text, photos, maps, and URLs that have already been present in Notes. Additionally, you can create instant checklists and even sketch in your notes. You can also share items to Notes using the Share feature in apps such as Photos. See Chapter 21 for more about Notes.

» **Improved Maps app:** With iOS 10, Maps gets a new look and major new features. You can now use it to find where you've parked your car, and there are significant new features added to show you what businesses and saved locations of your own are near your current location. These features add on to improvements in iOS 9, including a Transit view for finding information about public transit in select cities around the world. If you go to Settings and look at Maps in the left column, you'll see that you can enable extensions for Lyft, OpenTable, and Uber. This means that Maps may contain buttons to let you reserve a table or a ride (if you have the appropriate account). The extension architecture is widely promoted by Apple to developers so you'll probably start to see more services enabled directly from Maps. However, as is the case with Maps, the extensions that make this possible can be turned on and off from Settings for the app in question (Maps in this case).

» **Siri extensions for more functionality:** Siri, the iPhone's personal-assistant feature, can now interact with more apps such as Pinterest, WeChat, and Skype. This uses the extensions architecture that Maps also uses, and the Apple is promoting to developers. Expect to see Siri's ability to control apps broadened in the future as developers add their functionality.

Choose the Right iPad for You

The most obvious differences among iPad models are their thickness and weight, with the Pro being biggest, then iPad Air 2, and finally the smallest, iPad mini 4 (see **Figure 1-1**). All three models come in three colors: space gray, silver, or gold.

FIGURE 1-1

All three models come in Wi-Fi only for accessing a Wi-Fi network, or 3G/4G for connecting to the Internet through a cellular network as your cell phone does. The iPad models also differ slightly in available memory and price based on that memory:

» **iPad Pro:** $799 for 32 GB and $949 for 128 GB.

» **iPad Air 2:** $499 for 16 GB; $599 for 64 GB; $699 for 128 GB.

» **iPad mini 4:** $399 for 16 GB; $499 for 64 GB; $599 for 128 GB. Comparable Wi-Fi plus Cellular models cost about $130 more for each model.

Finally, there are variations in screen quality and resolution, camera quality, and so on. Logically, the bigger the iPad, the bigger the price and higher the quality.

Read on as I explain some of these variations in more detail.

Decide How Much Memory Is Enough

Storage capacity is a measure of how much information — such as movies, photos, and software applications (*apps*) — you can store on a computing device. Capacity can also affect your iPad's performance in handling tasks such as streaming favorite TV shows from the World Wide Web or downloading music.

REMEMBER

Streaming refers to watching video content stored on the web (or on other devices) rather than playing a file stored on your iPad. You can enjoy a lot of material online without ever downloading its full content to your iPad's memory — and given that every iPad model has a relatively small amount of capacity, that's not a bad idea. See Chapters 13 and 15 for more about getting your music and movies online.

Your storage capacity options are 32GB, 64GB, 128GB, and 256GB, depending on the model. You must choose the right amount for your needs, because you can't open the unit and add storage. Additionally, you can't insert a *flash drive* (also known as a *USB stick*) to add backup capacity because the iPad has no USB port — or CD/DVD drive, for that matter. But Apple has thoughtfully provided iCloud, a service you can use to save space by backing up content to the Internet. (You can read more about iCloud in Chapter 3.)

The biggest users of memory are movies, followed by photos and music. The bigger or longer the movies, photos, and songs are, the more memory you need. You can always back them up to iCloud to relieve the pressure on your iPad (as described in Chapter 3).

HOW BIG IS A GIGABYTE?

Do you know how big a gigabyte (GB) is? Technically, it's a billion bytes where a byte is the standard unit for digital information. A byte is typically 8 bits long where each bit is an on/off, yes/no, or 0/1 value (those terms are interchangeable in this context). So now do you know what a gigabyte is? Let's try another route.

A gigabyte can contain 60 minutes of standard TV video running a 2.2 megabits per second (2.2 Mbit/s). A gigabyte can also contain 7 minutes of high definition TV (HDTV) running at 19.39 Mbit/s. The difference between HDTV and SDTV has to do with the size of the image, but the storage also depends on the speed with which it runs: A faster speed makes for a smoother playback, and a larger image size makes for clearer images. Both the speed and the image size together determine how good the video looks.

When downloading or playing video on any computer, if you have a choice of HDTV or SDTV, pick the version that gives you the best results. In the best case, choose HDTV, but because the files are going to be larger than SDTV, if you're running out of storage space you might want to opt for SDTV.

If you are downloading video to view later (as opposed to viewing it now) you might want to do the download at an off-peak time and watch it in the best quality once it's downloaded.

Don't forget that downloading large files also costs you more if you're not using a Wi-Fi connection. So the choice is yours based on how much storage space you have, how long you have to download the file, and how much — if anything — you have to pay for the download itself.

Consider this: Just about any computer you buy today comes with a minimum of 250GB to 500GB of storage. Computers have to tackle larger tasks than iPads do, so that amount makes sense. The iPad, which uses a technology called flash for memory storage, is designed (to a great extent) to help you experience online media and email; it doesn't have to store much and in fact pulls lots of content from online sources. In the world of memory, 16GB is puny storage if you want to keep lots of content on the device.

CALCULATING CAPACITY

So how much capacity is enough for your iPad? Here are a few tips:

- If you like lots of media, such as movies or TV shows, and you want to store them on your iPad (rather than access them online on sites such as Hulu or Netflix), you need a lot of built-in memory. If you're just checking email and browsing the web, you generally need less memory; the minimum configuration is probably okay for you.

- Ask friends who are using an iPad how much memory they have and how much they think they need. Choose friends who do the same sorts of things you do. (To find memory usage, go to Settings and tap About. You'll see the numbers for capacity and available usage. Don't think that you can use all the available memory. Once you start using all your memory, performance can be degraded. There are no hard-and-fast guides to the amount of available memory you should have but just be aware that some of your memory is needed for the iPad itself.

- If you have an iPhone, use it as a guide. Look at how much memory you're using on your phone, and think about what you'll do on your iPad.

What can really, really, really push you into needing much more memory is using your iPad to create and edit content. If you're using iMovie to create your own movies from raw footage you shoot or collect, you're going need to be able to keep several clips as well as your being-built movie in memory at the same time. (iMovie from Apple is free from the App Store but you can also do a lot of video work with Photos, as described in Chapters 14 and 15.)

If you're creating complex drawings (large or detailed), you'll probably need more memory. If you're writing or editing text — even text with a few illustrations — you'll probably need less memory.

What Else You May Need: Internet and Computer

Although you can use your iPad on its own without any Internet or Wi-Fi access and without a computer to pair it with, it's easier if you have Internet access and a computer that you can (occasionally) use with your iPad.

Use basic Internet access for your iPad

You need to be able to connect to the Internet to take advantage of most iPad features. If you have an Apple ID, you can have an iCloud account, Apple's online storage service, to store and share content online, and you can use a computer to download photos, music, or applications from non-Apple online sources (such as stores, sharing sites, or your local library) and transfer them to your iPad through a process called *syncing.* You can also use a computer or iCloud to register your iPad the first time you start it, although you can have the folks at the Apple Store handle registration for you if you have an Apple Store nearby. If you don't have a store nearby, the Chat feature on apple.com can connect you to a representative; you can also use apple.com to request a phone consultation. These are free (but for Chat you'll need an Internet connection).

There are ways to set up your iPad without an Internet connection and without going to an Apple Store: The best way to find out more information is to contact support.apple.com through an Internet connection on another device or at a public library or Internet cafe.

Can you use your iPad without owning a computer and just use public Wi-Fi hotspots to go online (or a 3G/4G LTE connection, if you have such a model)? Yes. To go online using a Wi-Fi–only iPad and to use many of its built-in features at home, however, you need to have a home Wi-Fi network available. You also need to use iCloud or sync to your computer to get updates for the iPad operating system.

Pair your iPad with a computer

For syncing with a computer, Apple's *iPad User Guide* recommends that you have

>> A Mac or PC with a USB 2.0 port and one of the following operating systems:

- Mac OS X version 10.6.8 or later
- Windows 10, 8, 7, Windows Vista, or Windows XP Home or Professional with Service Pack 3 or later

>> iTunes 11 or later, available at www.itunes.com/download

>> An Apple ID and iTunes Store account

>> Internet access

>> An iCloud account

Apple has set up its iTunes software and the iCloud service to give you two ways to manage content for your iPad — including movies, music, or photos you've downloaded — and specify how to sync your calendar and contact information. There are a lot of tech terms to absorb here (iCloud, iTunes, syncing, and so on). Don't worry: Chapter 3 covers those settings in more detail.

Choose Wi-Fi Only or Wi-Fi + Cellular

You use *Wi-Fi* to connect to a wireless network at home or at locations such as an Internet cafe, a library, a grocery store, or a bus, train, plane, or airport that offers Wi-Fi. This type of network uses short-range radio to connect to the Internet; its range is reasonably limited, so if you leave home or walk out of the coffee shop, you can't use it anymore. (These limitations may change, however, as some towns are installing community-wide Wi-Fi networks.)

The *3G* and *4G-LTE* cellular technologies allow an iPad to connect to the Internet via a widespread cellular-phone network. You use it in much the same way that you make calls from just about anywhere with your cellphone. 4G-LTE may not always be available in every location. You can still connect to the Internet via 3G when 4G-LTE service isn't available, but without the advantage of the super-fast 4G technology.

A Wi-Fi + Cellular iPad costs an additional $130 when compared to the basic Wi-Fi only model, but it also includes GPS (Global Positioning System) service, which pinpoints your location so that you can get more accurate driving directions.

Also, to use your 3G/4G network in the United States, you must pay a monthly fee. The good news is that no carrier requires a long-term contract, which you probably had to have when you bought your cellphone and its service plan. You can pay for a connection during the month you visit your grandkids, for example, and get rid of it when you arrive home. Features, data allowance (which relates to accessing email or downloading items from the Internet, for example), and prices vary by carrier and could change at any time, so visit each carrier's website (see the following tip) to see what it offers. Note that if you intend to *stream* videos (watch them on your iPad from the Internet), you can eat through your data plan allowance quickly.

TIP

Go to these links for more information about iPad data plans: AT&T at `www.att.com/shop/wireless/devices/ipad.jsp`, Verizon at `https://www.verizonwireless.com/landingpages/ipad`, T-Mobile at `www.t-mobile.com`, and Sprint at `https://sprint.com`.

How do you choose? If you want to wander around the woods or town — or take long drives with your iPad continually connected to the Internet to get step-by-step navigation info from the Maps app — get Wi-Fi + Cellular and pay the price. If you'll use your iPad mainly at home or via a Wi-Fi *hotspot* (a location where Wi-Fi access to the Internet is available, such as an Internet cafe), don't bother with 3G/4G-LTE. Frankly, you can find *lots* of hotspots at libraries, restaurants, hotels, airports, and more.

If you have a Wi-Fi–only iPad, you can use the hotspot feature on a smartphone, which allows the iPad to use your phone's 3G or 4G connection to go online if you have a data-use plan that supports hotspot use with your phone service carrier. Check out the features of your phone to turn on the hotspot feature.

TIP

If you have CarPlay, chances are you have a mobile hotspot: It's called your car. Not all car dealers talk about technology in the same way that other people do: You may have to do a bit of poking around to find out what technology is behind "Super Duper Feature" in your car's advertising and documentation, but chances are you've got a mobile hotspot that you can use with your iPad. If you get a new car with a 2- or 3-month trial period for the built-in car Wi-Fi, use that time to monitor your usage per the instructions from your car dealer. See how much data you're using and, more important, keep track of what you've been doing.

TIP

Because 3G and 4G-LTE iPads are also GPS devices, they know where you are and can act as a navigation system to get you from here to there. The Wi-Fi–only model uses a digital compass and triangulation method for locating your current position, which is less accurate; with no constant Internet connection, it won't help you get around town. If getting accurate directions is one iPad feature that excites you, get 3G/4G-LTE and then see Chapter 17 for more about the Maps feature.

KNOW WHERE TO BUY YOUR IPAD

At this writing, you can buy an iPad at an Apple Store; at brick-and-mortar stores such as Best Buy, Walmart, Sam's Club, and Target; and at online sites such as MacMall.com. You can also buy 3G/4G-LTE models (models that require an account with a phone service provider) from Sprint, AT&T, T-Mobile, and Verizon, as well as at the Apple Store.

Apple Stores aren't on every corner, so if visiting one isn't an option (or you just prefer to go it alone), you can go to the Apple Store website (http://store.apple.com) and order an iPad to be shipped to you — even get it engraved, if you want. Typically, standard shipping is free, and if there's a problem, Apple's customer service reps will help you solve the problem or replace your iPad. Additionally, smaller stores that sell electronics can have an Apple Specialist designation that allows them to carry and sell Apple products. Check your local stores for this.

Consider iPad Accessories

At present, Apple offers a few accessories that you may want to check out when you purchase your iPad, including

» **iPad Smart Case/Smart Cover:** Your iPad isn't cheap, and unlike a laptop computer, it has an exposed screen that can be damaged if you drop or scratch it. Investing in the iPad Smart Case or Smart Cover is a good idea if you intend to take your iPad out of your house — or if you have a cat or grandchildren. The iPad Smart Cover (see **Figure 1-2**) costs $40 to $130 from various vendors, depending on design and material.

» **Printers:** Several HP, Brother, Canon, and Epson printers support the wireless AirPrint feature. At this writing, prices range from $129 to $399, and discounts are often available.

FIGURE 1-2

» **Smart Keyboard:** You can buy an attachable keyboard for your iPad Pro for $169, which will make working with productivity apps much easier. This keyboard connects to your iPad to provide power and transmit data between the devices. Also, the Magic Keyboard from Apple costs $99 and uses Bluetooth to connect to your iPad, a Mac, an iPhone, or any other device that works with a Bluetooth keyboard.

» **Apple Pencil:** For $99, you can buy the highly sophisticated stylus for use with the iPad Pro. The Apple Pencil makes it easy to draw on your iPad screen or manage complex interactions more precisely.

» **Apple Digital AV Adapter:** To connect devices to output high-definition media, you can buy this adapter for about $40 and use it with an HDMI cable. More and more devices that use this technology are coming out, such as projectors and TVs. But remember that wireless connections such as Bluetooth and Wi-Fi are less expensive and can eliminate all those cables and cords. In some circumstances, a wired connection is faster and more effective than wireless.

» **Stands, docks, and other accessories:** These are available from Apple Stores and from many third parties.

TIP

Don't bother buying a wireless mouse to connect with your iPad via Bluetooth; the iPad recognizes your finger as its primary input device, and mice need not apply. You can use a stylus or Apple Pencil to tap your input, however.

Explore What's in the Box

After you fork over your hard-earned money for your iPad, you'll be holding one box. Besides your iPad and a small documentation package, here's a rundown of what you'll find when you take off the shrink wrap and open the box:

» **iPad:** Your iPad is covered in a thick plastic sleeve-film that you can take off and toss (unless you think there's a chance that you'll return the device, in which case you may want to keep all packaging for 14 days — Apple's standard return period).

» **Documentation:** Notice, under the iPad itself, a small, white envelope about the size of a half-dozen index cards. Open it and you'll find

- *A single sheet titled iPad Info:* This pamphlet is essentially small print (that you mostly don't need to read) from agencies like the Federal Communications Commission (FCC).

- *A label sheet:* This sheet has two white Apple logos on it. (Apple has provided these for years with its products as a form of cheap advertising when users place stickers on places like their computers or car rear windows.)

- *A small card:* This card displays a picture of the iPad and call-outs to its buttons on one side, and the other side contains brief instructions for setting it up and information about where to find out more.

» **A Lightning-to-USB cable (fourth-generation iPad and later and all iPad mini models) or Dock Connector-to-USB cable (all earlier iPad models):** Use this cord (see Figure 1-3) to connect the iPad to your computer, or use it with the last item in the box: the USB Power Adapter.

» **USB Power Adapter:** The power adapter (refer to Figure 1-3) attaches to the Lightning-to-USB cable so that you can plug it into the wall and charge the battery. The iPad Pro 12.9-inch model comes with a 12W USB power adapter; others come with a 10W power adapter. You can use either one with either iPad, but using the 10W adapter with an iPad Pro will increase charging time.

That's it. That's all you'll find in the box. It's kind of a study in Zen–like simplicity.

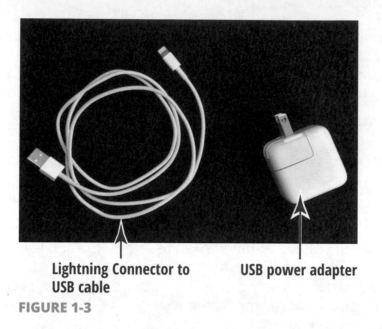

Lightning Connector to USB cable

USB power adapter

FIGURE 1-3

Take a First Look at the Gadget

The little card contained in the documentation that comes with your iPad gives you a picture of the iPad with callouts to the buttons you'll find on it. In this task, I give you a bit more information about those buttons and other physical features of the iPad. **Figure 1-4** shows you where each of these items is located on an iPad Air 2. The Pro model also has a Smart Connector slot in addition to items shown here.

Here's the rundown on what the various hardware features are and what they do:

» **(The all-important) Home/Touch ID button:** On the iPad, press this button to go back to the home screen to find just about anything. The home screen displays all your installed and pre-installed apps and gives you access to your iPad settings. No matter where you are or what you're doing, press the Home button, and you're back at home base. You can also double-press the Home button to pull up a scrolling list of apps so you can quickly move from one app to another. (Apple refers to this as multitasking.) If you press and hold the Home button, you open

Siri, the iPhone voice assistant. Finally, on the newest iPads, the Home button contains a fingerprint reader used with the Touch ID feature.

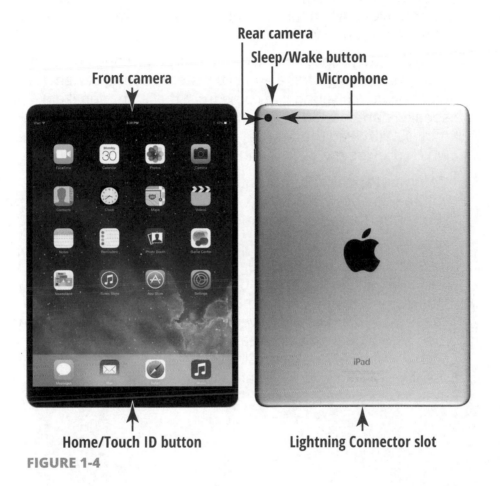

FIGURE 1-4

» **Sleep/Wake button:** You can use this button (whose functionality I cover in more detail in Chapter 2) to power up your iPad, put it in Sleep mode, wake it up, or power it down.

» **Lightning Connector slot:** Plug in the Lightning connector at the USB end to the power adapter to charge your battery or use it without the power adapter to sync your iPad with your computer (which you find out more about in Chapter 3).

» **Cameras:** iPads (except for the original iPad) offer front- and rear-facing cameras, which you can use to shoot photos or video. The rear one is on the top-right corner (if you're looking at the front of the iPad), and you need to be careful not to put your thumb over it when taking shots. (I have several very nice photos of my fingers already.)

» **(Tiny, mighty) Speakers:** One nice surprise when I first got my iPad was hearing what a great little stereo sound system it has and how much sound can come from these tiny speakers. The speakers are located along one side of the iPad Air 2 and iPad mini 4. With iPad Pro, you get four speakers, two on either side, which provide the best sound of all the models.

» **Volume:** Tap the volume switch, called a *rocker,* up for more volume and down for less. You can use this rocker as a camera shutter button when the camera is activated.

» **Headphone jack and microphone:** If you want to listen to your music in private, you can plug in a 3.5mm mini-jack headphone (including an iPhone headset, if you have one, which gives you bidirectional sound). A tiny microphone makes it possible to speak into your iPad to deliver commands or enter content using the Siri personal-assistant feature. Using Siri, you can do things such as make phone calls using the Internet, use video-calling services, dictate your keyboard input, or work with other apps that accept audio input.

Chapter **2**

Using Your iPad

I n this chapter, you turn on your iPad, charge it, and take your first look at the home screen. You also practice using the onscreen keyboard, see how to interact with the touchscreen in various ways, get pointers on working with cameras, and get an overview of built-in applications (called *apps*) and the Control Center.

Your iPad is pretty forgiving so go ahead and try things. Not sure what a button or another interface element does? Try it. Any action that will cause major changes to your data should be prefaced by a warning to that effect. Apple and third-party developers work hard to try to create apps (and the operating system) that not only work properly when you use them properly but that also work properly — or at least reasonably — when you use them incorrectly. So, go ahead and experiment. Remember you can always come back to this book to check out questions you may have.

See What You Need to Use the iPad

You need to be able, at a minimum, to connect to the Internet to take advantage of most iPad features, which you can do by using a Wi-Fi network (a network you set up in your own home or access in a public place such as a library) or by paying a fee and using a phone provider's network if you have a Wi-Fi+Cellular iPad model. You may want to have a computer so that you can connect your iPad to it to download photos, videos, music, or applications and then transfer them to or from your iPad through a process called *syncing.* An Apple service called iCloud syncs content from all your Apple iOS devices, such as iPhone, and your Mac and/or PC wirelessly, so anything you buy on your iPhone, for example, can be delivered to your iPad automatically. In addition, you can sync without connecting a cable to a computer by using a wireless Wi-Fi connection. You can control these options (and many more) by using Settings — it's on the home screen or in the Dock at the bottom of the screen.

Can you use the iPad if you don't own a computer and use public Wi-Fi hotspots to go online (or a 3G, 4G, or 4G LTE connection, if you have one of those models)? Yes. To go online using a Wi-Fi–only iPad and to use many of its built-in features at home, however, you need to have a Wi-Fi network available at certain times, and that includes the initial setup of your iPad.

IS YOUR IPAD USED?

More than 300 million iPads have been sold since the original model launched in 2010. Many (probably most) are still in use by their original owners. Some iPad owners have upgraded to newer models, however, and passed along their older iPads to other people. If you have a used iPad, the previous owner should have erased it before passing it along to you. (In case you're giving away or selling an iPad, Apple provides instructions for erasing an iPad here: `https://support.apple.com/en-us/HT201274`.) After that, you can continue with this chapter, because for all intents and purposes, your iPad will be "new" (at least on the software side).

If you have a previously owned iPad that hasn't been erased and you don't have the password for it, contact a nearby Apple Store or `https://support.apple.com`. The details of what to do next will depend on your exact circumstances.

If you're using an iPad that was configured by your employer or someone else, it should be set up for you, so you don't need to follow the setup steps in this chapter. When in doubt, contact the person who gave it to you.

Apple has set up both iCloud and its iTunes software to help you manage content for your iPad — which includes the movies, TV shows, music, or photos you've downloaded — and specify from where it should transfer your calendar and contact information. Chapter 3 covers iCloud in more detail.

Turn On the iPad for the First Time

When you're ready to get going with your iPad, try to be sure you're within range of a Wi-Fi network that you can connect with. You can set up your iPad without a Wii-Fi network, but some settings will be skipped. You can always come back to them by tapping Settings on the home screen, but it's easier to do it all at once when you first turn on your iPad. Hold the iPad with one hand on either side, oriented like a pad of paper. Plug the small end of the Lightning-to-USB cable that came with your device into your iPad, and plug the other end into a USB port on your computer or the USB power adapter that came in the box with your iPad just in case you lose your battery charge during the setup process. (The power adapter and Lightning-to-USB cable are shown in Figure 2-1.) Yes, if you use the power adapter, remember to plug it into the wall outlet. If you plug into a computer, it should either be powered on or have a battery charge of over 50%.

These steps help you get started, and I've tried to cover most of the items that might trip you up. The actual process of turning on your iPad and getting started can take all of 5-10 minutes.

Follow these steps to set up your iPad:

1. Press and hold the Sleep/Wake button on the top of your iPad until the Apple logo appears.

   In another moment, a screen with a cheery Hello on it appears.

2. Slide your finger to the right on the screen where you see the words Slide to set up.

3. Follow the onscreen prompts to make choices about your language and location, using iCloud (Apple's online sharing service), and so on.

   After you deal with all the setup screens, a Welcome to iPad screen appears.

4. Tap Get Started to display the home screen.

TIP

If you set up iCloud when registering (see Chapter 3), updates to your operating system can automatically be downloaded to your iPad without plugging it into a computer running iTunes. Until you provide an Apple ID, you don't have access to several features such as Find My iPad (which does just that), iCloud, email, and other features that are important to many people. These can be added later and turned on or off at any time from Settings.

Charge the Battery

Your first step in working with the iPad should be making sure that its battery is charged.

My iPad showed up in the box almost fully charged, and I hope yours did, too. Because all batteries run down eventually, however, one of your first priorities is knowing how to recharge your iPad's battery for when it needs charging. Go get your iPad and its Lightning–to–USB cable (iPad fourth generation and later, and iPad mini) and the Apple USB power adapter. Then follow these steps:

1. Gently plug the USB end of the Lightning-to-USB cable (or the Dock Connector-to-USB cable, for older models) into the USB power adapter.

2. Plug the other end of the cord (see **Figure 2-1**) into the Lightning Connector (or Dock Connector) slot on the iPad.

3. Unfold the two metal prongs on the power adapter so that they extend from it at a 90-degree angle; then plug the adapter into an electrical outlet.

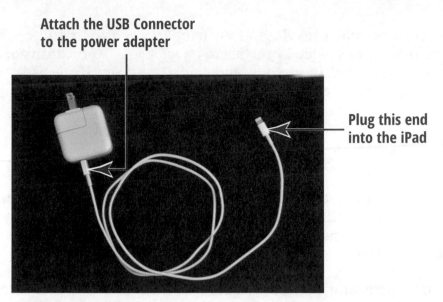

Attach the USB Connector to the power adapter

Plug this end into the iPad

FIGURE 2-1

Most people favor mobile devices that need recharging no more than once a day. If you've had other mobile devices, you may be used to carefully conserving your battery and checking it often during the day. You may be pleasantly surprised to find how long your iPad can run and how long it can retain its charge. I plug in my mobile devices (iPad, iPhone, and Apple Watch) at night. With very rare exceptions, such as using a great deal of navigation on an iPhone or Apple Watch, I have no trouble getting through the next day on a single charge. I typically plug in my iPad before I head out on a trip and recharge it overnight (which is where a multiple-port charger comes in handy).

TIP

BUYING A CHARGER

You can buy chargers from third parties to use to charge your iPad. Some of them plug into your car's accessory port, and some products have multiple ports. I use the Anker PowerPort 5, which is a five-port device that plugs into a wall outlet and recharges up to five devices at a time. The PowerPort 5 has a list price of $50, but you can find it and similar devices at lower prices.

It's a good idea to avoid low-price chargers from vendors you don't know, however. Some of the cheapest chargers have caused accidents.

The devices that I use less often usually keep their full charges for several days. It's a good practice to check the battery status of devices you haven't used in a while and recharge them if necessary before using them after a period of non-use.

Visit the Screens

When you press the Home button, you see the lock screen or the home screen. Notification Center appears when you swipe down from the top of the screen: It, too, is a type of home screen. Here's a guide to those screens.

In the upcoming section "Navigate the Multi-Touch Screen," you see how to move from one of these screens to another. You may want to flip back and forth between that section and this one if you're just getting started.

You can customize your iPad's screens with everything from the images in the background (*wallpaper*) to your time zone and language and the apps that are displayed on each screen.

Start from the lock screen

When you first pick up your iPad and press the Home button, you see the lock screen. (If the iPad is turned off, press the Sleep/Wake button at the top of the iPad (the edge opposite the Home button).

The lock screen, shown in **Figure 2-2**, displays the current date and time, but the iPad is locked; you can't do much of anything until you log in with your passcode or your fingerprint and Touch ID. The lock screen may have some very tiny app icons at the bottom of it. Like almost everything on a home screen, what you see can be configured using Settings.

FIGURE 2-2

Tour the home screen

The home screen (shown in **Figure 2-3**) appears after you've unlocked your iPad with Touch ID and your fingerprint or with a passcode. The main part of the home screen is taken up with icons for the apps installed on your iPad. The apps that are already installed for you may vary but typically include FaceTime (for video or audio conferencing), Photos, Camera, Videos, Notes, Reminders, and News.

Icons for other apps appear on the Dock at the bottom of the screen. (I cover all these apps in the section, "Take Inventory of Preinstalled Apps.")

FIGURE 2-3

Visit Today view

Today view (shown in **Figure 2-4**) is another of the views you can see when you press the Home button (for how to get to the Today view, see the following section). This view can contain events from your calendar, reminders, music, notes, and more. Tapping any of them gives you more information. As shown in Figure 2-4, you can add new widgets to Today view either by tapping the round Edit button below the left column or by tapping New Widget Available to see what it is and to install it if you want to.

Although it's called Today view, it's more of a Now view.

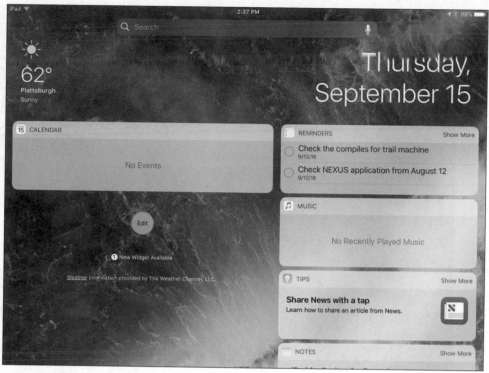

FIGURE 2-4

Check Notification Center

Swipe down from the top of the screen or from left to right to see Notification Center, shown in **Figure 2-5**. (For more on swiping, see the following section, "Navigate the Multi-Touch Screen.") Notification Center contains notifications from various apps such as Calendar and Reminders. (Notifications are just that — a notice from an app that something has happened, will happen, or might happen if you take an action.) It also can contain widgets that provide specific types of information, such as stock quotes and weather forecasts.

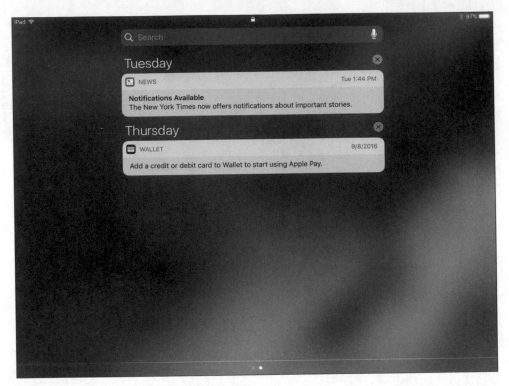

FIGURE 2-5

Navigate the Multi-Touch Screen

The iPad uses touchscreen technology. When you swipe your finger across the screen or tap it, you're providing input to the device just as you do when you use a mouse or keyboard with your computer.

WARNING

Despite a screen that's been treated to repel oils, you're about to deposit a ton of fingerprints on your iPad — one downside of a touchscreen device. DO NOT USE GLASS CLEANERS ON YOUR TOUCHSCREEN DEVICES. A soft cloth wipes off fingerprints. Never use aerosols or sprays. Although you can use a little water to clean your Apple Watch, your iPad is different. Don't get paranoid about this, but do be careful. If your hands are full, for example, don't use your iPad as a tray to carry three cups of hot coffee. (No further details about this disaster are available.)

Experiment with the touchscreen

Go ahead and play with the iPad's touchscreen for a few minutes; really, you can't hurt anything. Using the pads of your fingertips (not your fingernails), follow these steps:

1. Tap the Settings icon. The various settings (which you read more about throughout this book) appear, as shown in **Figure 2-6**.

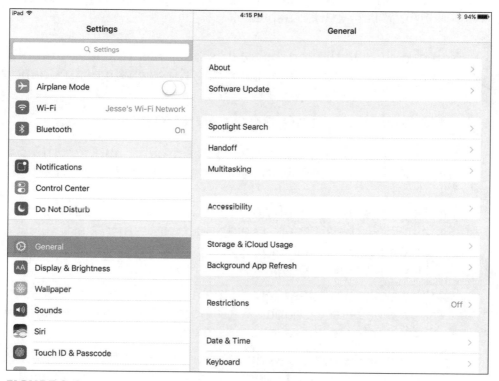

FIGURE 2-6

2. To return to the home screen, press the Home button.

3. Swipe a finger or two from right to left on the screen. This action moves you to the next home screen.

   The little dots at the bottom of the screen, above the Dock icons, indicate which home screen is displayed.

REMEMBER

4. To experience the screen-rotation feature, hold the iPad firmly with the Home button on one side and turn it sideways. The screen flips

to vertical orientation. To flip the screen back, just turn the device so that it's oriented horizontally again.

5. Drag your finger down from the top of the screen to reveal Notification Center, which contains items such as reminders, calendar entries, and so on (covered in Chapter 19).

6. Drag up from the bottom of the home screen to hide Notification Center and to display Control Center, which contains commonly used controls and tools. This feature is discussed in "Discover Control Center" later in this chapter.

You can change the touchscreen's *wallpaper* (background picture) and brightness. Read about making these changes in Chapter 4.

Try out tapping and swiping

You can use several methods to get around and get things done on the iPad by using its Multi-Touch screen, including the following:

» **Tap once.** To open an application on the home screen, choose a field (such as a search field), select an item in a list, select an arrow to move back or forward one screen, or follow an online link, tap the item once with your finger.

» **Tap twice.** Use this method to enlarge or reduce the display of a web page (see Chapter 6 for more about using the Safari web browser) or to zoom in or out in the Maps app.

» **Pinch and expand.** As an alternative to the tap-twice method, you can pinch your fingers together or move them apart (expand) on the screen when you're looking at photos, maps, web pages (see **Figure 2-7**), or email messages to quickly reduce or enlarge them, respectively.

You can use a three-finger tap to zoom your screen even more or use multitasking gestures to swipe with four or five fingers (see "Explore multitasking gestures" later in this chapter). This method is handy if you have vision challenges. Go to Chapter 4 to discover how to turn on this feature by using Accessibility settings.

FIGURE 2-7

» **Drag to scroll (swipe).** When you press your finger to the screen and drag to the right or left, the screen moves (see **Figure 2-8**). Swiping to the left on the home screen, for example, moves you to the next home screen. Swiping up while reading an online newspaper moves you down the page; swiping down moves you back up the page.

» **Flick.** To scroll a page quickly, flick your finger on the screen in the direction in which you want to move.

TIP

When you rock your iPad backward or forward, the home screen's background moves as well, via what is called the *parallax* feature. You can disable this feature if it makes you seasick. Tap Settings ⇨ General ⇨ Accessibility, and if the Reduce Motion setting is set to on (displaying the green section of the toggle switch), tap the switch to turn off the setting (hide the green part of the switch).

» **Tap the status bar.** To move quickly to the top of a list, web page, or email message, tap the status bar at the top of the iPad's screen.

» **Touch and hold.** If you're using Notes, Mail, or another application that lets you select text, or if you're on a web page, pressing and holding text selects a word and displays editing tools you can use to select, cut or copy, and paste the text.

Report: Court orders former Egyptian President Hosni Mubarak freed

By **Karl Penhaul and Laura Smith-Clark**, CNN
updated 1:35 PM EDT, Wed August 21, 2013

Ousted Egyptian President Hosni Mubarak is wheeled out of an ambulance following a hearing in Cairo on April 13, 2013.

FIGURE 2-8

Try out these methods as follows:

» Tap the Safari button on the Dock at the bottom of any iPad home screen to display the web browser. (You may be asked to enter your network password to access the network.)

» Tap a link (typically, colored text or a button or image) to move to another page.

» Double-tap the page to enlarge it; then pinch your fingers together onscreen to reduce it.

» Drag one finger around the page to scroll up, down, or side to side.

» Flick your finger on the page to scroll quickly.

» Press and hold — iOS's equivalent of right-clicking — black text that isn't a link. (Links usually are blue and take you to a location on the Internet.) The text is selected, and the toolbar containing Copy/Look Up/Share tools is displayed with relevant options, as shown in **Figure 2-9**. You can use this toolbar to get a definition of a word or copy it.

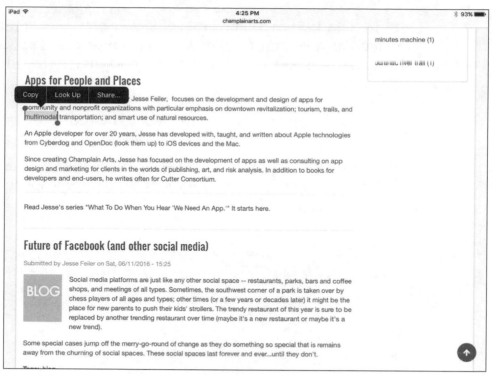

FIGURE 2-9

» Press and hold a link or an image. A contextual menu appears, with commands you select to open the link or picture, open it in a new tab, add it to your Reading List, or copy it. If you tap and hold an image, the menu also offers the Save Image command.

» Position your fingers slightly apart on the screen and then pinch them together to shrink the page. Then, with your fingers pinched together on the screen, move them apart to enlarge the page.

» Press the Home button to go back to the home screen.

Display and Use the Onscreen Keyboard

If you're entering data, you can use the iPad's onscreen keyboards. (Yes, there are several.) Or you can buy an Apple Pencil or Smart Keyboard for use with iPad Pro.

The built-in iPad keyboard appears whenever you're in a text-entry location, such as a search field or an email message. Tap the Notes icon on the home screen to open this easy-to-use notepad, and try out the keyboard:

» Tap the blank note page or (if you've already entered notes) tap a note; then tap anywhere on the note. The onscreen keyboard appears.

» Use the keyboard to type a few words. To make the keyboard display as wide as possible, rotate your iPad to landscape (horizontal) orientation, as shown in **Figure 2-10**.

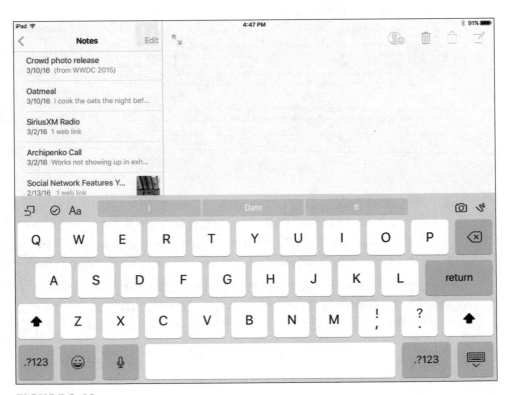

FIGURE 2-10

» If you make a mistake while using the keyboard — and you will when you first use it — tap the Delete key (it's in the top-right corner of the keyboard, with the little x on it) to delete text to the left of the insertion point.

» To create a new paragraph, tap the Return key just as you would on a computer keyboard.

» To type numbers and symbols, tap one of the number keys (labeled .?123) at either end of the spacebar (refer to Figure 2-10). The characters on the keyboard change. If you type a number and then tap the spacebar, the keyboard returns to the letter keyboard automatically. To return to the letter keyboard at any time, simply tap one of the letter keys (labeled ABC) at either end of the spacebar.

» Use the Shift keys (thick up arrows in the bottom-left and bottom-right corners of the keyboard) just as you would on a regular keyboard to type uppercase letters. Tapping a Shift key once causes only the next letter you type to be capitalized.

» Double-tap the Shift key to turn on the Caps Lock feature so that all letters you type are capitalized until you turn the feature off. Tap the Shift key once to turn off Caps Lock. (You have to turn this feature on by opening the Settings app and, in the General pane, tapping Keyboard.)

» To type a variation on a symbol (such as to see alternative currency symbols when you tap the dollar sign on the numeric keyboard), hold down the key. A set of alternative symbols appears (see **Figure 2-11**). Note that this trick works only with certain symbols.

» Tap the Dictation key (refer to Figure 2-10; it has a microphone symbol on it) to activate the Dictation feature (not available on the original iPad or the iPad 2) and then speak your input. Tap the Dictation key again or tap in a note to turn off the Dictation feature. This feature works in several apps, such as Mail, Notes, and Maps. You must be connected to the Internet for it to work.

» Tap the Emoji button (a smiley-face symbol to the left of the Dictation button) to display a set of smiley symbols to insert into your document. Tap tabs along the bottom to display other icon sets, such as pictures of nature or city skylines.

» To hide the keyboard, tap the Keyboard key in the bottom-right corner.

» Press the Home button to return to the home screen.

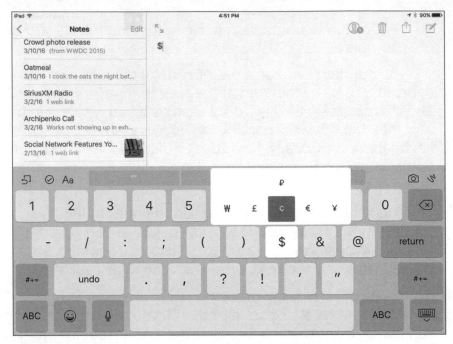

FIGURE 2-11

KEYBOARD TIPS

Here are some tips to help you get the most out of the onscreen keyboard:

- You can undock the keyboard to move it around the screen. To do this, press and hold the Keyboard key; then, from the pop-up menu that appears, choose Undock. Now, by dragging the Keyboard key up or down, you can move the keyboard up and down on the screen. To dock the keyboard at the bottom of the screen again, press and hold the Keyboard key, and choose Dock from the pop-up menu.

- In the Notes app, you can display a shortcut keyboard by using the General/Keyboard settings. This keyboard allows you to create a checklist, choose a font style, insert a photo, or create a drawing within a note. The onscreen keyboard also uses a feature called QuickType to provide suggestions above the keyboard as you type. See Chapter 21 for more about using the Notes app.

- To type a period and space, double-tap the spacebar. If you want to add punctuation, such as a comma, and then return immediately to the letter keyboard, simply tap the .?123 key and then drag up to the punctuation symbol you want to use.

You can buy a Smart Keyboard to go with an iPad Pro for $169. This physical keyboard from Apple attaches to your iPad and allows both power and data exchange. The connection for your keyboard is magnetic, so it's a snap to put it and the iPad together.

Use the Split Keyboard

The *split keyboard* feature allows you to split the keyboard so that each side appears nearer the edge of the iPad screen. For those who are into texting or typing with thumbs, this feature makes it easier to reach all the keys from the sides of the device — useful if you're holding your iPad with both hands. Open an application such as Notes in which you can use the onscreen keyboard and then follow these steps:

1. Tap an entry field or page to display the onscreen keyboard.

2. Place one finger on each side of the keyboard and drag them apart. (I put one finger on S and the other on K.) The keyboard splits, as shown in **Figure 2-12**. (This feature can be finicky, so you may have to try it a few times.)

3. Now hold the iPad with a hand on either side and practice using your thumbs to enter text.

4. To rejoin the keyboard, press and hold the Keyboard key, or drag the two parts together. You can position them at varying distances from one another as shown in **Figure 2-13**. You can dock or undock the keyboard to or from the bottom of the screen; you can also split or merge it.

When the keyboard is docked and merged at the bottom of your screen, you can simply drag the Keyboard key upward to undock and split the keyboard. To reverse this action, drag the Keyboard key downward. The keyboard is docked and merged.

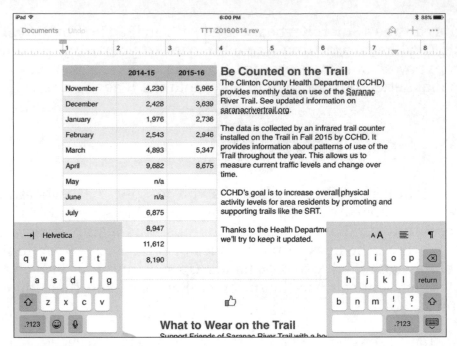

FIGURE 2-12

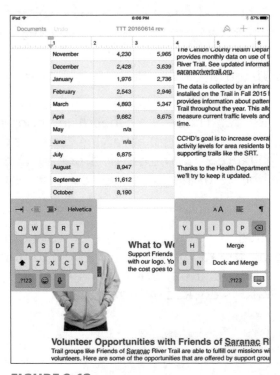

FIGURE 2-13

Flick to Search

The Spotlight Search feature of the iPad helps you find suggestions from the Internet, the Music app, iTunes, and the App Store, as well as suggestions for nearby locations, photos, music, emails, contacts, movies, and more. To use it, follow these steps:

1. Swipe down on any home screen (but not from the very top or bottom of the screen) to reveal the Search feature.

2. Tap in the Search iPad field. The keyboard appears.

3. Begin entering a search term. If you type the letter *c,* as shown in **Figure 2-14**, the iPad lists any contacts, built-in apps, music, and videos that you've downloaded, as well as items created in Notes that begin with *C.* As you continue to type a search term, the results narrow to match it.

FIGURE 2-14

4. Scroll down to the bottom of the search results, and tap Search Web, Search App Store, or Search Maps to check results from those sources.

5. Tap an item in the search results to open it in the corresponding app or player.

Update the Operating System

This book is based on the latest version of the iPad operating system at this writing: iOS 10. To make sure you have the latest and greatest features, update your iPad to the latest version of iOS now. If you've set up an iCloud account on your iPad, updates can happen automatically; otherwise, you can update over a Wi-Fi or 3G, 4G, or 4G LTE connection by tapping Settings⇨General⇨Software Update. You'll either see that your software is up to date (see **Figure 2-15**) or you'll get instructions for downloading a new version.

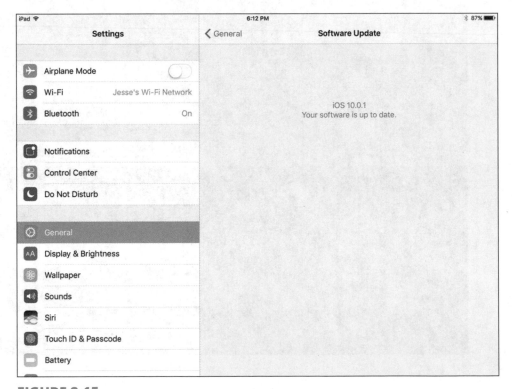

FIGURE 2-15

An iOS update may introduce new features for your iPad. If an update appears after you buy this book, go to my website at northcountryconsulting.com for details on new features introduced in the update.

Be a Multitasker

Multitasking lets you switch from one app to another without closing the first one. By default, iOS keeps the apps you open running. If you're not actively using an app, it may be suspended or its memory may be temporarily reused and restored later without you being involved. You can switch from one app to another by previewing all open apps and jumping from one to another, and quit an app simply by swiping upward.

Try out multitasking

To get acquainted with multitasking on the iPad, follow these steps:

1. Open two or more apps.

2. Double-tap the Home button.

3. On the app switcher screen that appears (see **Figure 2-16**), flick to scroll to the left or right, and locate another app that you want to move to.

4. Tap the new app to open it.

Tap the Home button to remove the multitasking bar from the home screen and return to the app you were working in. On your iPad, you can also slowly swipe from the right edge of the screen towards the center to open the Slide Over feature (described later in this chapter). It shows you all running apps and you can tap the one you want to switch to.

Explore multitasking gestures

Multitasking involves jumping from one app to another. Multitasking gestures let you maneuver through multitasking options. You can turn these gestures on or off by tapping Settings ⇨ General ⇨ Multi-tasking, and tapping the On/Off switch for Multitasking Gestures.

FIGURE 2-16

There are many gestures available on your iPad; many apps have their own gestures in addition to these. You can turn app-specific gestures on or off by using Settings for each app. Table 2-1 shows the most common gestures that you'll be using. Not all gestures can be used on all screens, so the table shows you the screens on which they work.

Table 2-1 contains a lot of information, and you'll probably refer to it often as you're getting started. Keep these points in mind:

>> Notifications appear in Notification Center. Where "Notification" is listed as the screen to start from, that means one notification, not Notification Center.

TABLE 2-1   Common iPad Gestures

From This Screen	Gesture	Result
Any (L)	Swipe up from bottom of screen.	Open Control Center.
Any (L)	Swipe down from top of screen.	Open Notification Center.
Any	Pinch four or five fingers together.	Go to home.
Home	Swipe down from middle of home screen.	Open search.
Any	Swipe up with four or five fingers.	Show App Switcher.
Any	Swipe left or right with four or five fingers.	Show next or previous app without going through App Switcher.
Home or Lock	Swipe right from left edge.	Show Today view.
Notification Center	Swipe up or press the Home button.	Close Notification Center.
Control Center	Swipe down, tap top of screen, or press the Home button.	Close Control Center.
Lock Screen	Swipe left.	Show Camera.
Notification	Swipe notification to right.	Open app that posted the notification.
Notification	Pull notification down from top of screen.	Respond without leaving current app (useful for Mail, Messages, and calendar invitations).
Notification	Swipe notification left.	Clear notification.

» When you can start from any screen, (L) indicates that includes the lock screen. Otherwise, you can start from any screen after you have unlocked your iPad.

> » Gestures that start from an edge or top/bottom of screen start from the *bevel* — the framing area beyond the main screen. It's part of the surface of the iPad but outside the screen area.
>
> » Unless otherwise mentioned, gestures can start from anywhere on the screen.

Use Slide Over and Split View

iPad Pro introduces two new interface features that take advantage of its large high-resolution touchscreen, allowing it to display more data on the screen. That can mean larger images with more detail, but it can also mean multitasking in new ways as you can see and work with several apps at the same time.

REMEMBER

Not every app supports these features yet. Most of the built-in apps do, and independent developers are gradually adopting the technology. If your favorite app doesn't yet support Slide Over or Split View, visit the app's web page or tap a Contact Us button to make your voice heard to the developer. In the future, when an app asks whether you want to receive notices about new features, opt in; then, if the developer presents a list of new features and lets users vote on them, you'll be able to make your opinion known. Developers do listen!

Starting with Slide Over

To use the Slide Over feature, follow these steps:

1. Open one of the apps you want to use. (Don't start from the home screen: You must start from an app.) **Figure 2-17** shows News, which is the starting point for this sequence of steps, but you can use any app you want.

2. With one finger, slowly drag from the middle of the right edge toward the center. Slide Over opens, as you see in **Figure 2-18**. If you haven't used Slide Over yet today, you may see the apps that are now running.

FIGURE 2-17

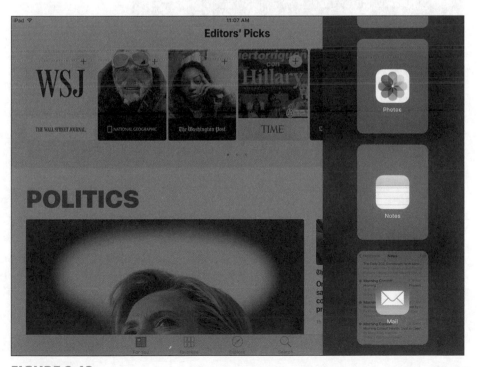

FIGURE 2-18

3. Tap an app to show it in Slide Over. (You can swipe up and down to see the apps.) If you tap Calendar, for example, you see it in Slide Over, as shown in **Figure 2-19**.

4. If you want to return to the list of running apps as shown in Figure 2-18, just drag down from the top of Slide Over. (Notice the small bar at the top of the screen in Figure 2-19.)

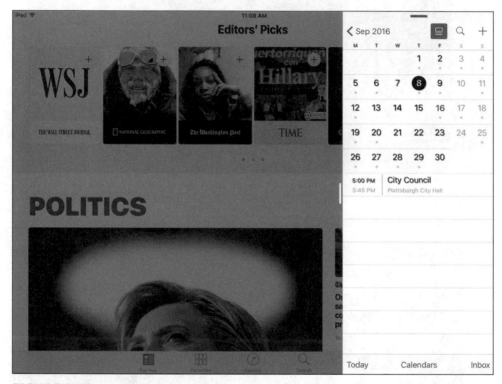

FIGURE 2-19

Slide Over is narrow. Both apps are running, but the main app has a bigger view for you to work with. Notice that at the top of the Slide Over in Figure 2-19, earlier in this chapter, you have a Back button (< Sep 2016) and other buttons from Calendar that allow you to search and add a new appointment. These buttons are a bit smaller, but they work.

Moving to Split View

If you want to use both apps at the same time, you can move on to Split View. With Slide Over open, continue dragging the small white handle toward the center of the screen to open Split View, as shown in **Figure 2-20**.

FIGURE 2-20

(In Figure 2-19, the handle is next to the 5:00 PM City Council calendar item.)

While you're in Split View, you can drag the heavy black divider left or right to change the sizes of the panes, or you can have equal space for both apps. Both apps are fully functional although in some special cases, the app may not show certain non-critical elements to adjust to the narrower width of the split view when compared to the full screen.

Discover Control Center

Control Center is a one-stop screen for common features and settings, such as muting or unmuting sounds, connecting to a network, increasing screen brightness, and turning Bluetooth on or off. To display Control Center, swipe up from the bottom edge of the screen.

At the bottom of the screen that appears, tap a button or slider to access or adjust a setting (see **Figure 2-21**).

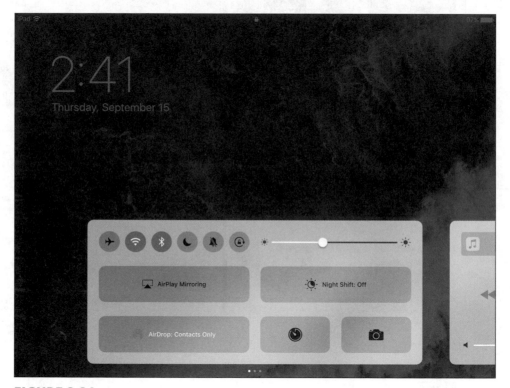

FIGURE 2-21

Control Center has several panes, and their contents depend on what apps and hardware you have installed. As you see in **Figure 2-22**, if there's another pane you can see, a small part will be visible. Swipe to move it into view.

FIGURE 2-22

The next pane, shown in **Figure 2-23**, shows accessories in HomeKit (described in Chapter 11). Again, the contents of this pane will vary depending on what you have installed. You can tap an accessory to turn it on or off.

Tap Scenes (or any other button) to explore the scenes, as shown in **Figure 2-24**.

Swipe down from the top of Control Center to the bottom of the screen to hide it.

REMEMBER

When another pane can be shown with a swipe, you see the edge of it (refer to Figure 2-22).

FIGURE 2-23

FIGURE 2-24

Understand Touch ID

In previous versions of the iPad, you had to set a password to protect the contents of your iPad and input that password to wake the device again every time it went to sleep. More-recent iPads sport a feature called Touch ID, which allows you to unlock your phone by touching the redesigned Home button. That button now contains a sophisticated fingerprint sensor. Because your fingerprint is unique, this feature is one of the most foolproof ways to protect your data.

If you're going to use Touch ID (it's optional), you must educate the iPad about your fingerprint on your finger of choice by tapping Settings ⇨ Touch ID & Passcode, entering your passcode, and choosing what to use Touch ID for: such as unlocking the iPad, using Apple Pay (Apple's electronic wallet service), or making purchases from the App Store and the iTunes Store. You can change these preferences from time to time.

Then, if you did not set up a fingerprint previously or want to add another one, tap Add a Fingerprint from inside Touch ID & Passcode. Follow the instructions and press your finger lightly on the Home button several times to allow Touch ID to sense and record your fingerprint. (You will be guided through this process and told when to touch and when to lift your finger.) With the iPad Unlock option turned on, press the power button to go to the lock screen and touch the Home button. The iPad unlocks. If you chose the option for using Touch ID with Apple Pay or purchasing an item in the Apple stores, you'll simply touch your finger to the Home button rather than entering your Apple ID and password to complete a purchase.

 There's a difference between touching and tapping your iPad. It's the ordinary every-day difference: Touching is a light touch without applying pressure. Tapping means you apply pressure — the same amount you would use in tapping people on their shoulder to get their attention.

Lock the iPad, Turn It Off, and Unlock It

Turning on your iPad is easy. It's just as easy to put it to *sleep* (a state in which the screen goes black, though you can quickly wake the iPad) or to turn off the power to give your new toy a rest. Here are the procedures you can use:

» **Sleep:** Press the Sleep/Wake button. The iPad goes to sleep. The screen goes black and is locked.

TIP

If you bought a Smart Cover or Smart Case with your iPad (or a third-party case with similar functionality), you can just fold the cover over the front of the screen to put the iPad to sleep. Open the cover again to wake the iPad. (See Chapter 1 for more about iPad accessories.)

» **Wake:** Press the Home button. If you didn't set up Touch ID (see "Understand Touch ID" earlier in this chapter), the iPad wakes when you press Home. Then press it again to unlock the iPad.

» **Sleep:** Press and hold the Sleep/Wake button until the Slide to Power Off bar appears at the top of the screen; then swipe the bar. You've just turned off your iPad.

TIP

The iPad automatically enters sleep mode after a few minutes of inactivity. You can change the time at which it sleeps by tapping Settings ⇨ Display & Brightness.

Explore the Status Bar

Across the top of the iPad screen is the *status bar* (see **Figure 2-25**). Tiny icons on this bar can provide useful information such as the time, battery level, and wireless-connection status.

iPad 🛜	2:19 PM	🔄 ✳ 65% 🔋

FIGURE 2-25

Table 2-2 lists some of the most common items you find on the status bar.

TABLE 2-2 **Common Status Bar Icons**

Icon	Name	What It Indicates
☀	Activity	A task is in progress — a web page is loading, for example.
🔋	Battery life	This icon shows the charge percentage remaining in the battery. The indicator changes to a lightning bolt when the battery is charging.
✻	Bluetooth	Bluetooth service is on, and the iPad is paired with a wireless device.
🔒	Screen orientation lock	The screen is locked and doesn't rotate when you turn the iPad.
12:07 PM	Time	You guessed it: You see the time.
📶	Wi-Fi	You're connected to a Wi-Fi network.

TIP

If you have GPS, 3G, 4G, 4G LTE, or Bluetooth service or a connection to a virtual private network (VPN), a corresponding symbol appears on the status bar whenever one of these features is active. The GPS and 3G. 4G, 4G LTE icons appear only on 3G- or 4G-enabled iPad models. (If you can't even conceive of what a VPN is, my advice is not to worry about it.)

Take Inventory of Preinstalled Apps

The iPad comes with certain functionality and applications — or *apps*, for short — preinstalled. When you look at the home screen, you see icons for each app. This task gives you an overview of what each app does. (You can find out more about every one of them as you read different chapters of this book.)

There's one important app that's not listed here, not shown in the Dock, and not shown on a Home screen: That's Siri, the intelligent personal assistant (technical name). Siri responds to spoken commands and questions using a voice that you choose. Chapter 5 is devoted to Siri, but remember that Siri can control almost all of the built-in apps.

Dock apps

You can add apps to the Dock (space permitting) and you can remove them as well. The Dock described here is probably what you will start out with, but it may differ. From left to right, the icons on the Dock (refer to "Navigate the Multi-Touch Screen," earlier in this chapter) are

» **Messages:** Using the Messages app, you can engage in live text and video conversations with others via their phones or other devices that use messaging. (Chapter 8)

» **Mail:** You use this application to access mail accounts that you've set up for the iPad. When you do, your email is displayed without your having to browse to the site or sign in. Then you can use tools to move among a few preset mail folders, read and reply to mail, and download attached photos to your iPad. (Chapter 7)

» **Safari:** You use the Safari web browser (see **Figure 2-26**) to navigate the Internet, create and save bookmarks of favorite sites, and add web clips to your home screen so that you can quickly visit favorite sites from there. You may have used this web browser (or another, such as Internet Explorer in the past or Edge now) on your desktop computer (see Chapter 6).

» **Music:** Music is your audio media player, which you can use to play music, podcasts, or audiobooks (see Chapter 13).

Home-screen apps

Apps with icons above the Dock on the home screen include

FIGURE 2-26

» **FaceTime:** The FaceTime video-calling app lets you use the camera of an iPad 2 or later to talk face to face with someone who also has an iPhone or iPad 2 or later. (Chapter 8)

» **Calendar:** Use this handy daybook to set up appointments and send alerts to remind you about them. (Chapter 18)

» **Photos:** The photo application in iPad helps you organize pictures in folders, email photos to others, use a photo as your iPad wallpaper, and assign pictures to contact records. You can also run slideshows of your photos, open albums, pinch or unpinch to shrink or expand photos, and scroll photos with a simple swipe. You can use the Photo Stream feature to share photos with your friends via iCloud. Photos displays images by collections, including Years and Moments, and offers filters you can apply to pictures to achieve different effects (see **Figure 2-27**).

» **Camera:** The Camera app is central control for the still and video cameras built into the iPad 2 and later (see Chapter 14).

FIGURE 2-27

» **Contacts:** In this address-book feature (see **Figure 2-28**), you can enter contact information (including photos, if you like, from your Photos or Cameras app) and share contact information by email. You can also use the search feature to find your contacts easily (see Chapter 20).

» **Clock:** This app allows you to display the time around the world, set alarms, and use timer and stopwatch features (see Chapter 18).

» **Maps:** In this cool Apple mapping program, you can view classic maps or aerial views of addresses; find directions from one place to another by bike, public transportation, car, foot, and in some areas, ride sharing like Uber and Lyft. You can also view your maps in 3-D. You can even get your directions read out loud by a narration feature (turn it on in Settings ⇨ Maps ⇨ Driving & Navigation ⇨ Navigation Voice Volume). Not all transportation modalities are available for all locations. Driving is the most common (see Chapter 17).

FIGURE 2-28

 » **Videos:** This media player is similar to Music but specializes in playing videos and offers a few features specific to this medium, such as chapter breakdowns and information about a movie's plot and cast (see Chapter 15).

 » **Notes:** Enter or cut and paste text into this simple notepad app. Draw sketches if you want, and organize notes with check boxes, headings, and some other formatting features. You'll notice that the sharing panel in many apps lets you automatically enter a note from other apps. (Sharing is the icon with the arrow pointing up out of a box). (For more information, see Chapter 21.)

 » **Reminders:** This useful app centralizes your calendar entries and alerts to keep you on schedule. It also allows you to create to-do lists (see Chapter 19).

 » **News:** This app is a news aggregator. When you select news sources, the News app displays top stories from those sources (see Chapter 22).

» **iTunes Store:** Tapping this icon takes you to the iTunes Store, where you can shop 'til you drop (or until your iPad battery runs out of juice) for music, movies, TV shows, audiobooks, and podcasts and then download them directly to your iPad (see Chapter 9).

» **App Store:** At the online App Store, you can buy and download applications that enable you to do everything from play games to build business presentations. Some of these apps are even free!

» **iBooks:** This outstanding e-reader app is similar to the Amazon Kindle. For details on working with iBooks, go to Chapter 12.

» **Settings:** Settings isn't exactly an app, but it's a feature you should know about anyway: It's the central location on the iPad where you can specify settings for various functions and perform administrative tasks such as setting up email accounts and creating a password.

» **Podcasts and iTunes U:** In the Extras folder, you'll find the Podcasts app (for playing audio broadcasts) and iTunes U (for tons of online courses).

You can add apps to populate as many as 11 home screens and move apps from one home screen to another. You can also nest apps inside folders. (Chapter 10)

Examine the iPad Cameras

The iPad has front- and back-facing cameras. You can use these cameras to take still photos (covered in detail in Chapter 14) or shoot videos (covered in Chapter 15). Switch between the front and rear cameras by tapping the Camera icon at the top of the right panel.

For now, take a quick look at your camera by tapping the Camera icon on the home screen. The Camera app opens, as shown in **Figure 2-29**.

FIGURE 2-29

You can use the controls on the screen to

» Take a picture or start recording a video.

» Turn the Time-Lapse feature on or off.

» Change from still-camera to video-camera operation by using the Camera/Video slider.

» Choose a 3- or 10-second delay with the new Timed Photos button.

» Use the Pano setting to shoot panoramic photos.

» Select the Square option to shoot in a format that's popular on photo-sharing services such as Instagram.

» Open previously captured images or videos.

When you view a photo or video, you can share it by posting it to a social media service, such as Facebook or Flickr, or send it in a tweet, message, or email by using AirDrop. You can also print the image, use it as wallpaper (your home-screen and/or lock-screen background image), assign it to a contact, or run a slideshow. See Chapters 14 and 15 for more details about using the iPad cameras, such as managing focus and lighting.

Chapter **3**

Apple IDs, iCloud, and Security

To get the most out of your iPad, you need an Apple ID to identify yourself. Fortunately, you already have one if you've made a purchase from iTunes or the App Store or the Mac App Store. And if you purchased your iPad from the online Apple Store, you've also already got an Apple ID.

With an Apple ID, you can share your content (such as songs from iTunes, apps from the App Store, and documents you create on your Apple ID–equipped devices, as long as the apps support that type of sharing. Your Apple ID can give you access to iCloud, which lets you store your data and other content with an Internet connection. It also is your passkey to connect your iPad with other devices (such as Apple TV) and your other Apple ID–equipped devices (such as a shared disk on AirPort Extreme).

As soon as you start thinking about sharing, you should think about security. Apple IDs, iCloud, and sharing all work together to make your data accessible wherever you want for whomever you want — and no one else.

Manage Apple ID Accounts

An Apple ID identifies you to Apple. It's the primary security mechanism for accessing any Apple resource that's not available to the public, including purchases of music, movies, and TV shows from iTunes, as well as your private iCloud storage area for your data.

In addition to giving you access to your data and resources, if you're a developer, an Apple ID identifies your developer account that lets you distribute your apps. If you're an iBooks author, an Apple ID identifies you to iBooks so you can publish your iBooks.

There's no right or wrong way to set up your Apple ID(s). My advice is to start (and stay) simple. For most people that means a single Apple ID for yourself. You can use Family Sharing (Chapter 9) to share with other people: That's preferable to having other people use your Apple ID. You may want a separate Apple ID for your media, or perhaps you want a separate ID for work, but that's enough complexity for most people.

Figure 3-1 shows part of the Settings screen on my iPad. I use separate Apple IDs for my iCloud account (jfeiler@champlainarts.com) and for iTunes & App Store, but you don't have to. Many people use the same Apple ID.

If you don't have an Apple ID, you can create one. Otherwise, sign in with an existing Apple ID. Both processes are described in the following sections.

Create an Apple ID

When you go through the standard iPad setup process (see Chapter 2), you're prompted to enter or create an Apple ID. (You can change that ID later, if you want to.) Here's how to create one.

1. Tap Settings on your iPad.
2. Tap iTunes & App Store or iCloud depending, on which service you want to create an Apple ID for. **Figure 3-2** shows the next screen if you're setting up an ID for iCloud.

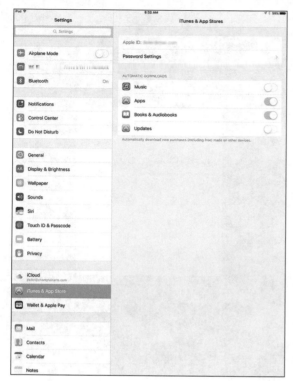

FIGURE 3-1

FIGURE 3-2

3. Tap Create a New Apple ID.

4. In the following screens, you answer a series of authentication questions, beginning with your birthdate, as shown in **Figure 3-3**. You can control the visibility of this information, but it's essential for Apple to make certain that minors don't access inappropriate information. You can fudge your age in other environments, but this item matters, and it's just between you and the Apple ID software.

Other verification questions allow you to prove your identity. The questions vary (the color of your first car, your favorite band, and so on). **Figure 3-4** asks for a critical piece of information: the email address you want to use for your Apple ID. You can change this address later, but you can't use the same email address for two Apple IDs.

FIGURE 3-3

FIGURE 3-4

Choose an existing Apple ID for a service

If you have an Apple ID, you associate it with a specific Apple service as you see in this section.

1. Tap Settings.

2. Tap the service with which you want to use the Apple ID: iCloud or iTunes & App Store.

3. Enter the Apple ID and password in the Sign In section (refer to Figure 3-2).

TIP

If you've forgotten your Apple ID or password, tap the Forgot Apple ID or Password? link below the Sign In field. The security questions you answered when you set up the account (see "Create an Apple ID" earlier in this chapter) may come into play in this situation.

4. Tap Sign In.

5. Enter your credit card information if you're prompted to do so (depending on the service).

Though it should be quite safe to do so, if you prefer not to leave your credit card info with Apple, you can buy an iTunes gift card and provide that as your payment information. You can replenish the card periodically through the Apple Store, but many people find it easier just to buy a new iTunes card. You can find them in many stores alongside other gift cards. (In some stores, there's a display of these cards near the cash registers so you can buy a new iTunes card the next time you buy a quart of milk.)

For details on Apple ID, go to `https://appleid.apple.com`. You can find more information on this page, as well as add security features.

Sync to iTunes Wirelessly

You can use the iTunes Wi-Fi Sync setting to allow cordless syncing of your data to iCloud or to a computer if you're within range of a Wi-Fi network that has a computer with iTunes installed connected to it. (You'll need to be logged into the same Apple ID on the computer's iTunes app as you use for your iPad.) To use this setting, you should have set up an Apple ID and chosen to sync with iTunes. (See "Manage Apple ID Accounts," earlier in this chapter.)

To install iTunes on your computer, go to `www.apple.com/itunes/download`.

To sync your iPad wirelessly, follow these steps:

1. Connect your iPad to your computer with the Lightning-to-USB cable.

2. Open iTunes on your computer.

3. Select your iPad in the Devices list.

4. On the Summary tab of iTunes, click Sync with This iPad over Wi-Fi, and then click Apply. You need to make this setting only once.

5. Disconnect your iPad from your computer.

6. Next, on your iPad tap Settings ➪ General ➪ iTunes Wi-Fi Sync.

7. In the pane shown in **Figure 3-5**, tap Sync to manually sync with a computer connected to the same Wi-Fi network. (Once you've set up Wi-Fi syncing, it happens on an as-needed basis, so instead of a massive backup and sync operation, it keeps up to date on both sides.)

FIGURE 3-5

If you have your iPad set up to sync wirelessly to your Mac or PC, and both devices are within range of the same Wi–Fi network, the iPad appears in your iTunes Devices list. Selecting iPad in your Devices list allows you to sync and manage syncing from within iTunes.

TIP You can tap any item on the left side of the iTunes window to handle settings for syncing items such as movies, music, and apps. In the Apps category, you can also choose to remove certain apps from your home screens. You can also tap the list of items On My Device (Music, Movies, TV Shows, Books, Audiobooks, and Tones) on the left side to view and even play contents.

Use iCloud

There's an alternative to backing up content with iTunes: iCloud. iCloud is a free cloud-based service that lets you store and share data among all your devices that use the same Apple ID. It also allows you to back up all your content and some of your settings (such as book-marks) to online storage. That content and those settings are pushed automatically to all your Apple devices that use the same Apple ID through a wireless connection. With iCloud, the primary data storage is in iCloud itself, and all your devices sync to iCloud. That's how you can buy a new device and, as part of the setup process, bring all your data and settings in from iCloud to the new device.

Syncing makes two different devices have the same data in the same condition (that is, the latest updates in both places). If you want to save a specific version of something, that's usually not syncing: You *copy* something to a secure location, and you usually don't want it to be synced. An example of this would be your year-end tax data: You may want to copy it to someplace safe, but you don't want it updated. You do want your ongoing checking account transactions to be updated over the course of the year.

All you need to do is create an iCloud account (go to https://www.icloud.com and click Create Yours Now) and then make settings on your devices to specify which types of content you want pushed to each device. After you've done that, any content that you create (except video) or purchase on one device — such as music, apps, books, and TV shows, as well as documents created in Apple's iWork apps, photos, and so on — can be synced among your devices automatically. (iWork is a very useful suite of apps for Mac and iOS devices. The apps are free, and you can find out more at http://www.apple.com/iwork/.)

When you get an iCloud account, you get 5GB of free storage. Content that you purchase through Apple (such as apps, books, music, and TV shows) isn't counted against your storage. If you want additional storage, you can buy an upgrade from one of your devices. You can buy 50GB of extra storage for 99 cents per month, 200GB for $2.99 per month, 1TB (terabyte) for $9.99 a month, and 2TB for $19.99 Note that these prices are subject to change. The good news is that like most cloud storage, the prices tend to go down. You can start with the free allotment and then monitor your usage to see when you need to update it.

To upgrade your storage, tap Settings ⇨ iCloud ⇨ Storage ⇨ Manage Storage. In the pane that appears, tap Change Storage Plan. Tap the amount you need and then tap Buy. You can also choose Buy More Storage in the Manage Storage section if you're willing to pay more to get a greater storage amount.

If you change your mind, you can get in touch with Apple within 15 days to cancel your upgrade.

If you pay $24.99 a year for the iTunes Match service, you can sync almost any amount of music in your iTunes library to your devices, which may be a less expensive way to go than paying for added iCloud storage. Tap Match in iTunes or visit https://support.apple.com/en-us/HT204146 for more information.

Turn on iCloud backup

Before you can use iCloud, you need an iCloud account. For most people, based on the Apple ID you set up at installation or afterward with Settings ⇨ iCloud as you see in Figure 3-1.

To set up iCloud Backup on your iPad, follow these steps:

1. Tap Settings ⇨ iCloud ⇨ Backup.

2. In the Backup screen, tap the on/off switch to turn on iCloud Backup (see Figure 3-6).

   You can also do an immediate backup from this screen by tapping Back Up Now (also shown in Figure 3-6).

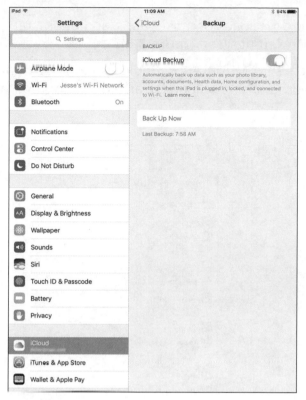

FIGURE 3-6

Make iCloud sync settings

The content you purchase and download from the iTunes Store can be synced among your devices automatically via iCloud. When you have an iCloud account up and running (refer to "Use iCloud," earlier in this chapter), you must specify which types of content should be synced with your iPad via iCloud.

TIP

If you need help with any of these features, you can always find and download the Apple manual in the iBooks Store (it's a free iBook).

1. Tap Settings ⇨ iCloud.

2. In the iCloud Settings pane, shown in **Figure 3-7**, tap the on/off switch for any item that's turned off that you want to turn on (or vice versa). You can sync iCloud Drive, Photos, Mail, Contacts, Calendars, Reminders, Safari, Home, Notes, News, Keychain, Backup, and Find My iPad (covered in the next section).

3. To enable automatic downloads of music, apps, and books, tap iTunes & App Store in Settings (see **Figure 3-8**).

4. Tap the on/off switches for Music, Apps, Books & Audiobooks, and Updates to set up automatic downloads of any of this content to your iPad via iCloud.

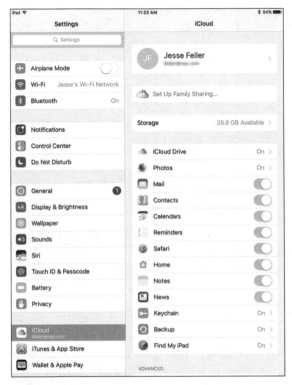

FIGURE 3-7

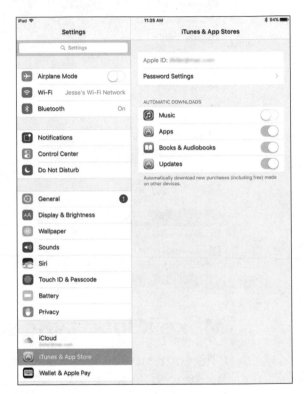

FIGURE 3-8

Find a lost or stolen iPad

If you want to allow iCloud to provide a service for locating a lost or stolen iPad, tap the on/off switch in the Find My iPad field (refer to Figure 3-7) to activate it. This service helps you use another device to locate, send a message to, or delete content from your iPad if it falls into other hands. I strongly recommend using this feature.

Once you're turned on Find My iPad, you can use another iOS or macOS to find it. Here's what you do.

1. On the other device, open Safari and log in with your Apple ID (if you have several accounts, use the one for the iPad that's lost). You'll see the screen shown in Figure 3-9.

FIGURE 3-9

2. Tap or click on Open Find My iPhone. (Use this to find any device.)

3. A map opens as you see in Figure 3-10.

4. Zoom in the map to see the device(s). Tap a device and you'll see its name at the bottom of the window, as you see in Figure 3-11.

5. Use the buttons at the bottom of the window to:

    • *Play a sound on the device.* This is useful if you or someone else is near where it might be. (Think of it as the lost-behind-the-sofa-cushion button.)

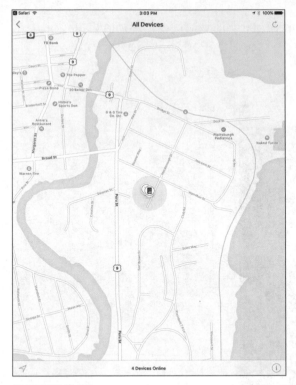

FIGURE 3-10

FIGURE 3-11

- *Set Lost Mode.* You can provide a message to be shown on the screen. (Maybe with your phone number in case someone finds the device.) No alerts for phone calls, messages, or notifications will be shown. If possible, credit and debit card you have set up for Apple Pay will be suspended. You must set a passcode if you don't have one. The passcode (new or old) will be required to unlock the device.

- *Erase.* You can erase the data from the selected device with the right-hand button. (Yes, it works with Apple Watch as well as iPad and iPhone.)

6. If you have CarPlay set up, your car may be located on the map as well. (This is useful for parking lots!)

Apple added a neat feature to Find My iPad. With this new feature, when the battery gets low, your iPad will send a message with its location to iCloud.

TIP

Chapter 4

Making Your iPad More Accessible

iPad users are all different; some face visual, motor, or hearing challenges. If you're one of these folks, you'll be glad to hear that the iPad offers some handy accessibility features.

To make your screen easier to read, you can adjust the brightness or change wallpaper. You can also set up the VoiceOver feature to read onscreen elements out loud. Then you can turn a slew of features on or off, including Zoom, Invert Colors, Speak Selection, and Large Type.

If hearing is your challenge, you can do the obvious thing and adjust the system volume. The iPad also allows you to use mono audio (useful when you're wearing headphones) and an LED flash when an alert sounds. Features that help you deal with physical and motor challenges include AssistiveTouch, for those who have difficulty using the iPad touchscreen; Switch Control, for working with adaptive accessories; and the Home Button and Call Audio Routing settings, which allow you to adjust how quickly you must tap the iPad screen to work with features.

The Guided Access feature provides help for those who have difficulty focusing on one task. It also provides a handy mode for showing presentations of content in settings where you don't want users to flit off to other apps, as in school or at a public kiosk.

iOS 10 offers two new accessibility features: Magnifier and Display Accommodations. These features help with visibility concerns. Magnifier is akin to a digital magnifying glass, and Display Accommodations helps users with color blindness and other vision issues more easily work with the iPad.

Use Magnifier

The newest accessibility feature is *Magnifier*. It's an accessibility feature, but almost everyone needs a magnifier at one time or another. To access Magnifier, tap Settings ⇨ General ⇨ Accessibility, as shown in **Figure 4-1**. Then press the Home button three times to turn it on. (I find it easiest to do that with my thumb while I'm holding the iPad.)

When Magnifier is on, you can use the back camera of your iPad just like a magnifying glass. In fact, it's like an illuminated magnifying glass. You see the magnified image on your screen. A slider lets you set the degree of magnification, as shown in **Figure 4-2**. You can also turn on a light (at the left of the bottom in Figure b) and lock the magnification level (also at the left). At the right, the three circles let you change the colors. Figure 4-2 shows a magnified close-up of the base of a bronze statuette. On the left, the artist's name is about two inches wide. You can enlarge the magnification even more as you see on the right. Use the round button (like a camera shutter) to have the iPad adjust its focus for what you're pointing at.

You can combine magnification with your iPad's portability so that you can reach up to (or behind) an object and magnify something that would not only be too small to see otherwise or would be out of view.

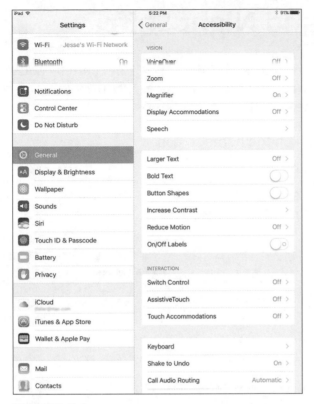

FIGURE 4-1

FIGURE 4-2

Set Brightness and Night Shift

Especially when you're using the iPad as an e-reader, you may find that a slightly less-bright screen reduces strain on your eyes. To adjust screen brightness, follow these steps:

1. Tap the Settings icon on the home screen.

2. Tap Display & Brightness.

3. To control brightness manually, tap the Auto-Brightness on/off switch (see **Figure 4-3**) to turn off this feature.

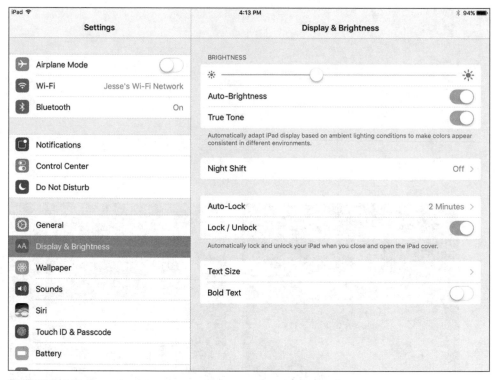

FIGURE 4-3

4. Tap and drag the Brightness slider (refer to Figure 4-3) to the right to make the screen brighter or to the left to make it dimmer.

5. Press the Home button to close Settings.

If glare on the screen is a problem for you, consider getting a screen protector. This thin film not only protects your screen from damage, but also reduces glare.

In the iBooks e-reader app, you can set a sepia tone for the page, which may be easier on your eyes. See Chapter 12 for more about using iBooks.

Night Shift can be set to be used during hours of darkness. It changes the colors to reduce the amount of blue in the images on your iPad. Bright blue light seems to interfere with sleep in some people, so turning on Night Shift if you read before bed (or in bed) may help you sleep better.

Change the Wallpaper

The default iPad's background image may be pretty, but it may not be the best for you. Choosing different wallpaper may help you see all the icons on your home screen more clearly.

To change the wallpaper, follow these steps:

1. Tap the Settings icon on the home screen.

2. On the left side of the Settings screen, tap Wallpaper (refer to Figure 4-3).

3. In the Wallpaper settings that appear, tap Choose a New Wallpaper and then do one of the following:

    - Tap a wallpaper category: Dynamic or Stills, as shown in **Figure 4-4**. View your options, and tap one to select it.

    - Tap an album in the Photos section, locate a picture to use as your wallpaper, and tap it.

4. At the bottom of the preview screen that appears (see **Figure 4-5**), tap Set Lock Screen, Set Home Screen, or Set Both to use the image for both the lock screen and home screen.

FIGURE 4-4

FIGURE 4-5

5. (Optional) You can tap Perspective Zoom to turn that feature on or off. When it's turned on, Perspective Zoom makes images move slightly as you move your iPad.

6. Press the Home button to return to your home screen, where (if you've set the new wallpaper to appear on your home screen) the new wallpaper is set as the background.

Set Up VoiceOver

VoiceOver reads the names of screen elements and settings to you, and changes the way you provide input to the iPad. In Notes, for example, you can have VoiceOver read the name of the Notes buttons to you, and when you enter notes, it reads words or characters you've entered. It can also tell you whether features such as Auto–Correction are on.

To set up VoiceOver, follow these steps:

1. Tap Settings ➪ General ➪ Accessibility.

2. In the Accessibility pane, shown in **Figure 4-6**, tap the VoiceOver on/off option to display the VoiceOver pane.

3. In the VoiceOver pane, shown in **Figure 4-7**, tap the VoiceOver on/off switch to turn on this feature. The first time you use it, you see a message that lets you know that enabling VoiceOver changes the gestures you use with iPad. Double-tap OK to proceed.

   When VoiceOver is on, you first tap to select an item such as a button, which causes VoiceOver to read the name of the item to you; then you double-tap the item to activate its function.

4. Tap the VoiceOver Practice button to select it and then double-tap the button to open VoiceOver Practice. (Double-tapping replaces the tapping action when VoiceOver is turned on.) Practice using gestures such as pinching or flicking left, and VoiceOver tells you what action each gesture initiates.

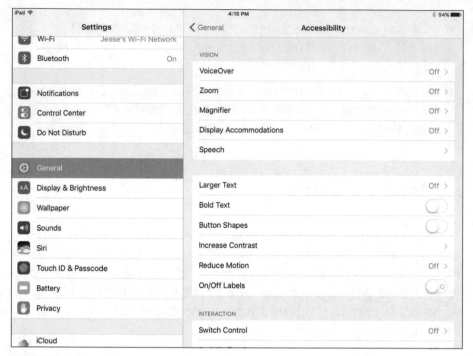

FIGURE 4-6

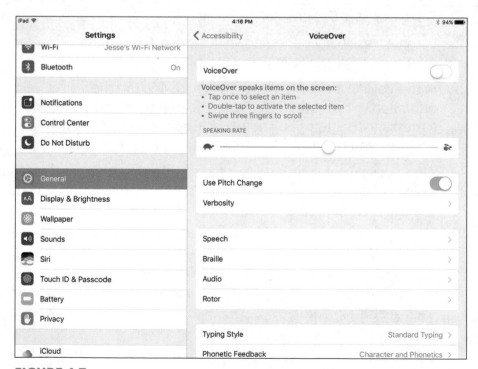

FIGURE 4-7

5. Tap the Done button and then double-tap the same button to return to the VoiceOver settings.

6. If you want VoiceOver to read words or characters to you (in the Notes app, for example), scroll down to tap and then double-tap Typing Feedback. In the Typing Feedback settings, tap and then double-tap to select the option you prefer. The Words option causes VoiceOver to read words to you, but not characters, such as the dollar sign ($). The Characters and Words option causes VoiceOver to read both, and so on.

7. Press the Home button to return to the home screen.

Read the next section to find out how to navigate your iPad after you've turned on VoiceOver.

You can change the language that VoiceOver speaks. Tap Settings⇨ General⇨International⇨Language, and select another language. This action also changes the language used for the labels of home-screen icons and various settings and fields on the iPad.

You can use the Accessibility Shortcut setting to toggle the VoiceOver, Zoom, Switch Control, AssistiveTouch, Grayscale, and Invert Colors features rapidly. Tap Settings⇨Accessibility⇨Accessibility Shortcut. In the right pane of the Accessibility Shortcut screen, choose what you want a triple-press of the Home button to activate. Thereafter, a triple press of the Home button opens the option you selected in this screen (such as Zoom or Invert Colors) wherever you go on your iPad.

Use VoiceOver

After VoiceOver is turned on, you need to figure out how to use it. I won't kid you — using it is awkward at first, but you'll get the hang of it!

Here are the main onscreen gestures you should know:

» **Tap an item to select it.** VoiceOver speaks the item's name.

» **Double-tap the selected item.** This action activates the item.

» **Flick with three fingers.** It takes three fingers to scroll around a page when VoiceOver is turned on.

Table 4-1 lists additional gestures that help you use VoiceOver.

TABLE 4-1   **VoiceOver Gestures**

Gesture	Effect
Flick right or left.	Selects the next or preceding item.
Tap with two fingers.	Stops speaking the current item.
Flick two fingers up.	Reads everything from the top of the screen.
Flick two fingers down.	Reads everything from the current position.
Flick three fingers up or down.	Scrolls up or down one page at a time.
Flick three fingers right or left.	Goes to the next or preceding page.
Tap three fingers.	Speaks the scroll status (such as "line 20 of 100").
Flick four fingers up or down.	Goes to the first or last element on a page.

If tapping with two or three fingers is difficult for you, try tapping with one finger of one hand and one or two fingers of the other hand. When you're double- or triple-tapping, you must perform these gestures as quickly as you can to make them work.

Check out all the settings for VoiceOver, including Braille and Language Rotor (for making language choices) here: https://www.apple.com/voiceover/info/guide/_1131.html#vo27992.

Make Additional Vision Settings

Several vision features are simple on/off settings, so rather than give you the steps to get to those settings repeatedly, I provide this useful list of additional features that you can turn on or off after you tap Settings ⇨ General ⇨ Accessibility:

» **Zoom:** The Zoom feature enlarges the contents displayed on the iPad's screen when you double-tap the screen with three fingers. The Zoom feature works almost everywhere on the iPad: in Photos, on web pages, on your home screens, in Mail, in Music, and in Videos. Give it a try!

» **Display Accommodations:** The Display Accommodations setting can reverse the colors on your screen so that white backgrounds are black and black text is white (invert colors), use color filters to help differentiate colors, and reduce the white point which has the effect of making bright colors a bit less so.

The Invert Colors feature works well in some places and not so well in others. In the Photos app, for example, pictures appear almost like photo negatives. Likewise, your home-screen image likewise looks a bit strange. And don't even think of playing a video with this feature turned on! If you need help reading text, however, White on Black can be useful in several apps.

» **Larger Text:** If having larger text in apps such as Contacts, Mail, and Notes would be helpful to you, you can turn on the Larger Type feature and choose the text size that works best for you.

» **Bold Text:** Turning on this setting first restarts your iPad (after asking you for permission to do so) and then causes text in various apps and on the Settings screen to be bold.

» **Increase Contrast:** Use these three settings to add greater contrast to backgrounds in some areas of the iPad and apps, which should improve visibility.

» **Reduce Motion:** If you turned this setting on but would rather have it off, tap this accessibility feature and then tap the on/off switch to turn off the parallax effect, which causes the background of your home screens to appear to float as you move the iPad around.

» **On/Off Labels:** If you have trouble making out colors and so have trouble telling when an on/off switch is on (green) or off (white), use the On/Off Labels setting to add a circle to the right of a setting when it's off and a white vertical line to a setting when it's on (see **Figure 4-8**).

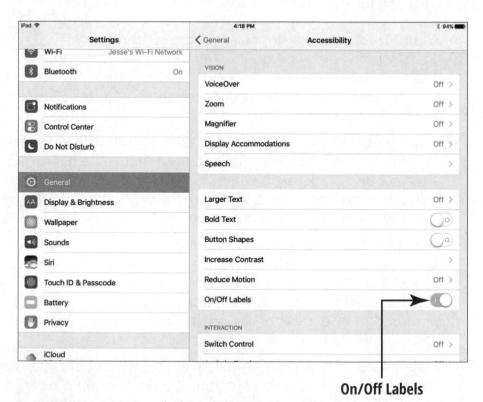

On/Off Labels

FIGURE 4-8

Adjust the Volume

Though individual apps such as Music and Video have their own volume settings, you can set your iPad's system volume for your ringer and alerts as well to help you better hear what's going on. To set the volume, follow these steps:

1. Tap Settings ⇨ Sounds.

2. In the Sounds pane that appears (see **Figure 4-9**), tap and drag the Ringer and Alerts slider to the right to increase the volume of these audible attention-grabbers or to the left to lower the volume.

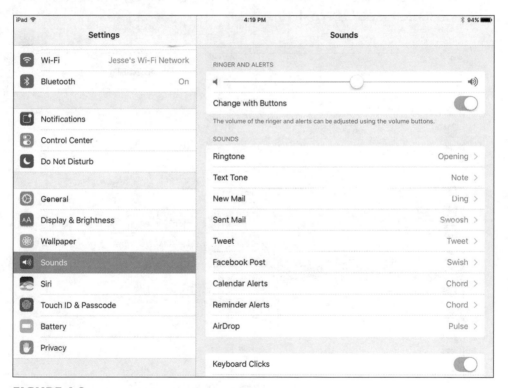

FIGURE 4-9

3. Press the Home button to display the home screen.

In the Sounds pane, you can turn on or off the sounds that the iPad makes when certain events occur (such as new mail or Calendar alerts). These sounds are turned on by default.

Set Up Subtitles and Captioning

Closed captioning and subtitles help folks with hearing challenges enjoy entertainment and educational content. To set up this feature, follow these steps:

1. Tap Settings ➪ General ➪ Accessibility to display the Accessibility screen (see **Figure 4-10**).

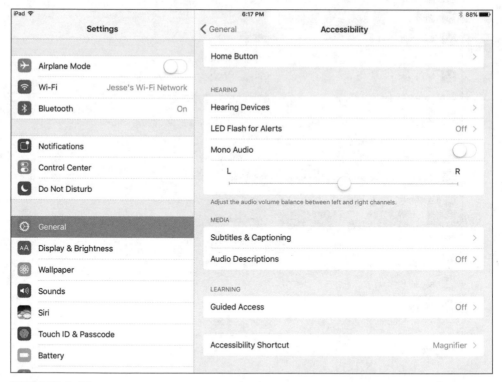

FIGURE 4-10

2. Scroll down to the Media section, and tap Subtitles & Captioning to display the Subtitles & Captioning screen (see **Figure 4-11**).

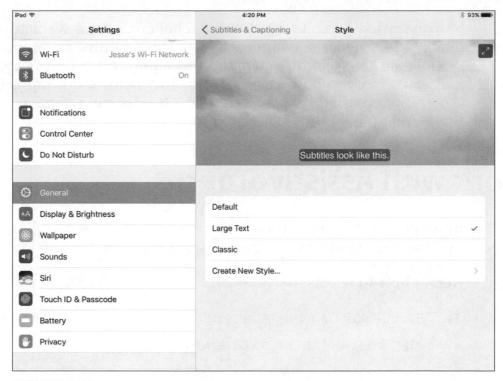

FIGURE 4-11

3. Tap the on/off switch to turn on Closed Captions + SDH (Subtitles for the Deaf and Hard of Hearing). If you like, you can also tap Style and choose a text style for the captions.

4. Tap the Style setting, and choose Default, Large Text, Classic (which looks like a typewriter font), or Create a New Style to personalize the font, size, and color for your captions.

Manage Mono Audio

Using the stereo effect in headphones or a headset breaks up sounds so that you hear a portion in one ear and a portion in the other ear, simulating the way that your ears process sounds. If there's only one channel of sound, that sound is sent to both ears.

If you're hard of hearing or deaf in one ear, however, you're picking up only a portion of the sound in your hearing ear, which can be frustrating. If you have hearing challenges and want to use the iPad with a headset connected, you should turn on Mono Audio. When that accessibility setting is turned on, all sound is combined and distributed to both ears. To turn this feature on, tap Settings⇨ General⇨Accessibility, scroll down to the Hearing section, and tap the Mono Audio on/off switch.

Work with AssistiveTouch

AssistiveTouch helps those who have challenges working with a touchscreen or who must use an assistive device for providing input.

Here's how to use AssistiveTouch:

1. Tap Settings⇨General⇨Accessibility.

2. In the Accessibility pane, scroll down to tap AssistiveTouch.

3. In the pane that appears, tap the on/off switch for AssistiveTouch to turn it on (see **Figure 4-12**).

   A gray square, called the AssistiveTouch button, appears onscreen. This square button now appears in the same location in whatever home screen or app you display on your iPad, although you can move it around the screen with your finger.

4. Tap the Home button to display the home screen and then tap the AssistiveTouch button to display its options, shown in **Figure 4-13**. You can tap Device or Custom on the options panel to see additional choices, tap Siri to activate the personal-assistant feature, tap Notification Center or Control Center to display those panels, or tap Home to go directly to the home screen.

Table 4-2 shows the major options available in AssistiveTouch and their purposes.

In addition to using Siri, don't forget about using the Dictation key on the onscreen keyboard to speak text entries and basic keyboard commands. See Chapter 2 for more information about the Dictation key.

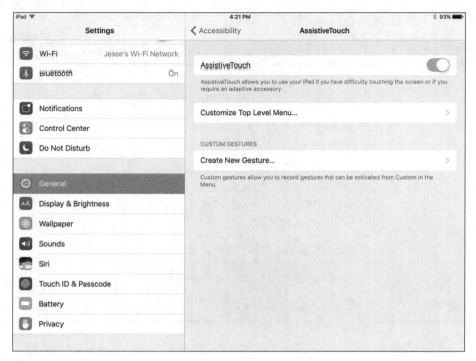

FIGURE 4-12

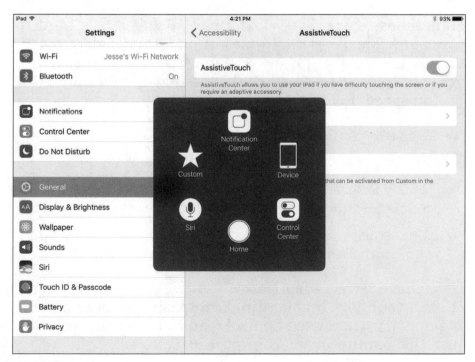

FIGURE 4-13

TABLE 4-2 **AssistiveTouch Controls**

Control	Purpose
Siri	Activates the Siri feature, which allows you to speak questions and make requests of your iPad.
Custom	Displays a set of gestures with only the Pinch gesture preset; you can tap any of the other blank squares to add your own favorite gestures.
Device	Allows you to rotate the screen, lock the screen, turn the volume up or down, mute or unmute sound, or shake the iPad to undo an action by using various presets.
Home	Sends you to the home screen.
Notification Center	Displays Notification Center.
Control Center	Displays Control Center.

Manage Home-Button Speed

Sometimes, if you have dexterity challenges, it's hard to double-press or triple-press the Home button fast enough to make an effect. Choose the Slow or Slowest setting when you tap this setting to allow you a bit more time to make that second or third tap. To set Home-button speed, follow these steps:

1. Tap Settings ⇨ General ⇨ Accessibility.

2. Scroll down to tap Home Button.

3. Tap the Slow or Slowest setting to change how rapidly you must double-press or triple-press the Home button to initiate an action.

4. You can also use the Rest Finger to Open option to open your iPad with Touch ID instead of pressing the Home button.

If you have certain adaptive accessories, you can use head gestures to control your iPad, highlighting features in sequence and then selecting one. Use the Switch Control feature in the Accessibility screen to turn this feature on and configure its settings.

Focus Learning with Guided Access

Guided Access is a feature you can use to limit a user's access to the iPad to a single app and even limit access to that app to certain features. This feature has many potential uses, ranging from a classroom to use by someone with attention deficit disorder and even to a public setting (such as a kiosk) where you don't want users to be able to open other apps. In a way, it's the opposite of accessibility because it limits what people can do with your iPad.

To use Guided Access, follow these steps:

1. Tap Settings ⇨ General ⇨ Accessibility ⇨ Guided Access.

2. On the screen that appears, tap the Guided Access on/off button to turn the feature on.

3. Tap Passcode Settings to display the Passcode Settings screen (see **Figure 4-14**).

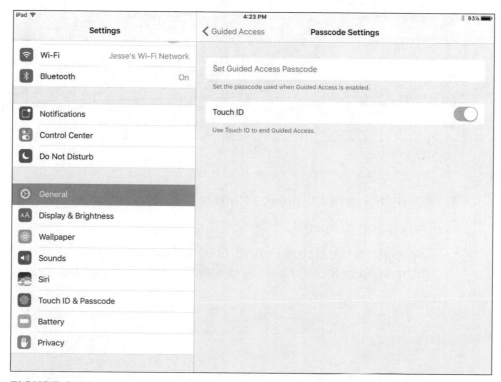

FIGURE 4-14

4. Tap Set Guided Access Passcode to activate a passcode so that those using an app can't return to the home screen to access other apps.

5. In the Set Passcode window that appears (see **Figure 4-15**), enter a passcode, using the numeric pad. Enter the number again when you're prompted to do so.

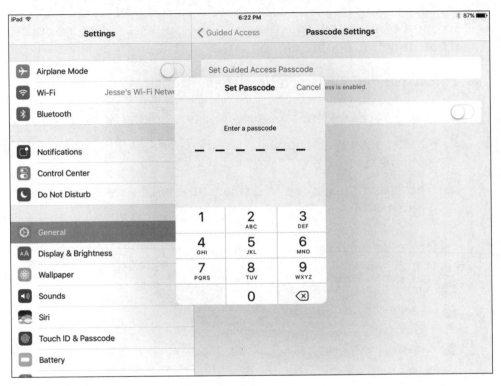

FIGURE 4-15

6. Press the Home button to return to the home screen.

7. Tap an app to open it.

8. Triple-press the Home button. Several buttons appear at the bottom of the screen, including a Hardware Buttons Options button.

9. Tap the Hardware Buttons Options button to display these settings:

- *Sleep/Wake Button:* You can put your iPad to sleep or wake it up with a triple press of the Home button.

- *Volume Buttons:* Tap Always On or Always Off. If you don't want users to be able to adjust volume by using the volume toggle on the side of the iPad, for example, use the Volume Buttons setting.

- *Motion:* Turn this setting off if you don't want users to disable the motion sensors — so that users can't play a race-car-driving game, for example.

- *Keyboards:* Use this setting to prohibit people from using the keyboard to enter text.

10. Turn on the Touch switch if you don't want users to be able to use this setting.

11. The Time Limit Options button lets you set a specific time limit for use.

12. After you have chosen your Guided Access options, tap Start in the top-right corner of the screen or Cancel in the top left.

13. You're now limited to the options you have set in Steps 9 through 12. When you want to get out of Guided Access, triple-press the Home button, and then enter your passcode (if you set one in Step 5) to return to the home screen. (In a classroom setting, you might do this for your students.)

2

Reaching Out with Your iPad

IN THIS PART. . .

"Hey Siri" — my wish is your command.

Log on to the web.

Send and receive email.

Tweet, use FaceBook, use Messages (and impress your loved ones!).

Chapter **5**
Talking to Siri

Siri is an "intelligent assistant." The assistant is built on voice recognition technology and a lot of what is called *artificial intelligence.* Both of those technologies work together to provide the useful experience you can have on your iPad (or iPhone or, with macOS Sierra, your Mac). The data that you provide on your iOS devices (particularly data in Contacts and your Calendar) is key to Siri's functionality along with data Siri retrieves from the web. Thus, to function properly, Siri needs to have an Internet connection.

This chapter shows you the basics of turning on Siri and using it. You'll also see more advanced tips for improving Siri's performance (and improving the way you ask Siri for results).

Turn on Siri on Your iPad

Siri is built into your iPad, but it needs to be turned on. You're asked during setup whether you want to turn it on, but you can always come back later to do that. To turn on Siri, follow these steps:

1. Tap Settings and then choose Siri, as you see in **Figure 5-1**.

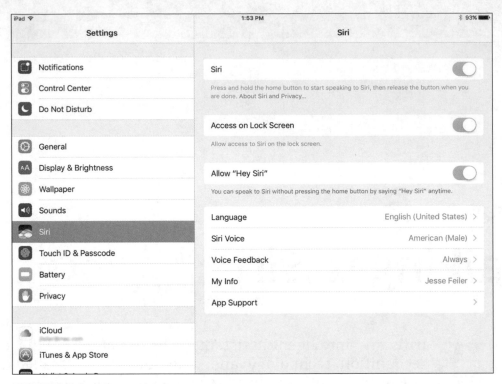

FIGURE 5-1

If Siri isn't on, tap the first button. You can then press and hold the Home button and begin speaking to Siri. Release the button when you have finished your question.

2. Using Settings, you can make Siri easier to use by enabling it from the lock screen. You also can allow "Hey Siri" to turn Siri on. This means you don't have to worry about pressing and holding the Home button.

TIP

If you regularly use your iPad in proximity to your iPhone, you might want to turn "Hey Siri" on only for your iPhone (or only for your iPad). That will avoid both devices responding to you.

3. Figure 5-1 shows that you can also choose the language for Siri — there are nine versions of English, by the way. You can choose a male or female voice. Voice Feedback gives you the options shown in **Figure 5-2.**

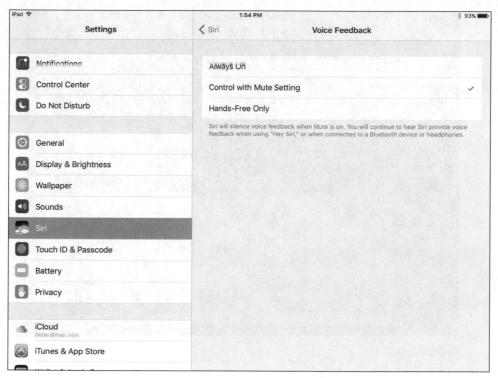

FIGURE 5-2

4. The Voice Feedback options shown in Figure 5-2 all rely on the Mute button, which you can turn on or off in Control Center. In **Figure 5-3,** the Mute button is on — it's the button with a bell on it and a line through it in that figure.

   The three options for Voice Feedback are:

   - **Always On.** Mute has no effect: Siri always uses the speakers.
   - **Control with Mute Setting.** If Mute is on (as it is in Figure 5-3), Siri is heard through Bluetooth headphones or another device but not through the iPad speakers. If you launch Siri with "Hey Siri," the speakers are enabled for Siri.
   - **Hands-Free Only.** You only hear Siri when you use "Hey Siri" or Bluetooth headphones or another Bluetooth device.

5. App Support (see **Figure 5-4**) reveals a list of the third-party apps that work with Siri. You can turn each one on or off. For example, if there are ride sharing services that work with Siri, you might want to use your favorite or you might not care.

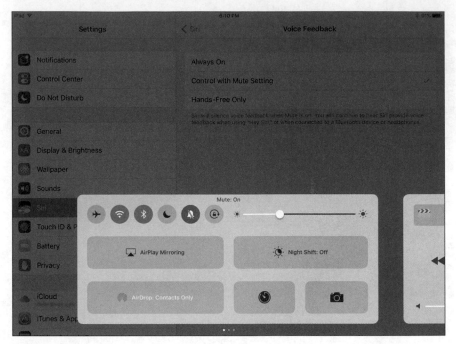

FIGURE 5-3

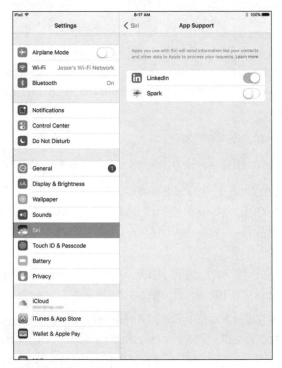

FIGURE 5-4

Work with Siri

Working with Siri is simple if you remember two things: You can ask questions of Siri, and you can tell Siri to do things.

Ask Siri questions

Siri's primary interactions with you are answering your questions and carrying out your commands. To ask Siri questions, follow these steps:

1. Press and hold the Home button or say "Hey Siri" if you've turned on that option as shown previously in Figure 5-1.

2. Ask Siri your question. As you speak, you can see the transcription. Siri may back up and revise the transcription as you are speaking and the meaning of your question becomes clearer.

3. Release the Home button when you finish your question.

4. Siri will respond. The response usually will tell you the source of the answer if Siri has looked it up. You can usually tap Siri's response on the screen to get more data.

You can customize Siri's response voice, as shown in Figure 5-1.

Following are some sample questions you can ask Siri:

» "What time is it?" Siri tells you the time and displays it onscreen. If you tap the time on the screen, you'll see that it comes from Clock (Clock is identified in the status bar at the top of the screen in this case).

» "What is the temperature?" Siri tells you and displays it onscreen. Again, if you tap the screen, you see that the temperature data came from the Weather app. (The source changes from time to time as Siri evolves.)

» "When is my next appointment?" (or "Do I have any appointments later today?") Siri displays your appointment(s) — if any — from Calendar.

After showing your appointments, Siri may ask whether you want to see the details. "Yes" or "No" is the perfect answer.

» "Does Bruce have a mobile number?" Siri looks in Contacts and shows you a list of all the mobile numbers for people in your Contacts whose first name is Bruce. It's interesting that it's not what you've actually asked, but it is likely to give you the result that you want. Then you can ask Siri to call the person you want to talk to.

» "Who is in the National League playoffs?" Siri shows the teams and the playoff schedule. As with most responses, you'll see where Siri found the data on the display (sometimes it's just a logo or some fine print).

» "What can you help me with?" If you remember only one Siri command, maybe it should be this one. That commands starts a conversation that can take quite a bit of time.

REMEMBER

Siri always asks you before doing anything irreversible or ambiguous. Gradually, you'll understand what you have to specify to Siri and what you don't.

Issue commands

You can ask Siri to open an app, but many of the most common interactions focus on actions, not on apps. This is important because over time, Siri may use different tools to fulfill your requests. It uses data from Calendar, Reminders, and Contacts by default, but sometimes it launches a web search for you, for example.

SMART ANSWERS

Apple has built some personality and cheekiness into Siri. Here's a sample interaction:

You: Can I watch "BBC Question Time" on Apple TV?

Siri: Allow me to direct you to Apple's rather fabulous website.

(At this point, you can tap the button that Siri presents or ask Siri to go there.)

Now you can see why entering data is so important. If you're going to want to be able to call people at their mobile numbers, you have to indicate in Contacts what is a mobile number for your contacts.

Siri commands don't have to specify a particular app on your iPad. You can issue commands that start with words or phrases such as these:

» Wake me up at. . .

» What song is this?

» Call [someone at. . .]

» Remind me. . .

» Schedule. . .

» What movies are playing near here?

» Play [song]

Experiment with these commands as well as the samples on Apple's Siri page (www.apple.com/ios/siri). The commands change both when there are new versions of iOS and as Siri learns more about you. And just to keep things moving, as you add or update apps that are enabled for Siri, new commands may appear. Fortunately, the structure of Siri commands is pretty constant: It starts with a command (wake me, call, what is, and so forth). Learn from kids using Siri to just try to see what happens.

Are we there yet? A Siri case study

If you spend time watching people use Siri, you'll recognize the characteristics of people who use Siri the best. Kids catch on to Siri very quickly. (Type "kids and Siri" into your favorite search engine for some anecdotes and suggestions.)

You can ask Siri to tell you a joke. You can tell Siri you don't feel too well, and Siri may ask what's wrong or, at the very least offer you sympathy.

Here is a useful Siri conversation that may be useful in the car. Here are the steps:

1. Start with "Hey Siri, get directions to home." (Or the address of someone or someplace in Contacts.)

2. When the directions appear, say "Hey Siri, go" (or tap the Go button).

3. Directions for the first leg appear.

4. Say, "Hey Siri, are we there yet?"

5. Siri will give you a time estimate for arriving.

6. As desired, go back to Step 4 ("Hey Siri, are we there yet?") Siri never tires of "Are we there yet?" You'll always get an answer based on your current location.

You might want to keep these steps in mind for your next car trip with the grandkids.

Use Siri with Third-Party Apps

iOS 10 lets developers create third-party apps that use Siri. These apps can use Siri to support VoIP calling, messaging, payments, photos, workouts, and ride booking. Aspects of CarPlay and restaurant reservations can be implemented by developers working directly with Apple, too.

Siri integration was rolled out to developers with iOS 10. It's there for developers and their apps to use, so you don't have to wait for periodic updates to iOS to get new Siri-enabled apps: They're available as soon as developers add them to the App Store. You can find the Siri-enabled apps that you have on your iPad by going to Settings ➪ Siri ➪ App Support, as shown previously in Figure 5-3.

As this is being written the list is growing rapidly. You can use a web browser to find Siri-enabled apps (or ask Siri to do the search for you). There are several areas that developers are particularly looking at Siri for:

- » Ride sharing. Apps that are useful to people on the go (either on foot, public transportation, or cars) are great candidates for Siri integration. You'll find the Lyft, Uber, Didi (China), and Tappsi (Colombia) apps with Siri interfaces. More are coming every day.

- » Restaurants. People on the go often get hungry, so Open Table and Yelp are now integrated with Siri.

- » Workouts and tourism. Siri is great at giving you directions and keeping track of where you are and how long you've been traveling or working out. Apps like Nike+ Run Club, Map My Run, Pocket Yoga, and Runtastic work with Siri.

- » Messaging. In addition to Messages, which is built into iOS, you'll find a variety of other apps such as WhatsApp, LinkedIn, Convo, WeChat, and Slack. It's really convenient to send a message without having to type on a screen or keyboard.

- » Scheduling apps. From movies to museums to food stores, apps let you find out when and where things are that you're interested in. More and more of these apps now work with Siri. You may find that you already have quite a few Siri-enabled apps on your iPad.

Improve Your Communication with Siri

Here are some steps to try to improve communication between yourself and Siri. Some are basic steps for handling questions and commands from people to computers (several of these will improve your search results no matter what search engine you use). Try any of these that seem appropriate:

- » **Be verbose.** Many people try to ask a search engine to do too little. They may say or type "date for snow tires," but the result will be better if you ask, "When should I put snow tires on?" Even simple questions of fact are answered better if you include "when is," "where is," or the like. Siri takes all these words into account in formulating an answer. Although you may be hesitant to type a long question, you're speaking to Siri, so speak up.

» **Don't let mistakes go by.** As you speak to Siri, you'll see the interpretation of your speech displayed as text. You can tap to edit the text. That will get you to the answer quickly, and in many cases Siri will learn how to interpret what you said properly.

» **Explain and things.** Siri can interpret a statement such as "Alice is my daughter." After that, you can say "Remind me to all Alice." Siri doesn't care what the role or relationship is. It also helps if the person or place is in Contacts. You should only have to do this once.

» **Correct things.** Siri got the pronunciation of my last name right on the first try (something many people don't do). However, I could have said, "That's not how you pronounce <whatever the word is>."

» **Ask Siri.** Siri responds correctly to the question, "What can I ask?" You might want to ask that question when you've got a new version of iOS. New commands are always being added. And even if you're a long-time user, you might have not noticed or forgotten some commands that you can use productively.

REMEMBER

Training Siri to become useful to you is not a process of practicing voice recognition. Rather, it's a process of reminding yourself to put data in Contacts, Calendar, and Reminders so that it's available to Siri. If Siri doesn't respond the way you expect, spend a moment or two to think about how it works and see if you can't train yourself in a few minutes to be more productive. The training works both ways: As you use Siri more and more, Siri also learns.

Chapter **6**

Browsing the Internet with Safari

Getting on the Internet with your iPad is easy thanks to its Wi-Fi or cellular capabilities. After you're online, the preinstalled *browser* (software that helps you navigate the Internet's contents) is your ticket to a wide world of information, entertainment, education, and more. This browser, Safari, will look familiar to you if you've used it on a PC or Mac computer, though the way you move around it on the iPad touchscreen may be new to you. If you've never used Safari, in this chapter, I take you by the hand and show you all its ins and outs.

In this chapter, you discover how to connect your iPad to the Internet, navigate web pages, and use iCloud tabs to share your browsing among devices that share your Apple ID. Along the way, you see how to place a bookmark for a favorite site, pin an active site to your Safari window, and place a web clip on your home screen. You also discover how to view your browsing history, save online images to your photo library, post photos to certain sites from within Safari, and email or tweet a link to a friend. You explore the Safari Reader and Safari Reading List features, and see how to keep yourself safer while you're online by using Private Browsing. Finally, you review the simple steps involved in printing what you find online.

Connect to the Internet

How you connect to the Internet depends on which iPad model you own:

» **Wi-Fi:** Every iPad can use a Wi-Fi network to connect to the Internet (or anything else that's available through that Wi-Fi network). You can set up this type of network in your own home by using your computer and some equipment from your Internet service provider. You can also connect over public Wi-Fi networks, referred to as *hotspots.* You'll probably be surprised to discover how many hotspots your town or city has. Look for Internet cafes, coffee shops, hotels, libraries, and transportation centers such as airports or bus stations, for example. Many of these businesses display signs alerting you to their free Wi-Fi.

» **Cellular:** If you own a cellular-enabled iPad, you can still use a Wi-Fi connection (in fact, when one is available, the iPad defaults to using Wi-Fi to save money), but you can also use the paid data network provided by your service provider (AT&T, Verizon, T-Mobile, or Sprint) to connect from just about anywhere you can get cellphone coverage via a cellular network with 3G or 4G LTE capability.

TIP

See Chapter 1 for more about the capabilities of iPad models and the costs associated with cellular service.

Connect via Cellular

If you have a Wi–Fi + Cellular iPad, you don't have to do anything. When you have a contract for data coverage, the connection is made on your iPad automatically wherever cellular service is available, just as it is on your cellphone.

Connect via Wi-Fi

To connect to a Wi-Fi network, you must complete a few steps for each network:

1. Tap Settings ⇨ Wi-Fi.

2. Make sure that Wi-Fi is set to On (see **Figure 6-1**).

FIGURE 6-1

3. Choose a network to connect to from the list under Choose a Network if more than one network is listed. Network names should appear automatically when you're in range of those networks.

You may also see one or more personal hotspots: These are Wi-Fi hotspots created by a cellphone or other device with hotspot capabilities. If you have an iPhone, here are the directions for setting it up as a personal hotspot: https://support.apple.com/en-us/HT204023.

After you select a network, you may see a message asking for a password. Ask the owner of the hotspot (such as a hotel desk clerk or business owner) for this password, or (if you're connecting to your home network) enter your home network password.

4. Your iPad automatically reconnects to this Wi-Fi network in the future when you come in range of it. Use the Ask to Join Networks switch at the bottom of Figure 6-1 to control whether your iPad asks you before joining a new network or just shows you a list of networks to choose from.

WARNING

Free public Wi-Fi networks typically don't require a password, or the password is posted prominently for all to see. These networks are *unsecured*, however, so it's possible for someone to track your online activities over these networks. Avoid accessing financial accounts or sending emails that contain sensitive information when you're connected to a public hotspot.

Depending on your carrier and your contract, you may also be able to use your iPhone or other mobile device as a mobile hotspot: From the Wi-Fi, it appears as just another Wi-Fi node, but it provides the connectivity through the iPhone's connection. What this means most to you is that most cell connections have a connection that you pay for as you use it (that's those GB — gigabits — on your bill). Most of the time, Wi-Fi connections do not charge in that way. But when you use a mobile hotspot through your phone, the connection from your iPad to the phone is typically free but the owner of the phone will get the bill for your web surfing. So, make certain that you and the owners of the mobile hotspots understand that you will be using their hotspot . . . and their data allowance!

Explore Safari

1. After you're connected to a network, tap the Safari icon on the Dock at the bottom of the home screen. Safari opens, possibly displaying the Apple home page the first time you go online (see **Figure 6-2**).

2. Put two fingers together on the screen and swipe them outward to enlarge the view, as shown in **Figure 6-3.** Double-tap the screen with a single finger to restore the default screen size.

FIGURE 6-2

FIGURE 6-3

3. Put your finger on the screen and flick upward to scroll the page contents and view additional contents lower on the page.

4. To return to the top of the web page, put your finger on the screen and drag downward.

 Using the expand or pinch gesture to enlarge or shrink a web page on your screen allows you to view what's displayed at various sizes, giving you more flexibility than the double–tap method.

 When you enlarge the display, you gain more control by using two fingers to drag the screen from left to right or from top to bottom. On a reduced display, one finger works fine for making these gestures.

Navigate Web Pages

1. With Safari open, tap the address field below the status bar. The onscreen keyboard appears (see **Figure 6-4**). You also see your favorites and recently visited sites. (See "Add and Use Bookmarks" later in this chapter to see how to add your own favorites.)

2. To clear the address field, if necessary, tap the X button at the far-right end of the keyboard or tap the Delete key.

3. Enter a web address.

4. Tap the Go key on the keyboard (refer to Figure 6-4). The website that you entered appears (see **Figure 6-5**).

FIGURE 6-4

FIGURE 6-5

5. If the page doesn't appear, tap the Reload icon (the circular arrow) at the right end of the address field.

6. If Safari is loading a web page, and you change your mind about viewing the page, you can tap the Stop button (the X icon), which appears at the right end of the address field during this process, to stop loading the page.

7. Tap the Back button (<) to go to the last page you displayed.

8. Tap the Forward button (>) to go forward to the page you came from when you tapped Back.

9. To follow a link to another web page (links typically are colored text or graphics), tap the link with your finger. To view the destination web address of the link before you tap it, touch and hold the link. A popover appears, displaying the address at the top, as shown in **Figure 6-6**.

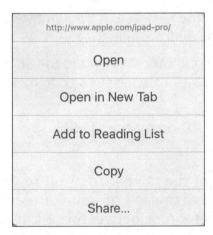

http://www.apple.com/ipad-pro/

Open

Open in New Tab

Add to Reading List

Copy

Share...

FIGURE 6-6

TIP

By default, AutoFill is turned on, causing entries that you make to display possibly matching entries automatically. You can turn off AutoFill by tapping Settings ⇨ Safari ⇨ AutoFill and then setting the Use Contact Info on/off button to off.

TIP QuickType is a feature that supports predictive text in the onscreen keyboard. This means that iPad identifies what you probably intend to type from text you've already entered and makes a suggestion to save you time typing. Tap a suggestion and iPad enters it for you.

Use Tabbed Browsing

Safari includes a feature called *tabbed browsing*, which allows you to have several websites open at the same time on separate tabs so that you can move among those sites easily.

1. To add a tab, tap the Add Tab button (a plus sign) near the top-right corner of the screen (refer to Figure 6-2). A new tab appears, displaying your favorites and frequently visited sites.

2. To open a new website, tap one of the favorites or frequently visited sites (refer to Figure 6-4), or tap the address field that appears.

3. Switch among open sites by tapping another tab, or tap the Show All Tabs button to see all open web pages. Tap a page to go to it, or tap Done to close All Tabs view.

4. To close a tab, scroll to locate the tab and then tap the Close button on the left side of the tab.

You can drag a tab to the left side of the tab bar to pin it to that window. Thus, you have one-tap access to each of your pinned tabs as well as the full tabs. The major difference between the tabs and the pins is the size of the tab or pin: You can get many more pins into a window than the number of tabs you can open. Note that the pin shows the first letter of the tab name (the website name). Gradually more and more websites are providing a small icon to use in these cases, so your user experience will change over the next few years as you use pins.

When you're using tabbed browsing, you can place not only a site on a tab, but also a search results screen. If you recently searched for something, those search results are in your Recent Searches list. Also, if you're displaying a search results page when you tap the + button to add a tab, the first ten suggested results are listed for you to choose among.

TIP

View Browsing History

As you move around the web, your browser keeps a record of your browsing history. This record can be handy when you want to visit a site that you viewed previously but whose address you've forgotten.

1. With Safari open, tap the Bookmarks icon. The Bookmarks sidebar slides in, as shown in **Figure 6-7**.

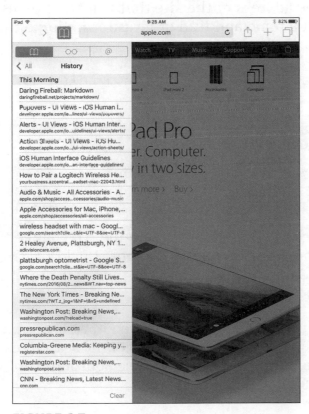

FIGURE 6-7

2. Tap the History option.

3. In the History list that appears, tap a date (if one is available) and then tap a site to navigate to it.

To clear the history, tap the Clear button in the bottom-right corner of the sidebar (refer to Figure 6-7). This button is useful when you don't want your spouse or grandchildren to see where you've been browsing for birthday or holiday presents!

You can tap and hold the Back button to quickly display your browsing history for the current tab during the current browsing session.

Search the Web

If you don't know the address of the site that you want to visit (or if you want to research a topic and find other information online), get acquainted with Safari's Search feature.

1. With Safari open, tap the address field. The onscreen keyboard appears.

2. Tap one of the suggested sites that appear, or enter a search word or phrase (such as a topic or a web address).

3. Tap the Go key on your keyboard (see **Figure 6-8**).

4. In the search results, tap a link to visit that site.

By default, Safari uses the Google search engine. To change your default search engine from Google to Yahoo!, DuckDuckGo, or Bing, tap Settings⇨Safari⇨Search Engine; then tap the option labeled Yahoo, DuckDuckGo, or Bing.

You can browse for specific items (such as web images or videos) by tapping the corresponding links at the top of the search results screen. Tap the More button in this list to see additional options and narrow your results.

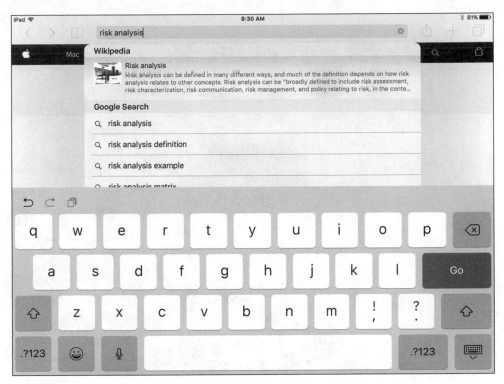

FIGURE 6-8

Share Items from the Web

The Share button lets you share something, such as the web page you're looking at or an image you selected.

1. Tap the Share button to open a sharing popover. In **Figure 6-9**, the popover points to the Share button. (Popovers usually point to the button that opens them.) The Share button works on the currently selected item or items (a whole paragraph or more of text can be the currently selected item).

2. Tap the round button in the top row of the sharing popover to share the selected item with another user using AirDrop. In Figure 6-9 only one nearby user is shown — initials JF, name Jesse, and on a device named "Mac Pro." There may be no nearby users or several.

FIGURE 6-9

3. Tap one of the colored icons in the second row to share the selected item with an app, social media account, or other service on your iPad. Refer to Figure 6-9.

4. Tap one of the gray-scale items in the third row to perform an immediate action on the selected item, such as printing it, or adding it to Favorites, Bookmarks, Home Screen, or Reading List.

5. You dismiss a popover by tapping anywhere outside it, but before you do, you can tap a button within it.

What you see in a sharing popover depends on two things: what type of thing you're looking at or have selected and what resources you have in your environment.

For example, in Safari, the Share button will have a Print button so you can print (if you have a printer). There's usually a Mail button. The page you're looking at will be printed or mailed.

If you've selected an image on the page, the image itself may be printed or emailed. In the case of a web page, usually the Mail message contains a link to the page rather than the contents of the page. A Mail message shared from an image may contain the actual image.

Exactly what is shared and how it is shared is determined by the app that's doing the sharing. The Share button asks the relevant apps to do the work.

In any row, you can flick across to see more buttons. Usually, you find a special button with an ellipsis (. . .), as you see in **Figure 6-10**.

» If you tap the ellipsis button in Safari, you see all your sharing choices in a text-based popover, as shown in **Figure 6-11**. You can rearrange the items in the list so that they appear in that new order in the sharing popover. Also, you can turn sharing choices on or off. (If you turn them off, you can always tap the ellipsis button again and turn them back on.)

FIGURE 6-10

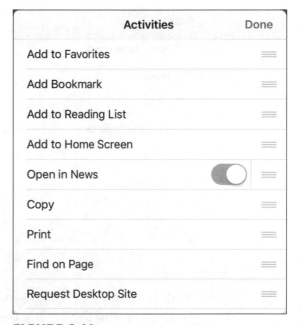

FIGURE 6-11

Add and Use Bookmarks

Bookmarks enable you to save favorite sites so you can easily visit them again.

Add a bookmark

1. With a site that you want to bookmark displayed, tap the Share button.

2. On the sharing popover, tap Add Bookmark. The Add Bookmark popover appears (see **Figure 6-12**).

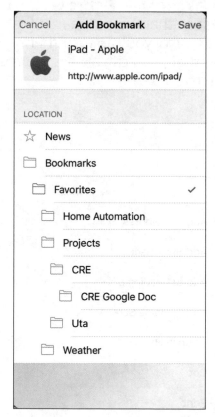

FIGURE 6-12

3. Edit the name of the bookmark, if you want to, by tapping the name of the site and then using the onscreen keyboard to edit its name.

4. Specify where you want to save the bookmark by tapping an item in the Location list. By default, new bookmarks are added to the Favorites folder and appear in the Favorites section of the Bookmarks menu.

5. Tap the Save button (or tap Cancel if you want to not add the bookmark).

Visit a bookmarked site

1. To go to a bookmarked site, tap the Bookmarks button (shaped like a little book) near the top-left corner of the sidebar. The Bookmarks list appears (see **Figure 6-13**).

FIGURE 6-13

2. Tap the bookmarked site that you want to visit. The site loads in Safari. (You'll notice in Figure 6-13 that the site bookmarked in Figure 6-12 is added at the end of the list of bookmarks.)

Organize bookmarks

When you tap the Bookmarks button, you can tap Edit at the bottom of the view and then use the New Folder option to create folders in addition to the existing Favorites folder to organize your bookmarks. When you next add a bookmark, you can choose the folder in which you want to save the new bookmark.

To set your default location for saved bookmarks, tap Location and then tap Bookmarks. Tapping Favorites adds saved bookmarks to the Favorites list.

Save Links and Web Pages to the Safari Reading List

Safari's Reading List feature lets you save web pages with content you want to read later. You can save not only links to sites, but also the sites themselves so you can read the content even when you're offline. Whereas a bookmark (refer to "Add and Use Bookmarks" earlier in this chapter) takes you to a live, updated page, adding an item to the Reading List simply saves a static copy of the item as it existed when you added it to the Reading List.

Add an item to the Reading List

1. With a site that you want to add to your Reading List displayed, tap the Share button.

2. On the popover that appears, tap Add to Reading List.

To save an image to your Reading List, tap and hold the image until a menu appears; then tap Add to Reading List. (This feature is available only for some images.)

View your Reading List

1. To view your Reading List, tap the Bookmarks button and then tap the Reading List tab (which sports a pair of reading glasses). The Reading List appears (see **Figure 6-14**).

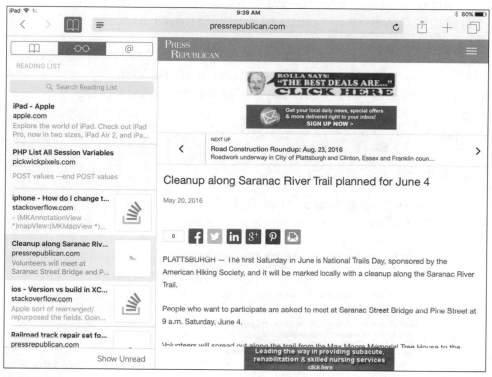

FIGURE 6-14

2. Tap the content you want to revisit, and resume reading.

TIP

If you want to see both Reading List material that you've read and material that you haven't read, tap Show All or Show Unread near the bottom of the Reading List. The option toggles between Show Unread and Show All as you tap it (refer to Figure 6-14).

TIP

To delete an item from the Reading List, swipe left over it; a Delete button appears. Tap this button to delete the item.

Enjoy Reading with Safari Reader

The Safari Reader feature gives you an e-reader experience within your browser, removing other stories and links as well as those distracting advertisements. When you're on a website article, Safari often displays the Reader button at the left end of the address field. (Not all web-page content can be shown in a reader.)

1. Tap the Reader button (see Figure 6-14). The content appears in Reader format (see **Figure 6-15**). You'll notice in Figure 6-15 that when you're in Reader format, the Reader button is highlighted.

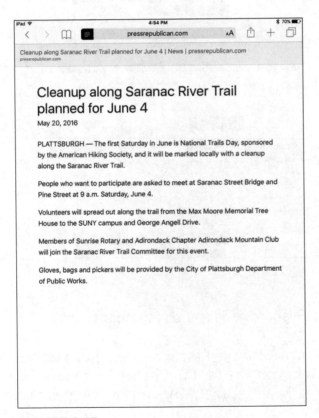

FIGURE 6-15

2. Scroll down the page to read the content.

3. When you finish reading the material, tap the Reader button in the address field again to return to the material's source.

TIP Reader view contains Next and Previous buttons that let you move to the next or previous Reader page, as well as left and right arrows at the top of the toolbar that let you move between Reader views.

Add Web Clips to the Home Screen

The web-clips feature allows you to save a website as an icon on your home screen so that you can go to the site at any time with one tap.

1. With Safari open and displaying the site that you want to add, tap the Share button.

2. On the sharing popover, tap Add to Home Screen. (If you don't see it, tap the ellipsis button and move it up in the list; refer to Figure 6-11 earlier in this chapter.) The Add to Home dialog appears (see **Figure 6-16**).

FIGURE 6-16

3. Edit the name of the site to be more descriptive, if you like, by tapping its name and using the onscreen keyboard to edit the text.

4. Tap the Add button. A button is added to your home screen along with your apps.

You can have as many as 11 home screens on your iPad to accommodate all the web clips and apps you download. For more information, see "Visit the Screens" in Chapter 2.

Send a Link

If you find a great site that you want to share, you can do so easily by sending a link to it in an email.

1. With Safari open and displaying the site that you want to share, tap the Share button.

2. On the sharing popover, tap Mail. A message form appears, containing the link (see **Figure 6-17**).

3. Enter the recipient's email address, a Subject line, and your message.

4. Tap Send, and the email containing the link is sent.

The email is sent from the default email account you set up on your iPad. For more about setting up an email account, see Chapter 7.

You can also send a link via the Message, Twitter, or Facebook apps, or even Reminders or Notes. For more information, see Chapter 10.

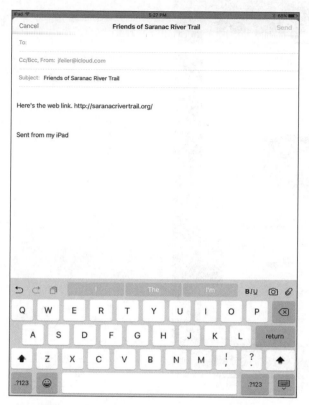

FIGURE 6-17

Print a Web Page

If you have a wireless printer that supports Apple's AirPrint technology (most manufacturers include AirPrint printers in their product lines), you can print web content via a wireless connection.

1. With Safari open and displaying the site that you want to print, tap the Share button.

2. On the sharing popover that appears, scroll to the right on the bottom list of buttons and then tap Print. Printer Options appears (see **Figure 6-18**).

3. Tap Select Printer.

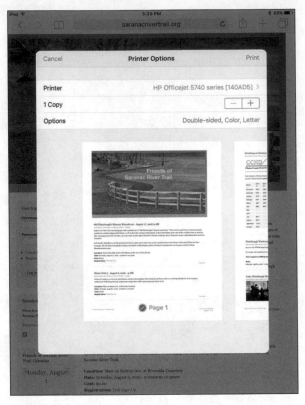

FIGURE 6-18

4. In the list of printers that appears, tap the name of your wireless printer.

5. Tap the plus or minus button in the Copy field to adjust the number of copies to print.

6. If you want to print only certain pages, tap Range and then select the pages to print.

7. Tap Print to print the displayed page.

TIP

If you don't have an AirPrint–compatible wireless printer or don't want to use an app to print wirelessly, just email a link to the web page to yourself, open the link on your computer, and print the page from there.

Save an Image to Your Photo Library

1. Display a web page that contains an image you want to copy or share.

2. Press and hold the image. From looking at the web page, it's not easy to tell if the image has a link connected to it or not. The following steps help you.

3. If a link is attached to the image, you'll see the choices shown in **Figure 6-19**. Those are your choice for sharing the image inside Safari. The final Share item opens the Sharing popover for you to share beyond Safari.

4. If there is no link attached to the image, your only choices are Save Image and Copy.

FIGURE 6-19

If you copy the image, you can paste it into a note, word processing document, or another place.

If you save the image, it's saved in your Photos gallery.

Be careful about copying images from the Internet and using them for business or promotional activities. Most images are copyrighted, and you may violate the copyright even if you simply use an image in, say, a brochure for your association or a flyer for your community group. Some search engines' advanced search settings offer the option of browsing only for images that aren't copyrighted.

Post Photos from Safari

You can post photos from Safari to sites such as eBay, Craigslist, and Facebook. For this example, go to Facebook and sign in. (To follow this example, you must have downloaded the Facebook for iPad app and created a Facebook account.)

1. In the Facebook app, tap Add Photos/Video, Upload Image/Video, or a link. (On Facebook, you may have to verify that you want to upload a photo or video rather than create a photo album.)

2. Tap the appropriate source for the image, such as an album in your Photos gallery or iCloud Drive.

3. Tap a photo on your iPad (see **Figure 6-20**).

4. Tap Done or Post, depending on the service, to post the photo or video.

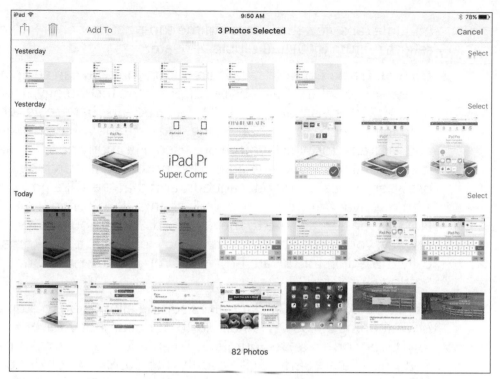

FIGURE 6-20

Make Private Browsing and Cookie Settings

Apple has provided some privacy settings for Safari that you should consider using:

» **Private Browsing:** This setting automatically removes items from the download list, stops Safari from using AutoFill to save information used to complete your entries in the search or address fields as you type, and erases some browsing history information. You turn Private Browsing on or off by tapping the multiple tabs view (the button in the top-right corner of Safari; refer to Figure 6-19) and tapping Private.

» **Do Not Track:** Do Not Track is an option that you can set in a browser like Safari. If a website supports the technology, it will not track your visit, and you will be spared ads that are generated in response to your browsing. That means you won't see ads for items for which you've browsed. For many people, that means that someone (the ad tracker probably) is watching their browser and selecting relevant ads, and that feels like an invasion of privacy. For other people, it seems like a convenience. Not all websites adhere to the standards, but if you value your privacy, you might want to turn on Do Not Track. It is automatically turned on for Private Browsing. You can turn it on and off in Settings for Safari.

» **Block Cookies:** The Block Cookies setting allows you to stop the downloading of *cookies* (small files that document your browsing history on a site) to your iPad. To enable this setting, tap Settings ➪ Safari ➪ Privacy & Security; tap the Block Cookies on/off button to turn the feature on (see **Figure 6-21**). Then turn on the option you want:

- Never allow cookies to be saved
- Always save cookies
- Allow cookies from the current website or visited third-party and advertiser sites
- Block cookies from the current website or visited third-party and advertiser sites

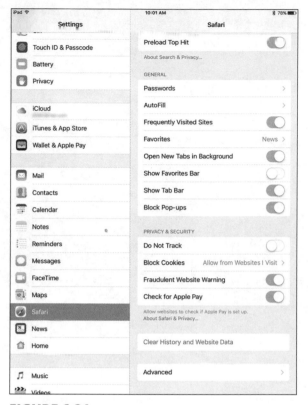

FIGURE 6-21

You can tap the Clear History and Website Data setting to clear your browsing history, saved cookies, and other data manually.

TIP

Chapter **7**

Keeping in Touch with Email

Staying in touch with others by using email is a great way to use your iPad. You can access an existing account by either using the handy Mail app supplied with your iPad or signing in to your email account by using the Safari browser (see Chapter 6). In this chapter, you look at using Mail, which involves adding one or more existing email accounts by way of Settings. Then you can use Mail to write, format, retrieve, and forward messages from one or more accounts.

Mail offers you the capability to mark the messages you've read, delete messages, organize your messages in folders, and use the handy search feature.

Mail also allows you to jump between a draft email and your inbox; swipe to mark an email as read or flag it for future action; and create an event or contact from information about a reservation, flight number, or phone number within an email.

In this chapter, you read all about Mail and its various features.

Add an Email Account

You can add one or more email accounts, including the email account associated with your iCloud account, on the Settings screen. If you have an iCloud, Google, Yahoo!, AOL, or Outlook account (including Microsoft Live and Hotmail), iPad pretty much automates setup. (If you're using your iPad at work — paid or volunteer — you may need to let an IT department set it up. Fortunately, today most of them are used to Apple devices. And if they're not, Apple has a web page dedicated to business and IT. It's at `http://www.apple.com/ipad/business/it/`.)

1. To set up the iPad to retrieve messages from your email account with one of these popular providers, tap Settings ⇨ Mail. The settings shown in **Figure 7-1** appear.

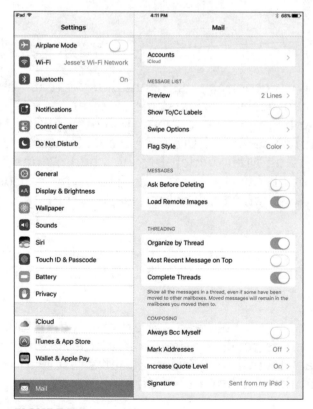

FIGURE 7-1

2. Tap Accounts at the top of the right column. The options shown in Figure 7-2 appear. (If you don't yet have any mail accounts set up, you see only Add Account.)

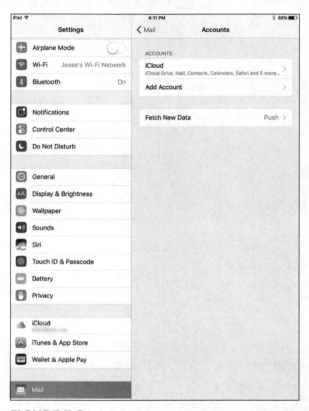

FIGURE 7-2

3. Tap Add Account to enter a new account. You see a list of popular email providers (see **Figure 7-3**). This list can change over time.

4. Tap iCloud, Exchange, Google, Yahoo!, AOL, Outlook.com, or Other to begin the setup process.

5. For some providers, such as Google, you see a customized login screen (see **Figure 7-4**). Enter the information that's asked for. In the Google login screen, you'll be able to create a new account or search for an existing account by tapping More Options.

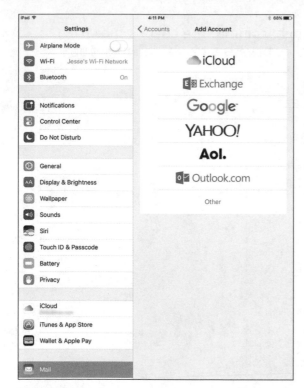

FIGURE 7-3

FIGURE 7-4

6. Enter your account information in the form that appears (see **Figure 7-5**), and tap Sign In or Next. (Note that the Next button won't be enabled until you enter data.)

7. Follow any additional prompts that are provided. (These prompts change from time to time.)

8. After the iPad takes a moment to verify your account information, tap any on/off switch to have Mail, Contacts, Calendars, Notes, or Reminders from that account synced with the iPad.

9. When you're done, tap Save or Next. The account is saved, and you can now open it by using Mail.

TIP

If you sync Calendars with Mail, any information you put in your calendar in that email account is imported into the Calendar app on your iPad and reflected in Notification Center (discussed in more detail in Chapter 19). This option is available only for certain types of email accounts, such as Exchange and Google.

FIGURE 7-5

Set Up a POP3 or IMAP Email Account ("Other")

You can set up most email accounts, such as those available through an Internet provider, by obtaining the host name from the provider. To set up an existing account with a provider other than Apple, Google, Microsoft, Yahoo!, or AOL, you must enter the account settings yourself.

1. Tap Settings ⇨ Mail to display the Mail settings screen (refer to Figure 7-1).

2. Tap Accounts at the top of the right column.

3. Tap Add Account.

4. On the screen that appears (refer to Figure 7-3), tap Other.

5. On the next screen (refer to Figure 7-5), enter your name and an account address, password, and description; then tap Next. The iPad takes a moment to verify your account and then returns you to the Mail page, where your new account is displayed.

6. To make sure that the Account field is set to receive email, tap Settings ⇨ Mail and then tap the account name (refer to Figure 7-2). On the screen that appears, tap the on/off button for Mail and then tap Done to save the setting. Now you can access the account through the Mail app.

   For some email services, after you set up the account, you must tap Settings ⇨ Mail, Contacts, and Calendars and then tap the account name to access the Mail on/off button.

TIP

If you have a less-mainstream email service, you may have to enter your password and what's called the mail server protocol. (Protocols are either POP3 or IMAP; ask your email provider for this information.) The iPad probably will add the outgoing mail server (SMTP) information for you, but if it doesn't, you may have to enter it yourself. Your Internet service provider can provide this information.

Open Mail and Read Messages

1. Tap the Mail app's icon, located on the home-screen Dock. A circled red number on the icon indicates the number of unread emails in your inbox.

2. In the Mail app, if the inbox you want isn't displayed, tap Mailboxes (or the name of the mailbox that's displayed) in the top-left corner to display your list of inboxes; then tap the inbox whose contents you want to display (see **Figure 7-6**).

FIGURE 7-6

3. Tap a message to open and read it (see **Figure 7-7**).

If you need to scroll to see the entire message, place your finger on the screen and flick upward to scroll down.

FIGURE 7-7

MAKING THE MOST OF MAIL

Here are some tips to keep in mind when working in Mail:

- You can swipe right while reading a message in portrait orientation to open the inbox list of messages and then swipe left to hide the list.

- Slide Over, Split View, and Picture in Picture all work with Mail.

- Email messages that you haven't read are marked with a blue circle in your inbox (refer to Figure 7-6). After you read a message, the blue circle disappears. You can mark a read message as unread to help remind you to read it again later. With your messages displayed, swipe to the right on a message and then tap Mark As Unread.

Reply to, Print, or Forward Email

1. With an email message open (see the preceding task), tap the Reply/Forward button, which looks like a left-facing curved arrow (refer to Figure 7-6).

2. Tap Reply, Reply All, Forward, or Print in the menu that appears (see **Figure 7-8**).

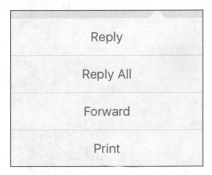

| Reply |
| Reply All |
| Forward |
| Print |

FIGURE 7-8

3. Take one of the following actions:

   - Tap Reply to respond to the sender of the message or (if the message had other recipients) tap Reply All to respond to the sender and to all recipients. The Reply Message form, shown in **Figure 7-9**, appears. Enter a message.

   - Tap Forward to send the message to somebody other than the sender. The form shown in **Figure 7-10** appears. Enter a recipient in the To field, tap in the message body, and enter a message.

   - Tap Print to print the email message (if you have a wireless printer connected).

4. Tap Send. The message is sent.

TIP

If you want to copy an address from the To field to the Cc or Bcc field, tap and hold the address, and drag it to the other field.

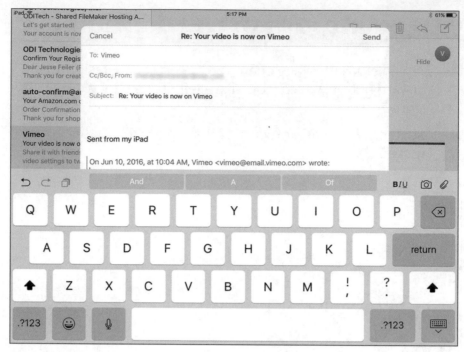

FIGURE 7-9

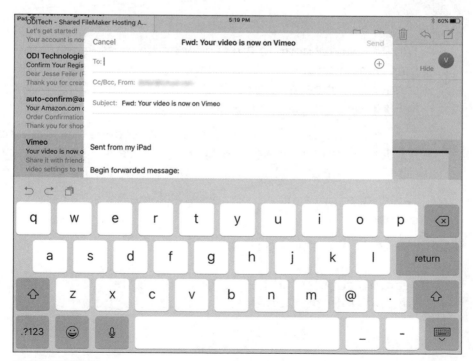

FIGURE 7-10

TIP If you tap Forward to send the message to somebody else, and the original message had an attachment, you're offered the option of including or not including the attachment.

Create and Send a New Message

 1. With Mail open, tap the New Message icon. A blank message form appears (see **Figure 7-11**).

 2. Enter a recipient's address in the To field by typing or by tapping the Dictation key on the onscreen keyboard and then speaking the address. If you have saved addresses in Contacts, tap the plus sign (+) in the Address field to choose an addressee from the Contacts list that appears.

FIGURE 7-11

3. If you want to send a copy of the message to other people, tap the Cc/Bcc field, and enter addresses in either Cc or Bcc or both. Use the Bcc field to specify recipients of blind carbon copies, which means that no other recipients are aware that that person received this reply.

4. Enter the subject of the message in the Subject field.

5. Tap in the message body and type your message.

6. If you want to check a fact or copy and paste some part of another message into your draft message, swipe down the email's title bar to display your inbox and other folders. Locate the message. When you're ready to return to your draft, tap the subject of the draft email that's displayed near the bottom of the screen to open it.

7. When you finish creating your message, tap Send.

Some people enter the address for the recipient at the end of the process. That way, if you accidentally tap Send too soon, you'll have a message that can't be sent because it's not addressed.

Format Email

You can apply some basic formatting to email text. You can use character formats (bold, underline, and italic) and indent text by using the Quote Level feature, though available formatting features may vary by the type of email account.

To use formatting, do any of the following:

» Press and hold a word in a new message that you're creating, and choose Select or Select All from the popover menu to select a single word or all the words in the email (see **Figure 7-12**). Then you can adjust the quote level, insert a photo or video, or add an attachment. If you select a single word, handles appear; you can drag the handles to add adjacent words to your selection.

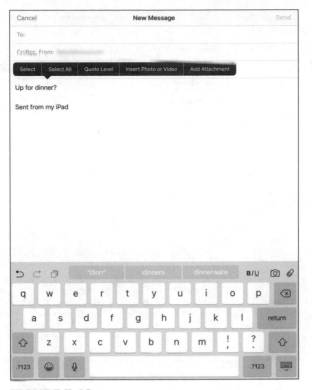

FIGURE 7-12

» To cut or copy text, replace it, apply bold, italic or underlining, look up a definition, or share via Facebook, Twitter, Message, or in other ways, press and hold the word to display the popover shown in **Figure 7-13**. Tap the appropriate option to apply the formatting.

» To change the indent level, tap and hold at the beginning of a line and then tap Quote Level.

» Tap Increase to indent the text or Decrease to move indented text farther toward the left margin.

» Tap the arrow at the right to see the additional options shown in **Figure 7-14**.

FIGURE 7-13

FIGURE 7-14

Search Email

What if you want to find all messages that are from a certain person or that contain a certain word in the Subject field? You can use Mail's handy Search feature to find these emails.

1. With Mail open, tap an account to display its inbox.

2. In the inbox, tap and drag down near the top of your inbox to display the Search field; then tap the Search field. The onscreen keyboard appears.

3. Enter a search term or name, as shown in **Figure 7-15.** Matching emails are listed in the results.

TIP

To start a new search, tap the Delete key in the top-right corner of the onscreen keyboard to delete the term or tap the Cancel button next to the Search field; then enter the new search term and tap Search. You also can use the Spotlight Search feature (see

Chapter 2) to search for terms in the To, From, or Subject lines of email messages.

TIP

You can reply to an email directly from the lock screen or Notification Center.

FIGURE 7-15

Mark Email as Unread or Flag for Follow-Up

You can use a simple swipe to access tools that mark an email as unread after you've read it (which places a blue dot before the message) or to flag an email (which places an orange circle before it). These methods help you remember to reread an email you've already read or to follow up on a message later.

1. With Mail open and an inbox displayed, swipe to the left to display three options: More, Flag, and Trash (see **Figure 7-16**).

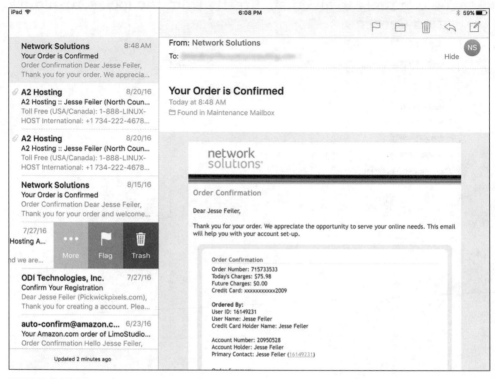

FIGURE 7-16

2. Tap Flag.

3. If you want, you can tap Trash to move the message to the Trash.

4. Tap Mark to flag a message (yes, the same as the Flag command in Step 2), mark it as read, or move it to the Junk folder.

5. Tap More if you want to use other options, as you see in **Figure 7-17**.

6. Tap Notify Me and you will be notified when anyone replies to this email thread. (That is, this email or any follow-up emails.)

7. Tap Move Message to move the message to another mailbox so you can keep your messages organized.

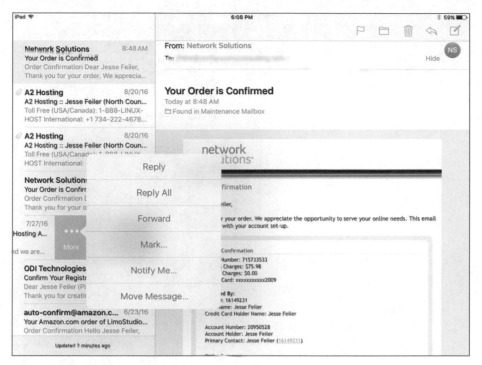

FIGURE 7-17

Create an Event from Email Contents

When you accept invitations sent to you in email, those events are placed in the Calendar app automatically. You can also create a Calendar event from certain information contained within an email.

1. To check out this feature, create an email to yourself mentioning a reservation on a specific airline on a specific date and time, or a dinner reservation, or just a phone number.

2. Send the message to yourself.

3. In your inbox, open the email. The pertinent information is displayed in blue underlined text.

4. Tap the underlined text. A menu appears, as shown in **Figure 7-18**.

5. Choose Create Event from the menu. A New Event form appears, as shown in **Figure 7-19**.

6. Enter information about the event and then tap Add.

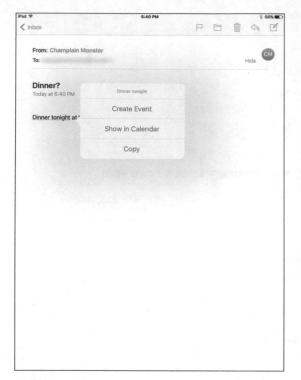

FIGURE 7-18

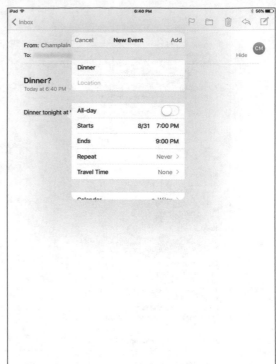

FIGURE 7-19

Delete Email

When you no longer want an email cluttering your inbox, you can delete it.

1. With the inbox displayed, tap the Edit button. A circular check box appears to the left of each message (see **Figure 7-20**).

2. Tap the circle next to the message you want to delete. (You can tap multiple items if you have several to delete.) A message marked for deletion has a check mark in its circular check box (refer to Figure 7-20).

3. Tap Trash at the bottom of the inbox. The message is moved to the Trash folder.

TIP

You can also delete an open email by tapping the Trash icon on the toolbar that runs across the top of Mail or by swiping left over a message displayed in the inbox and then tapping Trash.

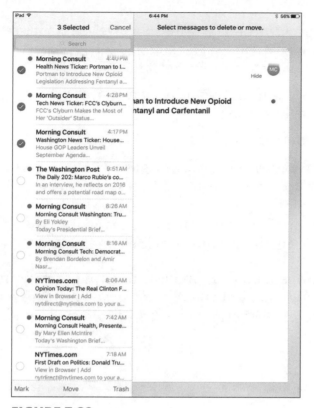

FIGURE 7-20

TIP

Mail keeps a copy of all deleted messages in the Trash folder for each email account for a time. To view deleted messages, tap Mailboxes (or the name of the mailbox that is displayed); then, on the screen that appears, tap the account name in the Accounts list. A list of folders opens. Tap the Trash folder to see the deleted messages. There is often an Advanced item under Settings ➪ Mail ➪ Accounts ➪ *your account* where you can adjust the time before deleted messages are truly deleted, but that's beyond the scope of this book.

Organize Email

You can organize messages by moving them into any of several pre-defined folders in Mail. These folders will vary, depending on your email provider and the folders you've created on its server.

1. After displaying the folder containing the message you want to move (such as Archive or inbox), tap the Edit button. A circular check box is displayed to the left of each message (refer to Figure 7-20).

2. Tap the circle next to the message you want to move. A check mark appears in its circular check box.

3. Tap Move at the bottom of the inbox.

4. In the list of mailboxes that appears (see **Figure 7-21**), tap the folder where you want to store the message. The message is moved.

TIP

If you receive a junk email, you may want to move it to the Spam or Junk folder, if your email account provides one.

TIP

If you have an email open, you can move it to a folder by tapping the Folder icon on the toolbar at the top of the screen. The mailboxes list appears (refer to Figure 7-21). Tap a folder to move the message.

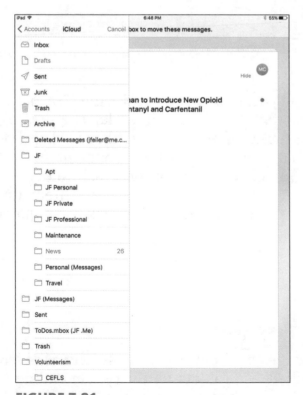

FIGURE 7-21

Chapter **8**

Getting Social with Your iPad

Your iPad provides a host of tools to help you keep in touch with your friends. They range from built-in support for your accounts at Twitter, Facebook, Flickr, and Vimeo, as well as FaceTime and Messages, which use your Apple ID to communicate with others using their Apple IDs. (Messages can send using SMS/MMS to phone numbers that accept text messages.)

These social media tools let you share text, photos, videos, and text messages that contain decorative and animated features. Your iPad and its camera are perfect for sharing photos of the grandkids or your own photos for them to share with others. A FaceTime session is perfect for a video session with your loved ones; you can show one another how to use the latest gizmo, for example, or help family members with their schoolwork.

FaceTime is also great for showing off your latest decorating and home improvement projects (but be careful about showing off how you've converted Bryce's bedroom to a guest room — he may be thinking about moving back if the latest romance or work gig doesn't work out).

And don't forget that an iPad or iPad Pro with its big screen is great for sharing. Wonderful though it can be to see a photo of a family get-together on an iPhone, it's much better on an iPad or iPad Pro.

This chapter shows you how to take advantage of the social media features of your iPad.

Use Social Media from Your iPad

You can access social media by using websites or apps such as Facebook, Twitter, Flickr, and Vimeo . . . and, it seems, more every week (SnapChat, Instagram, and WhatsApp, anyone?). This section covers how to work with the popular social media tools that have particularly tight integration with iPad. The list is likely to change over time, but for now, it's Facebook, Twitter, Vimeo, and Flickr.

The advantage of using the tightly integrated social media tools is that their apps on iPad can be accessed directly from the Share button, which is described later in this chapter.

 For more information on these services, see *Facebook For Dummies*, 6th Edition, by Carolyn Abram, or *Twitter For Dummies*, 3rd Edition, by Laura Fitton (both from John Wiley & Sons, Inc.).

Set up your account and password

Each social media tool requires a login account and password whether you use its web version, such as `facebook.com`, or an app such as the Facebook app for iPad that you can download from `http://itunes.apple.com/app/facebook/id284882215`.

You can set up your login from your iPad whether you already have created an account on the social media service you want to use or not. Here's how to handle both cases (you already have an account or not) for each of the four social media services.

Set up Facebook on your iPad

Here's how you set up Facebook:

1. Tap Settings on the home screen. Swipe down the left column and tap Facebook.

   - If the app is installed, it appears onscreen, as shown in **Figure 8-1**.

   - If the app is not installed, the button will read `Install`. Tap the button to install the app.

2. Tap Settings to customize your Facebook configuration. This is optional, and you can always revisit your settings by returning to Settings ⇨ Facebook.

3. If you want to customize your settings, tap Settings to reveal the appropriate options (see **Figure 8-2**). I suggest you leave the defaults to start with.

FIGURE 8-1

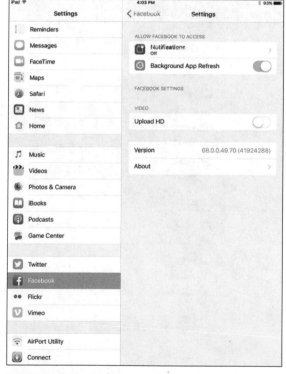

FIGURE 8-2

4. If you do not have a Facebook account from the website or an app on another device, tap Create New Account and follow the prompts. If you have a Facebook account (from the website or the app on another device), enter your username and password, and tap Sign In.

Set up Twitter on your iPad

Twitter is like Facebook but without customizable settings.

1. Tap Settings on the home screen to open it.

2. Swipe down the left column to find Twitter and tap it.

   - If the app is installed, it appears onscreen.

   - If the app is not installed, the button will read `Install`, as shown in **Figure 8-3.** Tap the button to install the app.

FIGURE 8-3

3. If you do not have a Twitter account from the website or an app on another device, tap Create New Account and follow the prompts. If you have a Twitter account (from the website or the app on another device), enter your username and password and tap Sign In.

Set up Flickr on your iPad

Here are the instructions for Flickr. They're almost the same as for Facebook and Twitter.

1. Tap Settings on the home screen to open it.

2. Swipe down the left column to find Flickr and tap it.

   - If the app is installed, it appears onscreen.

   - If the app is not installed, the button will read Install, as shown in **Figure 8-4.** Tap the button to install the app.

3. If you do not have a Flickr account create an account with the Flickr app (it is downloaded when you tap Install) or from Flickr.com.

4. Enter your username and password and tap Sign In.

Set up Vimeo on your iPad

Vimeo is like Flickr in that you need to create your account on the app.

1. Tap Settings on the home screen to open it.

2. Swipe down the left column to find Vimeo and tap it.

   - If the app is installed, it appears onscreen (see **Figure 8-5)**.

   - If the app is not installed, the button will read Install. Tap the button to install the app.

3. If you do not have a Vimeo account, create an account with the Vimeo app (it is downloaded when you tap Install) or from Flickr.com.

4. Enter your username and password and tap Sign In.

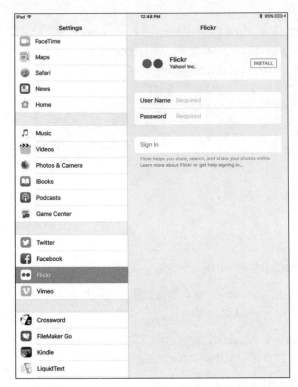

FIGURE 8-4

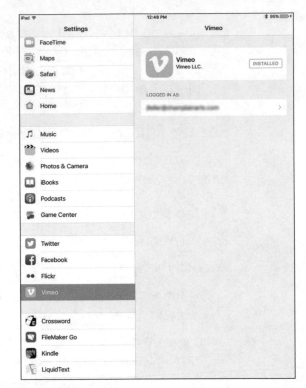

FIGURE 8-5

Use the Share button

If you configure your social media tools in Settings, iOS can use them to share articles you're looking at in Safari or text and pictures that you select in an app. Here's how you share.

1. Select the text your want to share or go to the web page in Safari you want to share.

2. Tap the Share button (the box with the arrow pointing up that you see at the right of the toolbar).

What you see in the Share popover depends on what you are looking at as well as what is installed on your iPad, so don't worry if this activity view looks different on your iPad.

3. Send your web page or selection to a nearby Mac or iOS device by tapping the AirDrop user button shown in the top row on **Figure 8-6**.

FIGURE 8-6

4. Send your web page or selection to an app like Message, Mail, Reminders, or Notes by tapping the button in the second row shown in Figure 8-6.

5. Send the web page or selection to iOS to have it create a copy, print it, or do something else with it (use the More button).

   What you can do depends on what you have selected and what apps you have installed on your iPad. If you have configured Facebook, Twitter, Flickr, or Vimeo, you'll have buttons in Share for them.

Use Messages

The iPad's Messages app lets you send short text messages. With iOS 10, Apple has refined Messages (formerly iMessage), adding new functionality. Now your messages can include videos and photos (even with handwritten annotations), a wide array of emojis, and stickers from the App Store. Messages has also become a quick (often one-tap) gateway to FaceTime as well as more traditional messaging services. (See "Use FaceTime" later in this chapter for details.)

Traditional messages (often called *text messages*) are sent over the phone network using either the SMS or MMS protocol. Most phone billing plans count messages separately from other data; many plans allow a certain number of messages, and a few allow unlimited messages.

Messages sent with the Messages app, however, are sent over your Wi-Fi or Internet data connection, so they may count against your combined data limit rather than a separate message category. Also, because messages sent over your data link are charged by size rather than number, messages that contain large attachments — generally media — can be more expensive.

Set up a Messages account

1. Tap Settings ⇨ Messages (see **Figure 8-7**).

2. Tap the iMessage on/off switch on the right side of the screen to turn it on. You see the screen shown in **Figure 8-8**.

3. To get started, you must have at least one address set, so click Send & Receive. You'll see the screen shown in **Figure 8-9**.

    You can set or change your Apple ID for Messages as well as several email addresses or phone numbers. Everything will be associated with Messages on your iPad.

TIP

When you set or change your Apple ID, the change is verified with Apple's servers. That means you need an Internet connection during the verification process. (Once you've been verified, you can use it offline.) Also, don't worry if it takes a while to complete the verification process. This is normal. If you happen to hit a time of very heavy traffic on Apple's servers (for example, the day a new iPhone goes on sale), you might have to wait a bit. Anything more than 2 minutes is probably a problem. But if you know from apple.com or the media that this is the day of an iPhone release, this is a good time to take a walk.

4. Choose which address in Figure 8-9 is used for outgoing messages (but you can change this for each message later).

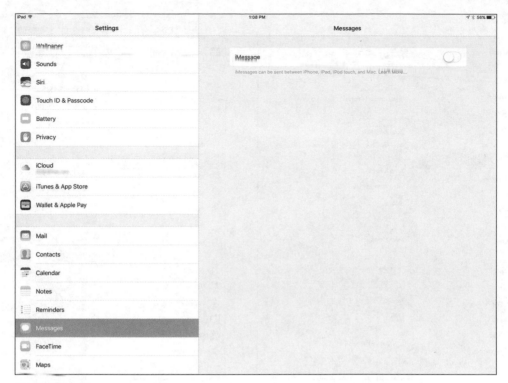

FIGURE 8-7

5. Experiment with any of the other settings, but these are the ones that must be set to get started with Messages. When you finish experimenting, you can move on to send and receive messages.

TIP

If you find yourself getting unwanted messages, you can turn Filter Unknown Senders on (refer to Figure 8-8). That will screen out messages from senders who are not in your Contacts.

Send a message

1. Open Messages from the home screen, and tap the New Message icon (the pencil diagonally placed in a square). A new message box appears (see **Figure 8-10**).

2. Tap the message box at the bottom of the message pane, and use the onscreen keyboard to enter your message.

FIGURE 8-8

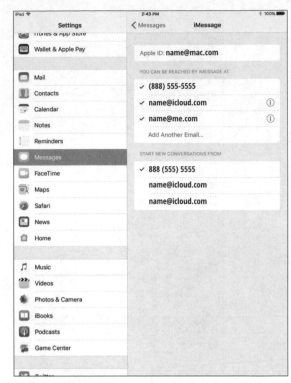

FIGURE 8-9

3. To address the message, enter a name in the To box at the top of the editing pane. You can send a message to one of your contacts using an email address or a phone number.

TIP

Addressing a message or email after you have typed it is a technique many people use. Because you can't send a message or email without a recipient, saving the address to be the last thing you do means that you can't accidentally send an incomplete message.

4. Tap the arrow to the left of the message box to display tools for sending photos and videos (camera); sketches, taps, kisses, or heartbeats (digital touches); and stickers from the App Store. They are described later in this chapter.

5. To send the message, tap the blue up arrow at the right end of the editing box.

New Message

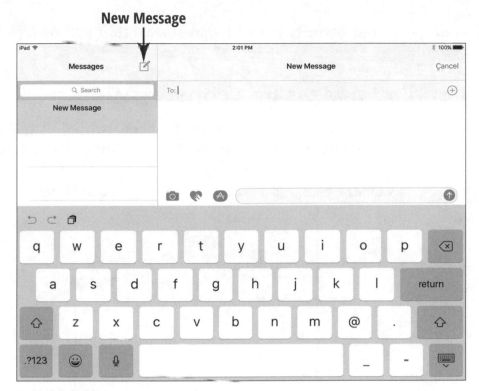

FIGURE 8-10

Read messages

1. Tap Messages on the home screen. When the app opens, you see a list of the text messages and attachments that have appeared in your Messages app.

2. Tap a message to see its message string, including any attachments. When you have selected a message, you see the sender's information at the top of the right-hand pane. Also, Messages lets you know if the message is from someone who's not in your contact list so it might be junk.

TIP

If you want the various junk and spam filters to work properly (not to mention helping Siri respond to your commands and making Maps as useful as possible), get yourself in the habit of storing names and addresses in Contacts. You can do this as a rainy–day project or just as it happens. If you add the name and address of your favorite markets and stores, that will reap many benefits.

Conduct a Messages conversation

Figure 8-11 shows a conversation that's been started. A friend asks me whether we should have coffee at 3. I said 3:10, and he said okay.

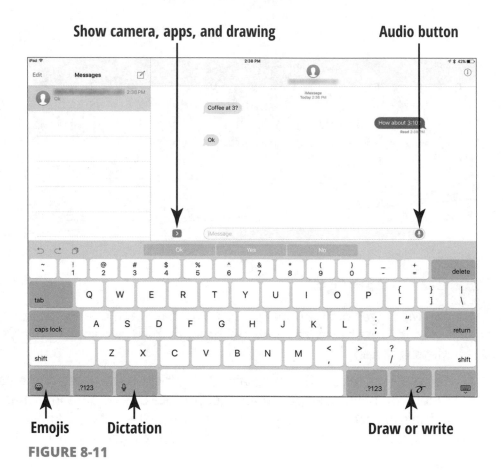

FIGURE 8-11

Now I want to add a handwritten note to reply. Here's how:

1. Tap the arrow to the left of the message box to show the tools for camera, digital touch, and apps.

2. Tap the App icon to display a writing/drawing pane.

3. Write your message in this pane with your finger or an Apple Pencil, as shown in **Figure 8-12**.

FIGURE 8-12

4. Tap Done. The writing/drawing pane collapses, but there's still space for you to type a message.

5. If you want, type a message (see **Figure 8-13**).

6. If you want, tap the emoji icon in the bottom-right corner of the keyboard; tap an emoji in the resulting pane (see **Figure 8-14**); and tap the blue up arrow to send the emoji.

7. Continue the conversation (see **Figure 8-15**).

8. To add an effect, tap and hold the up arrow shown in the message box in Figure 8-14 or 8-15 until the effect screen appears (see **Figure 8-16**). Then choose an effect by swiping the dots at the bottom of the message area. As you swipe, you see an animated preview (see **Figure 8-17**).

FIGURE 8-13

FIGURE 8-14

FIGURE 8-15

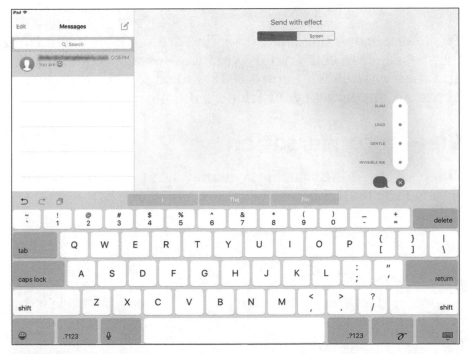

FIGURE 8-16

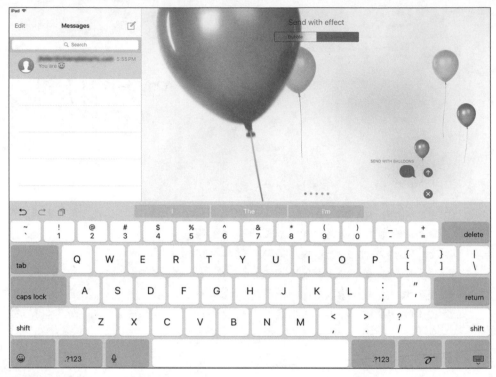

FIGURE 8-17

The features described in this section are available when you're send-ing messages to your friends who use Messages (that means your iOS and macOS friends). **Figure 8-18** shows the conversation described here as it appears on your friend's iPhone.

Clear a conversation

When you're done chatting, you may want to clear a conversation to remove the clutter before you start a new one.

1. With Messages open, swipe to the left on the message you want to delete.

2. Do one of the following:

- Tap the Delete button next to any item you want to clear (see **Figure 8-19**).

FIGURE 8-18

FIGURE 8-19

- Tap Edit at the top of the Message list. It changes to Cancel in case you want to stop editing. To continue, tap the circle next to the conversation you want to clear (see **Figure 8-20**), and then tap Delete in the bottom-right corner of the list of conversations.

Send an audio message

1. With Messages open, tap the New Message icon (refer to Figure 8-10).

2. Enter an addressee's name in the To field.

3. Tap and hold the Audio button. The audio tools appear (see **Figure 8-21**).

Delete conversation

FIGURE 8-20

FIGURE 8-21

4. Speak your message or record a sound or music playing near you.

5. Release the Audio button to stop the recording.

6. Tap the Send button (an up arrow at the top of the recording panel). The message appears as an audio track in the recipient's Messages inbox. To play the track, the recipient taps the Play button.

Send a photo or video message

1. With Messages open, tap the New Message icon.

2. Tap and hold the camera icon to the left of the message box. (If it's not shown, tap the arrow at the left of the box to show the camera, digital touch, and apps icons.)

3. Take a photo or video (see Chapters 14 and 15), or choose an image from your photo library, as shown in **Figure 8-22**.

FIGURE 8-22

4. To send multiple photos or videos, repeat Step 3.

5. Tap Send to send your message and attachments.

MESSAGING GROUPS

If you want to start a conversation with a group of people, you can use group messaging. Group messaging is great for keeping several people in the conversational loop.

You create a group message by addressing a message to more than one person and sending it.

When you participate in a group message, you see all participants in the Details section of the message. You can drop people you don't want to include any longer and leave the conversation yourself when you want to.

The ins and outs of group messaging are beyond the scope of this book, but if you're intrigued, go to https://support.apple.com/explore/messages for more information.

DON'T BE DISTURBED

If you don't want to get notifications of new messages for a while, you can use the Do Not Disturb feature.

1. With a message open, tap Details.

2. Tap Do Not Disturb to turn the feature on.

3. If you want to at another time, return to Details and tap Do Not Disturb again to turn the feature off.

You can turn on the Do Not Disturb feature for everyone by opening Control Center (drag up from the bottom edge of the screen to display it) and tapping the half-moon-shaped button. You can also allow selected callers to get through. Choose Settings ⇨ Do Not Disturb and select those callers.

Use FaceTime

The FaceTime app works with the cameras built into your iPad and lets you call other folks who have a device that supports FaceTime. You can use FaceTime to chat while sharing video images with another person. This app is useful for seniors who want to keep up with distant family members and friends and to see (as well as hear) the latest and greatest news.

You can't adjust audio volume from within the app or record a video call.

You can use your Apple ID and email address or phone number to access FaceTime, so it works pretty much right away. See Chapter 3 for more information about getting an Apple ID.

Activate FaceTime

1. Tap Settings ➪ FaceTime.

2. Enter your Apple ID and password, if requested, and then tap Sign In.

3. Tap the on/off switch to turn FaceTime on, if it's not already on.

Make a FaceTime call

1. Tap the FaceTime icon on the home screen.

2. The first time you use the app, you may be asked to select the phone number and email accounts you want to use for FaceTime calls; select them and then tap Next.

3. On the screen that appears, tap to choose a video or audio call. Video includes your voice and image; audio only includes your voice.

4. Tap the Enter Name, Email, or Number field and begin to enter a contact's name; a list of matching contacts appears. Tap the correct contact's name to display his information (see Chapter 20).

If you haven't saved this person in your contacts and you know his email address, you can enter that information in the Enter Name, Email, or Number field.

5. On the contact's information page, tap a phone number or email address that the contact has associated with FaceTime, and then tap the FaceTime button (shaped like a video camera). You've just placed a FaceTime call!

When the person you're calling accepts the call, you see the recipient's image and a small draggable box containing your image.

When you use an email address to call somebody, that person must be signed in to her Apple ID account and must have verified that the address can be used for FaceTime calls. iPad and iPod touch (fourth-generation and later) users can make this setting by tapping Settings ⇨ FaceTime and signing in with an Apple ID.

You can make audio-only FaceTime calls, which cuts down on the data streaming that can cost you when you share video. In the preceding Step 5, simply tap the Call button (shaped like a phone handset) instead of the FaceTime video button to initiate your audio-only call.

Accept and end a FaceTime call

If you're on the receiving end of a FaceTime call, accepting the call is about as easy as it gets.

1. When the call comes in, tap the Accept button to take the call, or tap the Decline button to reject it.

2. Chat away with your friend, tapping the FaceTime button if you want to view video images.

3. To end the call, tap the End button, which is shaped like a phone receiver.

To mute sound during a call, tap the Mute button, which looks like a microphone with a line through it. Tap the button again to unmute your iPad.

Switch views

When you're on a FaceTime call, you may want to use the iPad's built-in camera to show the person you're talking to what's going on around you. (There's more on the camera in Chapter 14.)

1. Tap the Switch Camera button to switch from the front-facing camera that's displaying your image to the back-facing camera that captures whatever you're looking at.

2. Tap the Switch Camera button again to switch back to the front camera, which displays your image.

3
Treating Yourself to Apps and Media

IN THIS PART. . .

Buy music, movies, and TV shows from the iTunes Store.

"There's an app for that" — How to find apps and put them on your iPad.

Throw out your timers and extensions cords: Use your iPad to control your home.

Chapter **9**

Shopping the iTunes Store

T he iTunes Store app that comes preinstalled on iPad lets you easily shop for music, movies, and TV shows.

In this chapter, you discover how to find content in the iTunes Store. The content can be downloaded directly to your iPad or to another device and then synced to your iPad. With the Family Sharing feature, which I cover in this chapter, up to six people in a family can share purchases and make new purchases with the same credit card.

Explore the iTunes Store

REMEMBER

To make purchases in the iTunes Store and other Apple stores, you need to use an Apple ID (see Chapter 3). You can create a second Apple ID to use for purchases in the various stores, and the music, TV shows, movies, and books you buy will be linked to that Apple ID (and to any related Apple IDs in Family Sharing). You can also set whether purchased music, apps, books, or updates should be downloaded automatically to all your devices sharing the Apple ID you used to purchase them (see **Figure 9-1**).

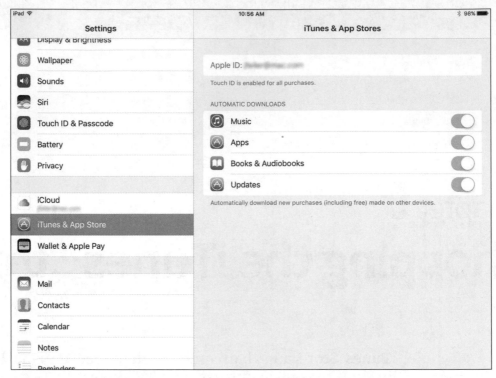

FIGURE 9-1

Visiting the iTunes Store from your iPad is easy with the built-in iTunes Store app. To do so, follow these steps:

1. Tap the iTunes Store icon on the home screen.

2. If you're not already signed in to an Apple store with your Apple ID and password, enter them when you're asked for them.

3. Tap the Music button in the row of buttons at the bottom of the screen, if it's not already selected, to view selections, as shown in **Figure 9-2**. You can browse various sections and display more music selections. (Both the sections and the items within them change periodically.)

4. Tap the Genres button in the top-left corner of the screen to display a display a list of music categories (see **Figure 9-3**).

5. Tap one genre. Items that are displayed are organized by criteria such as New Music and Hot Tracks.

6. Tap any listed item to see more details about it, as shown in **Figure 9-4.**

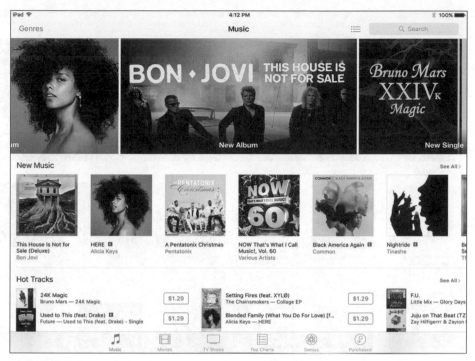

FIGURE 9-2

FIGURE 9-3

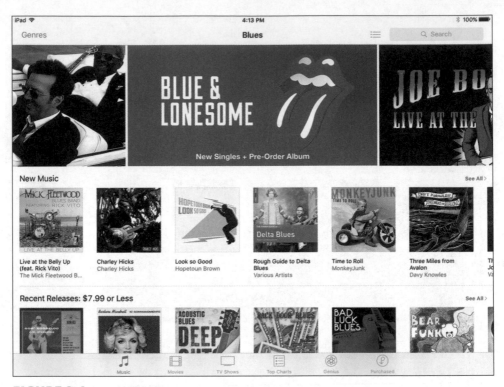

FIGURE 9-4

TIP

The navigation techniques in these steps work essentially the same way in any of the content categories (the tabs at the bottom of the screen), which include Music, Movies, and TV Shows.

TIP

If you want to use the Genius playlist feature, which recommends additional purchases based on the contents of your library, tap the Genius button at the bottom of the screen. If you've made enough purchases in iTunes, song and album recommendations appear based on those purchases as well as on the content in your iTunes Match library (a fee-based music service), if you have one.

The Share button in Figure 9-5 opens the usual options (Mail, Facebook, and Twitter if you have those accounts) as well as iTunes Store–specific buttons for sending the item as a gift or putting it on your own wish list.

FIGURE 9-5

Find an Item

You can look for an item in the iTunes Store by following these steps:

1. In the Search field shown in **Figure 9-6**, enter a search term with the onscreen keyboard, such as a genre of music, the name of an album or song, or an artist's name. A list of suggestions appears as you type.

2. If a suggestion in the list of search results appeals to you, tap it, or tap Search on the keyboard.

3. Tap a result.

On the description page that appears when you tap a selection, you can find the results sorted by albums and songs (see **Figure 9-7**). You can purchase any of the result items by tapping the price box.

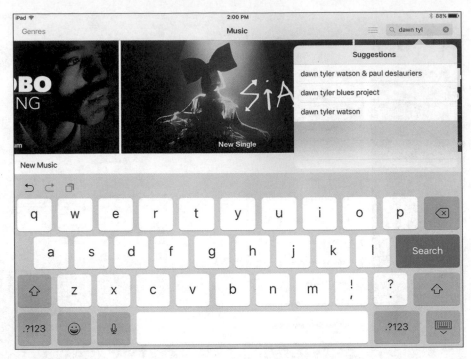

FIGURE 9-6

FIGURE 9-7

Preview an Item

Before deciding whether to buy a song or a movie, for example, you may want to preview it. To preview an item in iTunes, follow these steps:

1. Tap the name of the item shown in Figure 9-7 to see detailed information about it, as shown in **Figure 9-8**.

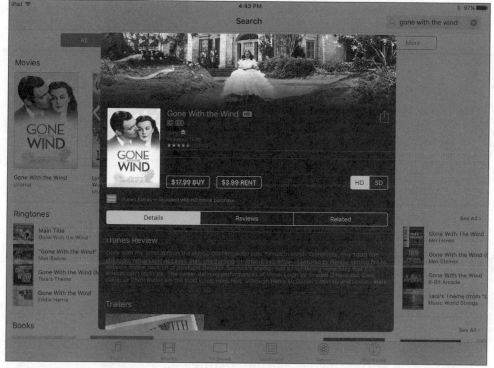

FIGURE 9-8

2. If you want to listen to a sample of a music selection, tap the track number on the left side of the list — not the price on the right side (refer to Figure 9-8). A small square preview appears in place of the track number, and the track plays. Tap the square to stop the preview.

    If the item is a movie, tap the Play button to view the theatrical trailer, if one's available. If the item is a TV show, tap an episode to get further information.

Buy or Get an Item

You can get both free and priced items in the iTunes Store. An item that you pay for has a Buy button on its detail page; a free item has a Get button.

To buy a priced item or get a free one, follow these steps:

1. Tap the Price or Get button.

2. If you're not already signed in to the iTunes Store, enter your Apple ID and password when prompted.

   The item begins downloading, and the cost (if any) is automatically charged against your account.

TIP

If you don't want to allow purchases from within apps (such as Music or Videos) and want to allow purchases only through the iTunes Store, tap Settings ⇨ General ⇨ Restrictions ⇨ Enable Restrictions, and enter a passcode. After you've set a passcode, you can tap individual apps to turn on restrictions for them, as well as for actions such as installing apps, sharing via AirDrop, or using Siri.

Rent a Movie

You can rent some movies instead of buying them. If you rent, you have 30 days from the time you rent the movie to begin watching it. After you've begun to watch it, you have 24 hours remaining to watch it on the same device as many times as you like.

To rent a movie from iTunes, follow these steps:

1. With the iTunes Store open, tap the Movies button.

2. Search for and select the movie you want to rent (refer to "Find an Item" earlier in this chapter).

3. On the movie's detail page, tap the Rent button (refer to **Figure 9-8**). The tapped button's name changes to Rent Movie.

4. Tap the Rent Movie button to download the movie to your iPad.

5. When the download is complete, use the Music or Videos app to watch the movie. (See Chapters 13 and 15, respectively, to read about how these apps work.)

Set Up Family Sharing

Family Sharing allows up to six people to share whatever anybody in the group has purchased from the iTunes, iBooks, and App Stores, even if the group members don't share an Apple ID. Group members must use the same credit card to purchase items, but you can approve purchases by younger children.

To set up Family Sharing, follow these steps:

1. Tap Settings ⇨ iCloud ⇨ Set Up Family Sharing. The pane shown in **Figure 9-9** opens.

FIGURE 9-9

2. Tap Get Started.

3. On the next screen, add a photo for your family, if you want. Tap Add Photo to choose one from your photos or to take a new one as you see in Figure 9-10.

FIGURE 9-10

4. Tap Continue. The current payment method associated with your Apple ID appears.

5. Review the payment information and either correct it or tap Continue.

6. On the next screen, tap Share Your Location.

7. On the next screen, tap Add Family Member to add people to your group as you see in **Figure 9-11**. Enter a person's name or email address and then tap Next. An invitation is sent to that person's email. When the invitation is accepted, the person is added to your family.

Cancel   **Add Family Member**   Next

To:

Enter a family member's name or email address.

Want to add a child who doesn't have an account?
Create an Apple ID for a child.

FIGURE 9-11

TIP

SHOPPING APPLE STORES FROM YOUR IPAD

You can access the Apple Store and several other stores by using their apps on your iPad. Here's a guide to the stores you can access this way:

- iTunes Store (the topic of this chapter) is where you can buy movies, music, and TV shows to play on your iPad or other devices.

- App Store (described in Chapter 10) is where you buy apps.

- Apple Store is the app you use to purchase items from a bricks-and-mortar Apple Store. It also helps you manage Genius appointments. You can buy Apple products as well as selected third-party accessories.

- iBooks is the app you use to purchase and read iBooks. Find out more in Chapter 12.

- You can buy music and videos directly from the Music and Videos apps, respectively. For more on Music, see Chapter 13; for details on Videos, see Chapter 15.

- The Games app lets you purchase and play the wide variety of games that are available for the iPad and other iOS devices.

TIP

If you want to add a child under age 13, note the separate link, Create an Apple ID for a Child, at the bottom of the pane shown in **Figure 9-11** This method is provided here because kids younger than 13 can't set up their own Apple IDs.

TIP

You can also share calendars and photos through Family Sharing. See Chapter 18 for information about sharing calendars and Chapter 14 for information on sharing photos.

Chapter **10**

Working with Apps

Some apps come preinstalled on your iPad, such as Contacts and Videos. But you can get a world of other apps for your iPad, some for free and some for a price. (Typically, paid apps cost 99 cents to about $10, though some can top out at $90 or more.)

Apps range from games and travel planners to financial tools such as loan calculators and productivity applications, including the iPad versions of Pages, the Apple software for word processing and page layout; Keynote, the presentation software; and Numbers, the spreadsheet software.

In this chapter, I suggest some apps you may want to check out and explain how to use the iPad's App Store to find, purchase, and download apps.

Understand App Store Apps

The App Store is curated, which means that only developers who have registered with Apple can upload their apps. The curation process also entails review of the actual apps. Apps that don't pass the tests are returned to the developers for further work.

The App Store offers five types of apps:

» **Free:** Apple is insistent that *free* means free. No "free" app that charges for basic functionality is accepted in the App Store.

» **Freemium:** Under the *freemium* model, the app is free, but certain functions are available as in-app purchases. Freemium apps often provide advanced levels in games, clues for solving a puzzle, or access to advanced formatting in certain graphics and business apps.

» **Subscription:** Subscriptions are relatively new for apps. Sometimes, initial subscriptions are free, and charges are made only for subsequent periods. (This model is a try-before-you-buy model.)

» **Paid:** Paid apps cost money and provide a license to the buyer for the right to use it.

» **Paymium:** Paymium is like freemium except that the initial purchase is paid.

Search the App Store

1. Tap the App Store icon on the home screen. The site shown in **Figure 10-1** appears. Note that there are five tabs at the bottom of the screen: Figure 10-1 shows Featured apps. Also, remember that apps are always coming and going to and from the App Store, so use the figures in this chapter only as a general guide.

2. Use one of several options for finding apps:

   • Tap the Search field at the top right, enter a search term, and then tap the Search button on the onscreen keyboard to see results.

   • Swipe the screen downward to scroll down, or swipe to the right to see more selections.

   • Tap the Featured tab at the bottom to see currently featured apps, as is the case in Figure 10-1.

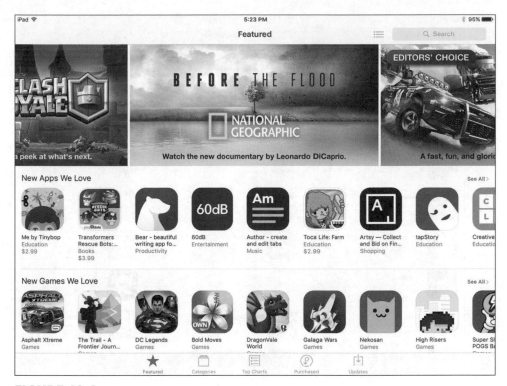

FIGURE 10-1

- Tap the Categories tab at the bottom of the screen to see different categories of apps.

- Tap the Top Charts tab at the bottom of the screen to see which free and paid apps other people are downloading most.

- Tap the Purchased button at the bottom of the screen to view apps you've already purchased, as shown in **Figure 10-2.** An item with a cloud symbol to the right of it means that you need to download it to use it. (You may have purchased and installed this app on another device but not on your iPad.)

- Tap the Updates tab to see updates to apps you've already purchased.

- In Top Charts tab, use the Paid, Free, and Top Grossing tabs to narrow your search.

FIGURE 10-2

Buy or Get Apps from the App Store

Getting apps or buying apps requires an Apple ID, which I cover in Chapter 3. After you have an Apple ID, you can use your saved payment information to buy apps or download free apps in a few simple steps.

To buy or get apps from the App Store, follow these steps:

1. Locate an item in the App Store that you want to download (see "Search the App Store" earlier in this chapter).

2. Tap the Buy (paid) or Get (free) button for the app you want to download (see **Figure 10-3**). The button name changes to Install.

3. Tap the Install button (see **Figure 10-4**).

4. If you're not already signed in to the App Store, enter your Apple ID and password.

FIGURE 10-3

FIGURE 10-4

5. If you've set up Touch ID, touch the Home button when you're prompted (see **Figure 10-5**).

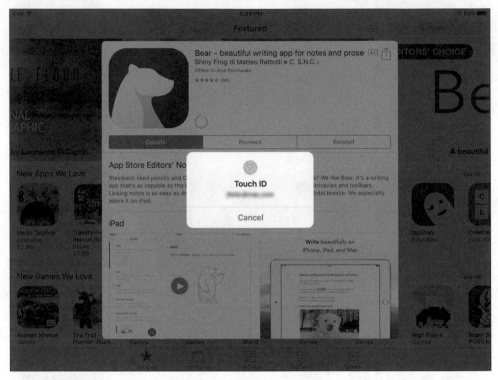

FIGURE 10-5

The first time you launch an app, you may be asked for some configuration settings, as shown in **Figure 10-6**. In almost every case, you can come back later and use Settings to change these initial choices, so don't agonize over them too much. (The very few cases in which the settings are permanent will be identified to you.)

TIP

If you've opened an iCloud account, anything that you purchase on your iPad can be set up to be pushed to other iOS devices automatically. See Chapter 3 for more about iCloud.

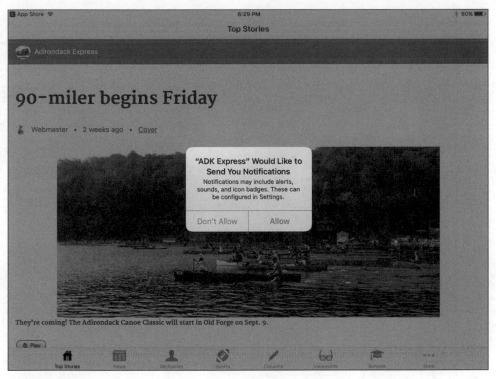

FIGURE 10-6

Organize Apps

The iPad can display up to 11 home screens. By default, the first screen contains preinstalled apps; other screens are created to contain any apps you download or sync to your iPad. At the bottom of any iPad home screen (just above the Dock), dots indicate the number of home screens, and a solid dot specifies the home screen you're on, as shown in **Figure 10-7.**

The most basic way of organizing apps is moving them from one home screen to another. Another way to organize them is to move them into folders that you create. (And then, you can combine both techniques to move some folders to certain home screens.)

FIGURE 10-7

Organize apps on your iPad's home screens

To reorganize apps on a home screen, follow these steps:

1. Press and hold any app on that screen. The app icons begin to jiggle, and any apps you've installed sport a Delete button (a gray circle with a black *X* on it).

Some preinstalled apps can't be deleted and so have no Delete button on them; see "Delete Apps" later in this chapter.

2. Press, hold, and drag an app icon to another location on the screen.

3. Press the Home button to stop all those icons from jiggling!

TIP To move an app from one screen to another while the apps are jiggling, you can press, hold, and drag an app to the left or right to move it to the next screen.

Organize apps in iTunes for your iPad's home screens

You can use iTunes to manage what app resides on what home screen. This process may be easier for some people and allows you to rearrange home screens, which you can't do from the iPad.

TIP

If you decide to do a wholesale rearrangement of apps on your iPad, you may find that using iTunes is the fastest way to do it.

To organize apps on home screens using iTunes, follow these steps:

1. Connect your iPad to your Mac or PC running iTunes (either via a cable or wirelessly).

2. Tap the small iPhone button in the top left of the screen as shown in **Figure 10-8** and choose your iPad from the list of devices.

3. Tap Apps under settings for your iPad at the left of the screen, and you'll see the list of apps and then your home screens and folders at the right.

4. Rearrange the apps on home screens just by dragging them.

5. If you need a new home screen, create it with the + at the top right. (You don't delete home screens manually: Empty home screens are automatically deleted for you.)

6. Drag entire home screens back and forth to change their order.

7. When you've finished rearranging folders and home screens, tap Sync and then Done at the lower right of the screen, as you see in Figure 10-8.

Organize apps in folders

iPad lets you organize apps in folders so that you can find them more easily. There's no limit on the number of apps you can store in a folder. The process is simple:

1. Tap and hold an app icon until all apps do their jiggle dance.

FIGURE 10-8

2. Drag one app on top of another app. The two apps appear in a folder with a placeholder name in a strip above them (see **Figure 10-9**). (The placeholder name is derived app categories: It just looks like magic.)

3. To change the folder name, tap the bar above the box. The onscreen keyboard appears. Tap the Delete key to delete the placeholder name, type one of your own; then tap Done. Tap anywhere outside the bar to save the name.

4. Press the Home button to stop the icons from dancing around.

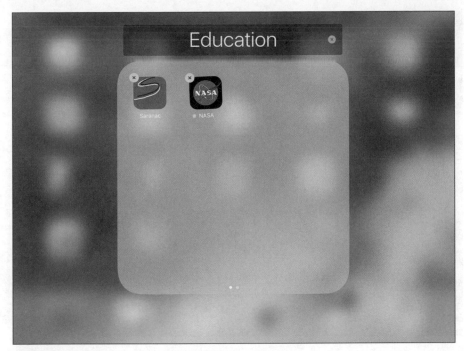

FIGURE 10-9

Delete Apps

When you no longer need an app that you installed, it's time to get rid of it. If you use iCloud to push content across all Apple iOS devices, note that deleting an app on your iPad won't affect that app on other devices.

REMEMBER

You can't delete apps that are preinstalled on the iPad, such as Notes, Calendar, and Photos.

To delete an app you no longer need, follow these steps:

1. Display the home screen that contains the app that you want to delete.

2. Press and hold the app's icon until all apps begin to jiggle.

3. Tap the app's Delete button. A confirmation message like the one shown in **Figure 10-10** appears.

4. Tap Delete to proceed with the deletion.

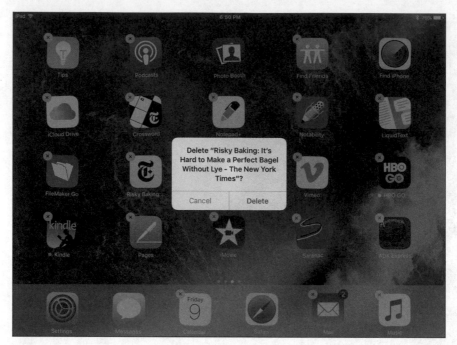

FIGURE 10-10

Don't worry about wiping out several apps by deleting a folder. When you delete a folder, the apps that were contained within the folder are placed back on home screens.

TIP

If you have several apps to delete, you can delete them by using iTunes, which makes the process a bit more streamlined. See "Organize apps in iTunes for your iPad's home screens" earlier in this chapter.

Update Apps

Developers update their apps all the time to fix problems or add new features. When app updates are available, the App Store icon displays the number of those updates in a red circle.

You can also use the Updates switch in Settings to automatically download updates to your apps, as shown in **Figure 10-11**.

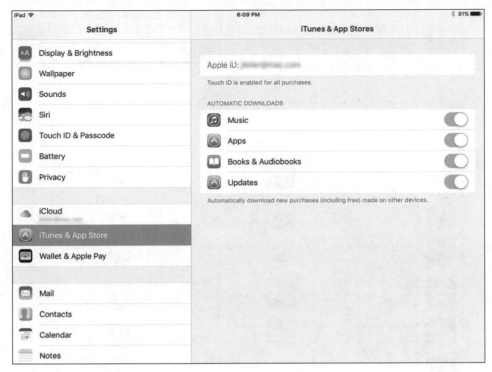

FIGURE 10-11

Apple, developers, and I all recommend very strongly that you automatically install updates. Many them fix security holes in apps. If you want to spend a scary few minutes search the Internet for "security flaws in old software versions." I just did it and got 130,000,000 results. Just the first few items are enough to cause you to run to turn on the Updates switch.

If you'd rather get updates manually, here's how:

1. Tap the App Store icon.

2. Tap the Updates button to access the Updates screen and then tap any item you want to update.

3. On the screen that appears, tap Update.

4. If you're not already signed in to the App Store, enter your Apple ID and password.

5. If you're asked to confirm that you're over a certain age or agree to terms and conditions, read the message and then tap Agree.

If you have Family Sharing turned on (see Chapter 9), you can tap My Purchases in the top left of the Purchases tab to view apps and updates for each person, as you see in **Figure 10-12**.

FIGURE 10-12

TIP

You can download multiple app updates simultaneously. If you choose more than one app to update, all items will download in parallel.

If you have an iCloud account that you've made active on various devices, when you update an app on your iPad, it also updates automatically on any other Apple iOS devices you have (and vice versa).

Chapter 11
Apps for You and Your Home

Have you heard about *home automation*? What about *smart homes*? Automation and the digital lifestyle have moved into your home with you. A few years ago, we were all rather amazed, and per–haps somewhat bewildered, to be able to purchase a new refrigerator with an Internet connection. "Pardon me a moment while I open the fridge door to check my email" — or something like that.

Home Automation offers products from a variety of manufacturers and vendors. You can find HA sections in stores such as Lowes and Home Depot (yes, "HA" is the code word in many places). Whether you're jumping on the bandwagon yourself or profiting from an eager neighbor or relative who wants to change your life, HA and Apple's HomeKit are your ticket.

In fact, as is often the case, the technology precedes the widespread useful applications of it that make our lives easier. Turning on the furnace or air conditioner when you're half an hour away from home is certainly a convenience, and we could do that (albeit somewhat awkwardly) for a few years now.

What company is it that takes technology and makes it understand-able, easy to use, and, before long, indispensable to us in our daily lives?

Yes, that company is Apple, maker of your iPad. This chapter intro-duces you to HomeKit and the Home app for iPad (they're both built into iPad automatically).

Get to Know HomeKit

HomeKit is a database that's built into iOS 10 as well as an app (called "Home") that's installed on your iPad along with iOS 10. Together, the database and app let you automate your home. For that you need three things:

» *Home*. That's your home, be it a house, a condo, an apartment, or a tent (equipped with power and Wi-Fi). You can actually have several homes inside HomeKit (maybe a weekend home and another home if you're lucky).

» *Room*. A home contains rooms. Most of the time these are the rooms you live in every day, but you can create special "rooms" such as a dining area within a main room. To get started, just think about guiding a friend through your home: What are the rooms you would point out?

» *Accessories*. These are Wi-Fi-enabled devices such as light bulbs, a thermostat, door and window locks, a garage door opener, or a smoke alarm. Each accessory has its own power supply and is connected to your Wi-Fi network. Note that if you're using Wi-Fi-enabled light bulbs, a light fixture with three bulbs in it is three accessories.

The rest of this chapter shows you how you put them together.

TIP

HomeKit relies on one device in your home being on all the time and connected to the Internet. For many people, that's an Apple TV that is on your local Wi-Fi connection. It can also be an iPad (even an old one) that you keep running and plugged in. There is a very minimal amount of setup work the first time you launch Home on your iPad. Just follow the directions on the screen.

Set Up Accessories

Accessories are the lights, door locks, automated window shades, switches, thermostats, sensors for temperature and intrusion, and other items that do the work of HomeKit. They are manufactured by various manufacturers, and, if they are compatible with HomeKit, Apple certifies them with the logo shown in **Figure 11-1**.

FIGURE 11-1

Accessories communicate with HomeKit wirelessly. Some accessories (the Philips Hue bulbs and other devices, for example) communicate wirelessly to a small device that in turn connects to HomeKit. The device is normally called a *hub* or *bridge* and it may come with a starter kit of your first bulbs. Other manufacturers sell accessories that include bridge-type functionality: iDevices sells accessories that don't require an external bridge. In this section, you'll see an iDevices Switch set up with HomeKit: That's the simplest method.

Elsewhere in this book, you'll see a Philips Hue Bridge used. Several bulbs connect to the bridge. Once you add an accessory directly to HomeKit as described in this chapter, you can add it to rooms, scenes, and your home. If you use a bridge, you add the bridge itself to a room or scene, and then its accessories become available. Whether added directly or via a bridge, accessories work the same way with HomeKit.

The following sections cover adding and adjusting accessories.

Add an accessory

Here's how to set up an accessory. The accessory in question is an iDevices Switch. At the time of this writing, it sells for $49.95 at `https://store.idevicesinc.com/idevices-switch/` and elsewhere on the web (search for "iDevices Switch"). The iDevices switch is two devices in one: It contains a night light as well as a regular plug into which you can plug lamps, fans, heaters, or other devices. The steps here work the same way for any accessory.

If you follow these directions, you'll set the iDevices Switch up in the default home and room that come with Home. You can rename them later.

The only part of setting up HomeKit that may be a bit tricky is connecting third-party accessories such as bulbs and thermostats to the HomeKit network. Because it's all wireless, you may need to try it a couple of times. Take your time and remember that you're dealing with a network. While you're setting things up, if a device like a bulb doesn't respond immediately, give it some time and try again. The old turn-it-off-and-turn-it-on-again routine may solve several problems, particularly if you pause between off and on.

1. Tap Home on your iPad to open the app (it comes with iOS 10). You'll see the view shown in **Figure 11-2**. (If you have never run it before or have not set up your iCloud account, you'll be prompted to do so, and the view shown in **Figure 11-2** may look a little different. See Chapter 3 for more on iCloud.)

2. Power on your new accessory. Make sure it is fairly close to your iPad. For the next steps, it will use the short-range Bluetooth communication technology so keep it within about 10 meters (32.8 ft.) of your iPad. This is just for the initial discover step — you'll add it to Wi-Fi in Step 4.

3. Tap + in the upper right to add a new scene or accessory (**Figure 11-3**).

4. Tap Add Accessory.

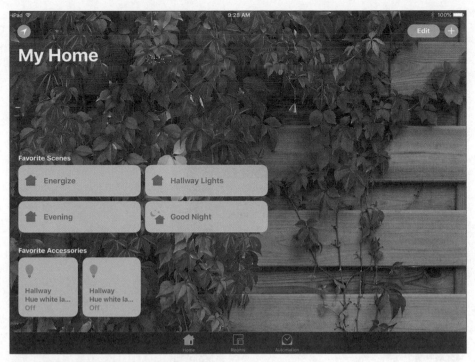

FIGURE 11-2

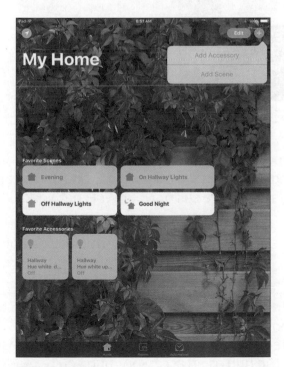

FIGURE 11-3

If you choose to add a new accessory, you should see it on the next screen. If you don't see it (as shown in **Figure 11-4**), there are several reasons and several solutions to try (in this order):

FIGURE 11-4

1. The accessory must be powered on (not just plugged in), and it should be near your iPad. Once it is *discovered*, you can move it or move your iPad as long as both are still on your Wi-Fi network.

2. The accessory might need a minute or two to power on and connect to the network. So Step 2 is: Have patience and consider a cup of coffee or tea.

3. Some accessories connect to what is called a *bridge* — a hub such as one from Philips or Lutron. In those cases, the accessories are set up for the hub using the instructions that come with the hub and accessory. Then, the hub itself is connected to HomeKit. If you move your iPad close to the hub, it often recognizes the hub as an accessory, and you're ready to go.

4. You may need to reset the accessory and/or the hub.

5. If all else fails, consult the documentation for the accessory and/or the hub. In this case, you might find helpful advice on the Internet or on *support.apple.com*. If there is something like *support. yourhubmanufacturer.com*, try that, too.

6. Once the accessory is located, you'll be prompted to add it to your network as shown in **Figure 11-5**. Tap Allow.

7. You'll be prompted to add the new accessory to your home, as shown in **Figure 11-6**. Tap the accessory (if you have several new accessories, tap the one you want to add).

8. You may be prompted to enter the HomeKit code from the device or its packaging. If so, do so either manually or by positioning the code from the device or packaging in the iPad frame as shown in **Figure 11-7**. (Note that as the camera focuses, the code will appear blurry, but it will be adjusted automatically. If it isn't, tap Enter Code Manually and do so.)

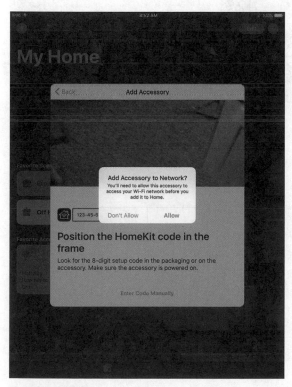

FIGURE 11-5

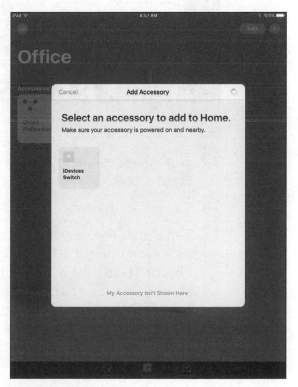

FIGURE 11-6

9. After you have verified the code, you can complete the add process as shown in **Figure 11-8**. Tap Identify Accessory to flash its light (or beep depending on the accessory) so that you're sure which one you're working with.

FIGURE 11-7

FIGURE 11-8

10. Tap the accesssory name to change it with the keyboard, as shown in **Figure 11-9**.

11. Tap Location to choose another location if you want.

12. Tap Done. The new accessory will apear on your home screen, as shown in **Figure 11-10**. The other rooms and scenes shown in **Figure 11-10** will be any that you have created. Tap the new accessory to turn it on or off. With the iDevices Switch, you'll see the night light go on and off. If you plug in a fan or lamp, you'll see it go on or off as you tap the switch (remember, you have two accessories in the iDevices Switch).

FIGURE 11-9

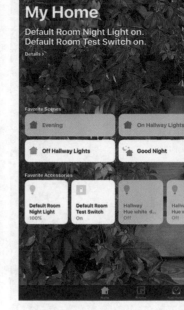

FIGURE 11-10

Adjust an accessory

Setting up an accessory is a one-time task. You frequently adjust accessories.

1. To adjust an accessory, tap and hold it from the home screen (as shown in **Figure 11-10**). You can start with the night light.

2. The details view shown in **Figure 11-11** appears. It shows you the status (Powered On/Powered Off for the switch outlet).

3. Tap Details to adjust the details shown in **Figure 11-12**.

The most common accessory to be adjusted is a bulb. When you have added a bulb as an accessory, you can touch and hold the accessory icon to open the view shown in **Figure 11-13**.

You can drag the brightness indicator up or down with the little handle at the top. For example, in **Figure 11-13**, the bulb is at 63% brightness. Drag the handle all the way up to change that to 100%; drag it to the bottom and it will be off.

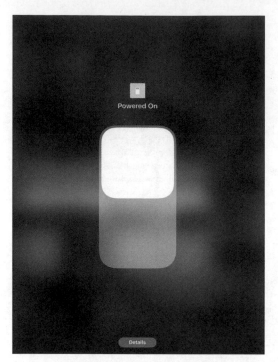

FIGURE 11-11

FIGURE 11-12

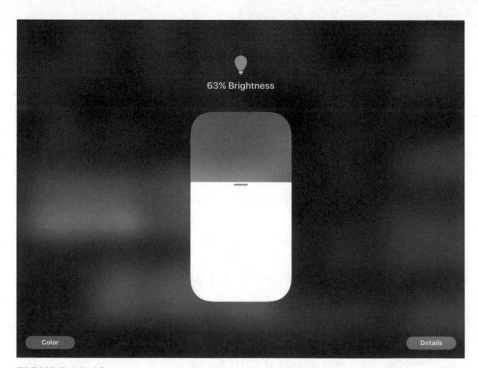

FIGURE 11-13

The Details button at the bottom of the bulb opens the view shown in **Figure 11-14**.

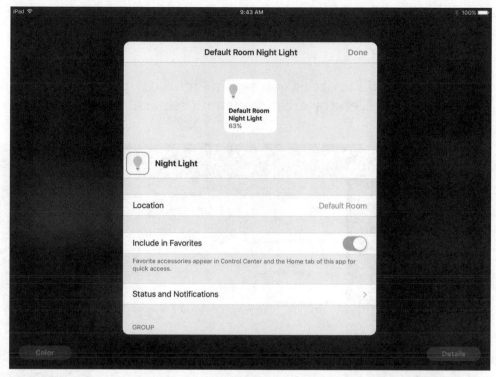

FIGURE 11-14

You can name the bulb and choose its location. You can also indicate if you want it to be shown as a favorite as well as if it's part of a bridge.

TIP

Yes, you can create a lamp and then choose its location. Or, you can start from the location and add the lamp. Either way is fine with HomeKit.

Work with Scenes

Scenes are collections of accessories. You may want to group accessories into rooms (that's not HomeKit-speak: It's normal English). But you also may want to group accessories into scenes that may or may not be confined to a room. For example, you can create a Go To Bed scene that turns on bedside lights, turns off the switch for a fan in the living room, and locks the outside door. My advice is to start with just one or two accessories and one or two rooms or scenes.

Add a Scene

If you tap Add Scene as you saw in Figure 11-3, you'll be able to choose an existing scene or create a custom scene as you see in **Figure 11-15**.

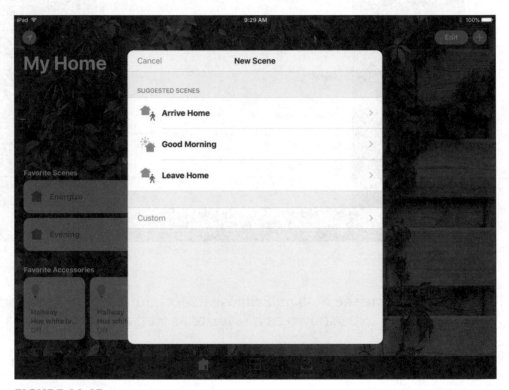

FIGURE 11-15

It's easy to create and modify scenes and you don't have to get on ladders to "move" things around. Remember that falls are one of the major risks for everyone and particularly for seniors, so being able to set up and rearrange your home with your iPad when you've got both feet on the floor is a bonus.

A FEW WORDS ABOUT FALLS

TIP

While you're sitting down, you might want to take a break from setting up HomeKit to browse `http://www.cdc.gov/homeandrecreationalsafety/falls/adultfalls.html`, which is the Centers for Disease Control and Prevention page about senior falls. It starts by saying that more than one out of four older people falls each year. You can set up HomeKit without climbing many ladders unless you're connecting a ceiling bulb or fixture as an accessory. Perhaps more important, using automation in Home can turn lights on and off at appropriate times, which can help you avoid reaching for light switches that are a bit out of reach.

If you choose Custom, you'll be able to name the new scene as you see in **Figure 11-16**.

FIGURE 11-16

TIP

You may want to make the names for your scenes distinct from other names. Nothing prevents you from naming the bulb in a lamp Living Room, but you'll soon run into conflicts when you try to name the room Living Room. And if you decide to create a Living Room Scene, you'll have a conflict if you just try to name it Living Room. The purpose of HomeKit and home automation in general is to make your life easier, and not to give you something else to annoy you.

In addition to naming the scene, you can tap Add Accessories to do just that.

Combine accessories into scenes

You can combine HomeKit accessories into *scenes*. A scene can consist of accessories in several rooms. You do this because you want Home-Kit to manage them together. Which brings us to *automation*.

You use Home to automate your accessories and scenes. You can set up an automation to turn the hall light on at a certain time (or at sunset) and off at another time (perhaps at sunrise when it's no longer needed). Alternatively, you can create a scene with the upstairs hall light accessory and the dining room window shades so that at 7PM, the hall light goes on and the shades are drawn for the evening.

HomeKit automation can build on accessories (individual light bulbs, for example), rooms (groups of accessories in a room), and scenes (groups of accessories in various rooms).

Even though you use automation a lot with HomeKit, keep in mind that with Home you can always tap a scene or accessory to turn it on or off.

As you set up HomeKit, you may have to work a bit out of sequence. You need to connect the accessories before you can combine them into scenes or place them into rooms. However, it may be easier for you to set up your rooms (or at least name them), connect the accessories, and then come back to place them into rooms.

Adjust a scene

Adjusting a scene is much like adjusting an accessory. You start by locating the scene — it may be in a room where it is used (as shown in **Figure 11-17**), or it may be on your Home screen (as shown in Figure 11-3).

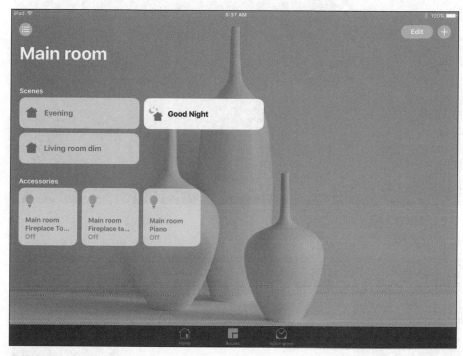

FIGURE 11-17

1. Touch and hold the scene. As shown in **Figure 11-18**, you'll see the scene name and image if you've provided one as well as a Details button.

2. Tap details. You'll see the details shown in **Figure 11-19**.

3. Edit the name if you want (as soon as you tap in the name field, the keyboard appears).

4. Touch and hold an accessory to edit it, as you saw in Figure 11-12. (The most common settings for an accessory are brightness and color for bulbs.)

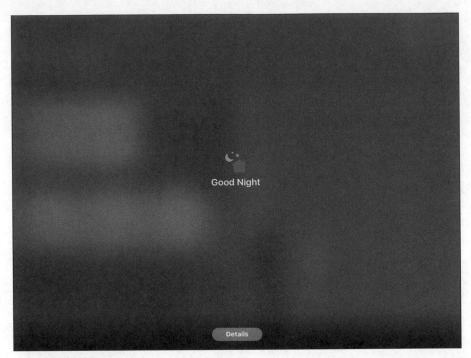

FIGURE 11-18

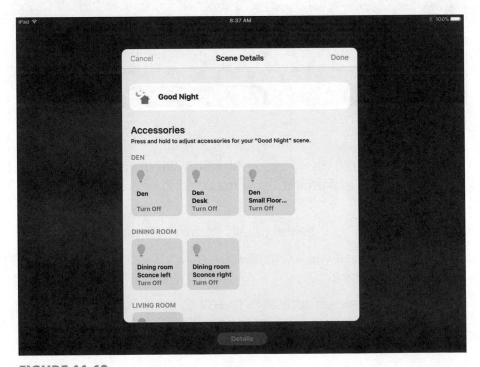

FIGURE 11-19

5. When you've finished adjusting your accessories, swipe down to the bottom to test your scene, as shown in **Figure 11-20**.

6. Tap Done in the top right.

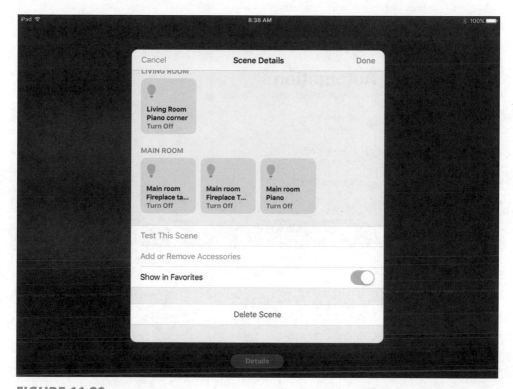

Set up a room

Tap the Rooms tab at the bottom of Home to start working with rooms. You'll see any scenes that the room participates in, and you can tap the scene to turn it on or off. You'll also see the accessories in the room. You can tap to turn them on or off. As shown in Figure 11-17, you'll also see the current status of the accessories.

Use Automations

Tap the Automations tab at the bottom to manage automations, as you see in **Figure 11-21**.

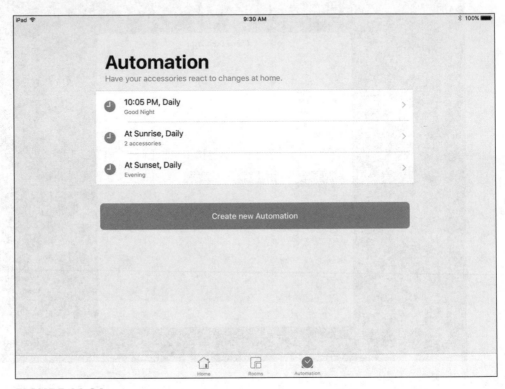

FIGURE 11-21

You can work with one of the built-in automations or you can create your own. (Most people probably use a combination of both.) It may be easiest to start with one of the built-in automations. Remember that you can always come back and redo this, do put your feet up (remember: no ladders needed!) and experiment to your heart's content.

1. Tap an automation to open it, as you see in **Figure 11-22**.

2. Make sure it's enabled. (You may want to disable automations at some time in the future so that you can set up automations to enable while you're on vacation, for example.)

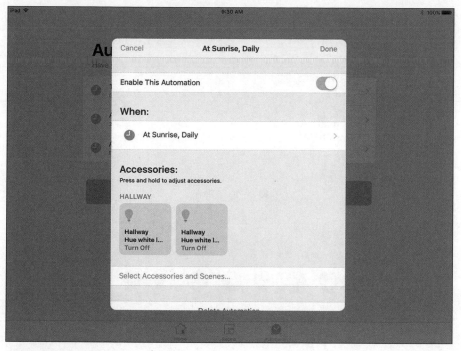

FIGURE 11-22

3. Tap When to set a time for the automation to run. You can choose sunrise or sunset and HomeKit will figure that out for you. You can also tap Time of Day to set a specific time, as you see in **Figure 11-23**.

4. Also note that you can tap the days of the week when you want the automation to run. Tap any day to turn it off.

5. Tap Select Accessories and Scenes to open the view shown in **Figure 11-24**.

6. Choose the scenes you want to use when the automation starts.

7. Swipe down to choose accessories to use, as shown in **Figure 11-25**.

8. For both scenes and accessories, touch and hold to edit the details to be used in this automation.

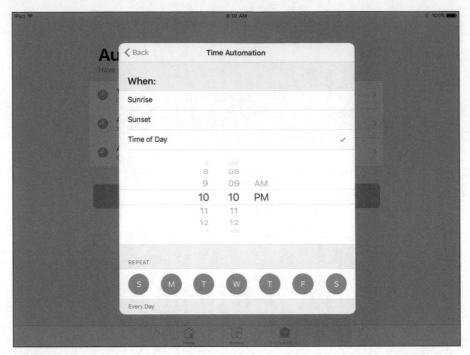

FIGURE 11-23

FIGURE 11-24

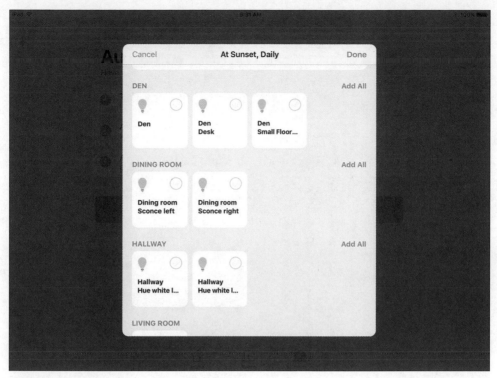

FIGURE 11-25

4

Having Fun and Consuming Media

IN THIS PART. . .

Read ebooks on your iPad.

Listen to music.

Take photos (and fix them up).

Play and record video.

Take on all comers with games on your iPad.

Get around with Maps.

Chapter 12

Using Your iPad as an E-Reader

This part of the book focuses on media: books, music, photos, videos, and more. E-books appeared in the late 1990s and were popularized by Amazon's Kindle in 2007. When iPad launched in 2010, it also supported e-books (although, as you'll see, in a different format from Kindle's).

An *e-reader* is any electronic device that enables you to download and read books, magazines, PDF files, and newspapers. These devices typically are portable and designed only for reading the electronic versions of published materials.

Apple's free, preinstalled app that turns your iPad into an e-reader is *iBooks*, which enables you to buy and download books from Apple's iBooks Store. You can also use one of several other free e-readers, such as the Kindle app.

REMEMBER

Although e-book readers such as iBooks are free, e-book devices, such as the Kindle, are not. The iPad is a bit different from most e-readers: It allows you to use iBooks or other e-reader apps (which typically are free).

In this chapter, you discover the options available for buying books and subscribing to publications. You also see how to navigate an e-book, interactive book, or periodical; adjust brightness and type; search books; and organize your iBooks library.

What Is an E-Book?

E-books come in two basic types:

» **Basic:** Basic e-books are essentially printed books reformatted for reading on an e-reader — a dedicated device like Amazon's Kindle or a device like the iPad or iPhone (yes, many people do read books on their phones). The software on the device supports *pagination* — formatting the text so that it appears in pages and providing support to go the next or previous page. Typically, you can search for words or phrases, and you may be able to annotate or highlight sections of the book.

Most e-book readers allow you to change the font size to your preference. In general, when you change the font size, the e-book reader repaginates the text so that the pages appear in the correct font. The consequence of this is that as the font and page size change, the page numbers change as well. All that is handled automatically on the device as part of its pagination. Thus, page 35 of an e-book on one device with one font size setting may be page 52 on another device.

You can buy basic e-books from online stores such as Apple's iBooks Store and Amazon's Kindle Store, as well as from publishers.

» **Enhanced:** Enhanced e-books can include features such as animation, audio, and video that can't be included in a printed book. Like basic e-books, they're available from online stores and publishers.

TIP

Apps can be also used to present book content. The text of a book along with enhanced features (animation, audio, and video) can be presented alongside interactive features (particularly useful in textbooks) and other advanced features in an app. The same content is available in different formats for many books on the App Store (as apps) and on the iBooks Store (as iBooks). To see the differences search for a book that's a classic like *A Tale of Two Cities* in both stores and compare the descriptions of the iBook and the app versions.

Find Books with iBooks

To shop in the iBooks Store, follow these steps:

1. Tap the iBooks icon on the home screen to open the app, as shown in **Figure 12-1**.

2. Tap the Featured tab at the bottom to show books currently featured in the iBooks Store. (In this figure and most of the others in this chapter, the actual books you see will vary over time.) You'll be able to buy any of these books as described in the "Buy Books" section later in this chapter.

3. On the Featured tab, tap Categories at the top left to see the categories of books, as shown in **Figure 12-2**.

4. Explore the iBooks Store:

   a. *Tap My Books to see the books you've purchased.*

   b. *Tap NYTimes to see the current New York Times best-sellers.*

   c. *Tap Top Charts to see what's selling in the iBooks Store.*

   d. *Tap Top Authors to see the best-selling authors in the iBooks Store.*

   e. *Tap Purchased to see any books you've bought on devices signed in with the same Apple ID.* You can tap the All tab to show content from all devices or tap the Not on This iPad tab to see only content purchased on your other devices.

FIGURE 12-1

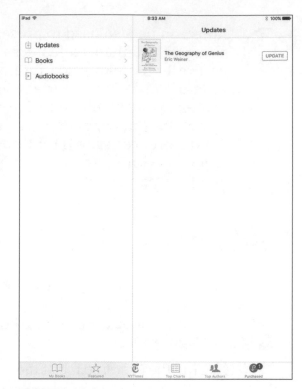

FIGURE 12-2

When there is a badge on the tab as there is in Figure 12-1, the number in the badge indicates the number of books for which updates are available. Yes, one of the key advantages of an e-book over a printed book is that it can be updated for you at no cost. (A new edition of a book such as the 2019 guide to Europe is typically not a free update but a priced separate edition. It's up to the publisher.)

TIP

My Books includes books you've purchased from the iBooks Store as well as PDF files that you have added on your own. Your PDF files are not included in the Purchased tab.

TIP

You can download samples before you buy. You get to read several pages of the book to see whether it appeals to you, and it doesn't cost you a dime! Look for the Sample button when you view details about a book. If you like the book, you can buy it from within the iBooks app by tapping the sample and then tapping

Buy. Hmmm, this is just like buying music, movies, and music on iTunes, isn't it?

Explore Other E-Readers

You can use other e-reader apps on the iPad to display content from bookstores other than the iBooks Store.

1. Download an e-reader application, such as Kindle from the App Store. (See Chapter 10 for details on how to download apps.)

2. Read the books you've purchased from Amazon or another publisher for your Kindle account on your iPad.

   Today, many publishers automatically publish e-book versions of most of their titles for iBooks and for Kindle and often other formats. The formats are not transferrable.

Buy Books

Many books in the iBooks Store are free, but we still refer to the process of obtaining them as "buying" them. Here's how you do that.

Get books from the iBooks Store

If you've set up an account in the iTunes Store, you can use the iBooks app to buy books at the iBooks Store. This store is available through iTunes (see Chapter 9) and the iBooks app on your iPad.

1. Tap the iBooks icon to open iBooks (refer to Figure 12-1).

2. Tap Featured at the bottom of the screen to open the iBooks Store.

3. When you find a book you want to explore, tap it to open its details page, as shown in **Figure 12-3**.

4. (Optional) If a Sample button is available, you can tap it to download a sample of the book.

Price

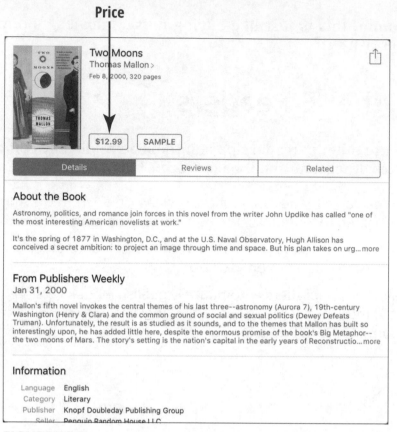

About the Book

Astronomy, politics, and romance join forces in this novel from the writer John Updike has called "one of the most interesting American novelists at work."

It's the spring of 1877 in Washington, D.C., and at the U.S. Naval Observatory, Hugh Allison has conceived a secret ambition: to project an image through time and space. But his plan takes on urg...more

From Publishers Weekly
Jan 31, 2000

Mallon's fifth novel invokes the central themes of his last three--astronomy (Aurora 7), 19th-century Washington (Henry & Clara) and the common ground of social and sexual politics (Dewey Defeats Truman). Unfortunately, the result is as studied as it sounds, and to the themes that Mallon has built so interestingly upon, he has added little here, despite the enormous promise of the book's Big Metaphor-- the two moons of Mars. The story's setting is the nation's capital in the early years of Reconstructio...more

Information

Language	English
Category	Literary
Publisher	Knopf Doubleday Publishing Group
Seller	Penguin Random House LLC

FIGURE 12-3

5. When you're ready to purchase, tap the book's price button (see **Figure 12-3**). The button changes to the Buy Book button (see **Figure 12-4**). If the book is free, these buttons are labeled Get and Get Book, respectively.

6. Tap the Buy Book or Get Book button. If you haven't already signed in, iTunes asks for your Apple ID and password; if you're signed in, your purchase downloads immediately. The book appears on the bookshelf in your iBooks library, and the cost is charged to whichever credit card you specified when you opened your iTunes account.

Buy Book

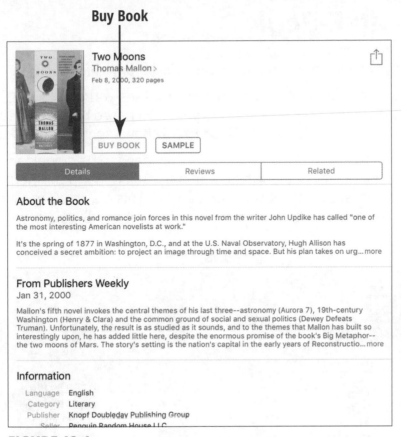

FIGURE 12-4

Get books from other sources

Content is available from a variety of other sources, such as Project Gutenberg (www.gutenberg.org) and Google.

TIP

Many public libraries allow you to borrow e-books and sync them to your iPad. Certain formats may need to be associated with the apps for those formats, such as the Mobi and AZW formats for the Kindle.

Navigate an E-Book

1. Tap the iBooks icon to open your iBooks library (refer to Figure 12-1).

2. Tap the My Books tab at the bottom. You'll see your books. (Remember that My Books shows your purchased books as well as PDFs you may have added.) **Figure 12-5** shows some of my books.

Some of the book images show that they need to be downloaded from iCloud, others show the cover of a traditionally published book, and others show PDF books I have added. This is a scrolling view so you see parts of some of the books at the top and the bottom.

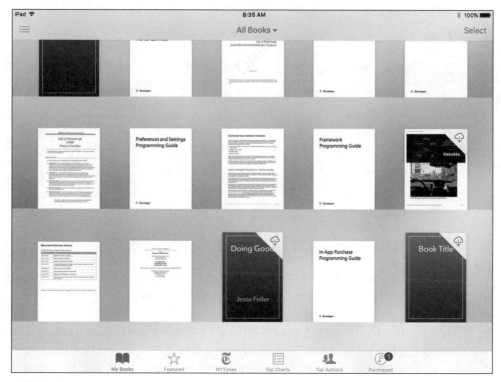

FIGURE 12-5

3. Tap a book's cover. (If it's stored in iCloud, it may take a few moments to download.) The book opens, as shown in **Figure 12-6**. If you hold your iPad in portrait orientation (short side on top), it shows one page; in landscape orientation (long side on top), it shows two. Note that Figure 12-6 shows the iBooks edition of *iPad User Guide for iOS 10*.

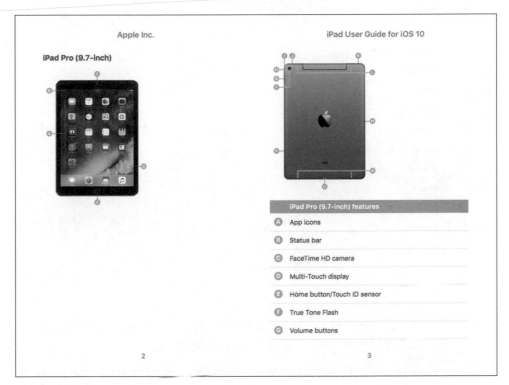

FIGURE 12-6

4. Take any of the following actions to navigate the book:

- *To go to the book's table of contents:* Tap the screen to display various tools; tap the Table of Contents button at the top of the page (it looks like a little bulleted list); and then tap the name of a chapter in the table of contents (see **Figure 12-7**) to go to it. Tap Resume in the upper left to leave the Table of Contents.

- *To turn to the next page:* Tap your finger anywhere on the right edge of the page or flick to the left from the right edge.

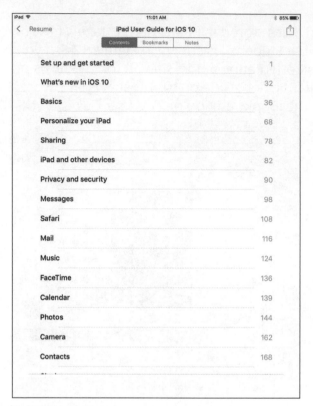

FIGURE 12-7

- *To return to the preceding page:* Tap your finger anywhere on the left edge of the page or flick to the right.

- *To move to a nonadjacent page:* Tap anywhere on the page to show the slider at the bottom of the page, as shown in **Figure 12-8**. Then drag to the right or left to go to another page.

TIP

- *To return to the library* to view another book at any time, tap the left-pointing arrow at the top left of the page. If the button isn't visible, tap anywhere on the page, and the tools appear. Note that the tools, including the left-pointing arrow, are visible in Figure 12-8 but not in Figure 12-6.

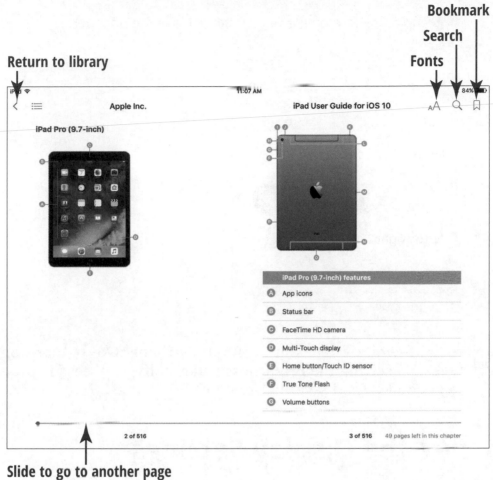

Return to library

Bookmark

Search

Fonts

Slide to go to another page

FIGURE 12-8

Adjust Brightness

iBooks offers an adjustable brightness setting that you can use to make your book pages more comfortable to read.

1. With a book open, tap the Font button (shown in Figure 12-8). The Font popover opens (see **Figure 12-9**).

2. Tap and drag the Brightness slider at the top of the popover to the right to make the screen brighter, or tap and drag the slider to the left to dim the screen.

3. Tap anywhere on the book page to close the popover.

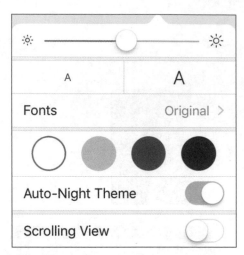

FIGURE 12-9

TIP

Bright-white screens are commonly thought to be hard on the eyes, so setting the Brightness slider halfway or less is probably a good idea (and saves battery life).

Change the Display Settings

If the type on your screen is a bit hard for you to make out, you can change to a larger font size, choose a different font for readability, or adjust the display theme.

1. With a book open, tap the Font button (refer to Figure 12-8).

2. In the Font popover (refer to Figure 12-9), tap the button with a small *A* on the left to use smaller text, or tap the button with the large *A* on the right to use larger text.

3. Tap Fonts. The list of fonts shown in **Figure 12-10** appears.

4. Tap a font name to select it. The font changes on the book page.

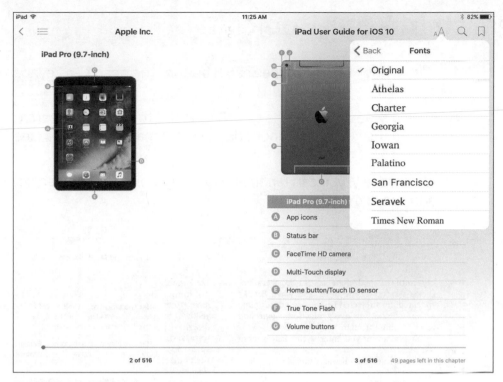

FIGURE 12-10

5. If you want to add a sepia tint to the pages or to reverse black and white, which can be easier on the eyes, tap the White, Sepia, Gray, or Black icon (refer to Figure 12-9) to choose the theme you want to display. Black causes the iPad to detect a dark environment and automatically display the page in Night mode, even if another theme is set.

6. Tap outside the Font popover to return to your book.

TIP

Some fonts appear a bit larger on your screen than others because of their design. If you want the largest font, use Iowan.

REMEMBER

If you're reading a PDF file, you're reading a picture of a document rather than an e-book, so you can't modify the page's appearance by using the Font popover.

Search in Your Book

1. With a book open, tap the Search button. The onscreen keyboard appears.

2. Type a search term in the search field and then tap the Search key on the keyboard. iBooks displays any matching entries (see **Figure 12-11**).

Alternatively, you can tap the Dictation key on the onscreen keyboard and speak the term.

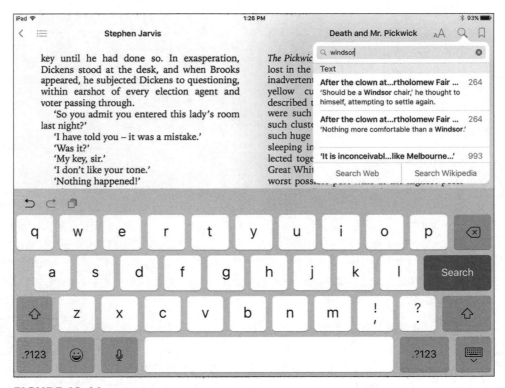

FIGURE 12-11

3. Scroll down the entries and tap the one you want.

TIP

You can tap the Search Web or Search Wikipedia link at the bottom of the Search popover to search for information about the search term online.

Add Bookmarks, Highlights, and Notes

Bookmarks and highlights enable you to revisit a favorite passage or refresh your memory about a character or plot point.

1. To bookmark a page, display the page and then tap the Bookmark button in the top-right corner. A ribbon appears in the top-right corner of the page.

2. To highlight a word or phrase, press a word until the toolbar shown in **Figure 12-12** appears.

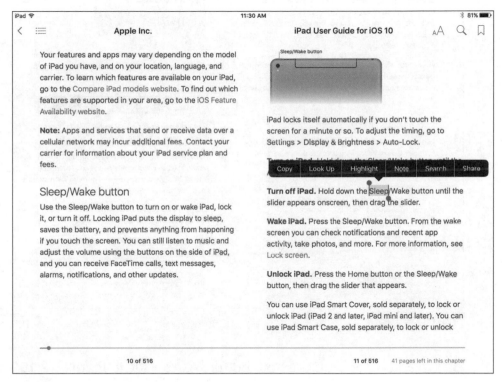

FIGURE 12-12

3. Tap the Highlight button to show the menu shown in **Figure 12-13**.

4. Tap the button with three colored circles. A colored highlight is placed on the word, and the color palette shown in **Figure 12-14** appears.

5. Tap the color for the highlight you want to use.

Highlight Trash Note Share

FIGURE 12-13

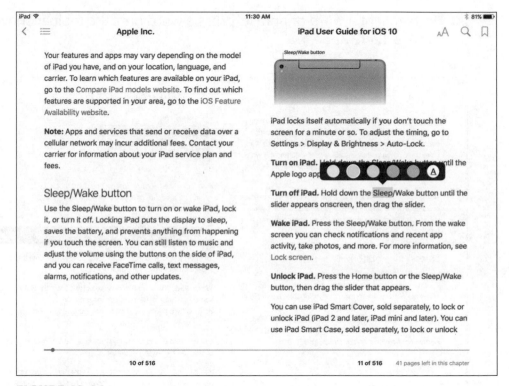

FIGURE 12-14

6. To add a note, tap the note button. As you see in **Figure 12-15**, the keyboard appears and you can type a note.

7. To delete a highlight or note, tap the highlight itself and then tap the trash can in the choices shown in Figure 14-13.

8. Tap outside the menu in Figure 12-13 to close it.

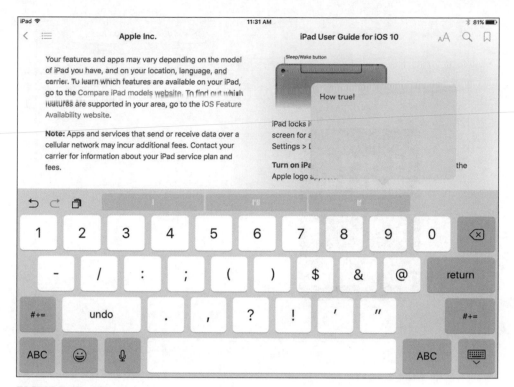

FIGURE 12-15

View a Bookmark or Note

 1. To go to a list of bookmarks and notes, tap the Table of Contents button on a book page, as shown in Figure 12-7.

2. On the table of contents page, tap the Bookmarks or Notes tab to see a list of your bookmarks and notes (see **Figure 12-16**). A highlight without a note or bookmark isn't kept.

3. Tap a bookmark or note to go to that location in the book.

4. If you encounter a bookmark or note as you're reading, it will be marked in the margin, as you see in **Figure 12-17**. You can tap it to read the note.

TIP

The iPad automatically bookmarks the place where you left off reading in a book, so you don't have to do it manually. Because that information is stored in the iTunes Store, you can pick up where you left off on a Mac or any other iOS device you own.

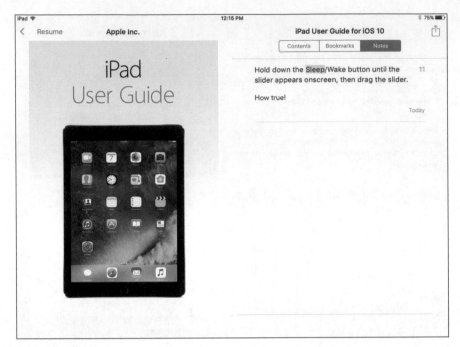

FIGURE 12-16

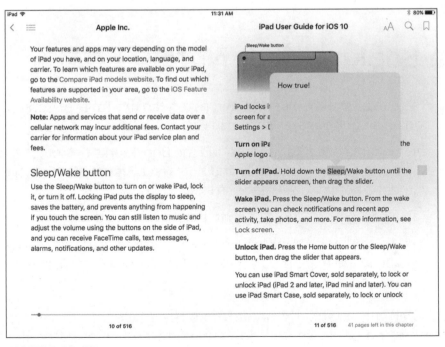

FIGURE 12-17

Check Words in the Dictionary

1. With a book open, tap a word to highlight it.

2. Lift your finger; then press and hold the word until the toolbar shown in Figure 12-12 appears.

3. Tap the Look Up button. You see a popover with definition and other references, as shown in **Figure 12-18**.

4. Tap Done to close the popover.

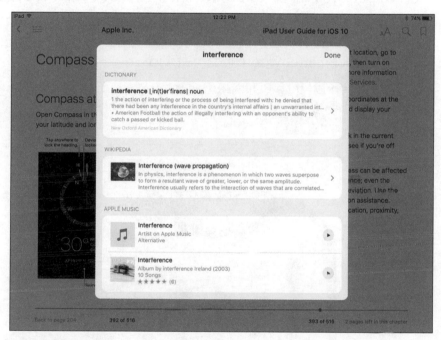

FIGURE 12-18

Adding a PDF

Adding a PDF to your iBooks collection is very simple today. It wasn't this simple in some of the earlier versions of iBooks, so be careful following complicated directions you may find from the past on the web.

Here's how you add a PDF.

1. Open the document you want to share. It can be a PDF document, or it can be something like an image document that iOS can convert to a PDF. (The easiest way to find this out is to follow these steps.)

2. If a Share button is shown (it's usually in the top-right of the view), tap it. If it is not shown, you can't share the document, but if you can share it, the Sharing view appears, as shown in **Figure 12-19**.

3. Look for an option to share with iBooks. If there isn't one, you can't share it. But if you can, the document will be added to iBooks as a PDF.

4. Tap to open a PDF file you want to add to iBooks. It might be a PDF file on your iCloud Drive, or it might be one saved by one of your apps. It doesn't matter where it came from.

5. If someone sends you a PDF in email (or you send it to yourself), you can just tap the PDF in Mail to add it to your iBooks library.

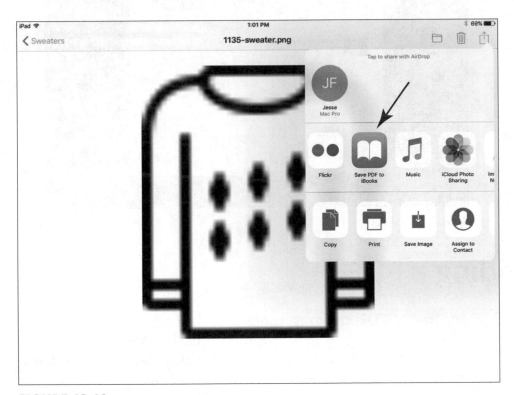

FIGURE 12-19

Chapter 13
Playing Music on the iPad

iPad includes an app called Music that allows you to take advantage of the iPad's amazing sound system to play your favorite music.

In this chapter, you get acquainted with Music and its features. You also get an overview of AirPlay, which you can use to access and play your music over a home network or any connected device. Finally, I introduce you to iTunes Radio for your listening pleasure.

View the Library Contents

You'll see how to view your music library's contents in this section. But if there's nothing there, you might want to head to Chapter 9 to see how you can buy some music from the iTunes Store. Then you can come back here and carry on.

1. Tap the Music app's icon to launch the app, which opens to display the Music library. **Figure 13-1** shows the library in Albums view.

2. Tap the Library menu (see **Figure 13-2**) to sort your music by Recently Added, Playlists, Artists, Albums, and Songs.

FIGURE 13-1

FIGURE 13-2

Create a Playlist

You can create your own playlists to put tracks from various sources in collections of your choosing.

1. With Music open, tap Playlists on the Library menu (refer to Figure 13-2). Your playlists appear, as shown in **Figure 13-3**. Sometimes the playlist has an icon that reflects its contents; other times, its a default icon, as are most of them in Figure 13-3.

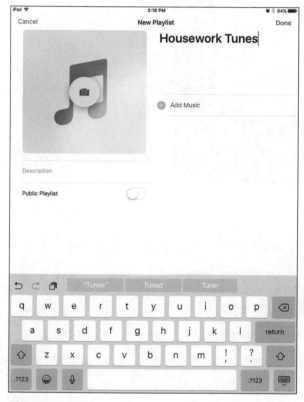

FIGURE 13-3

2. Tap the New button in the top-right corner. The New Playlist screen appears (see **Figure 13-4**).

3. Type a new playlist name over the default playlist name (refer to Figure 13-3).

FIGURE 13-4

4. (Optional) Enter a description of the playlist in the Description field, if you want.

5. Tap Add Music to start adding content to your playlist. The Library dialog opens (refer to **Figure 13-4**).

6. Tap Genres to open the Genres dialog (see **Figure 13-5**).

7. Tap the genre of music you want to use. You see the albums in your Music library that are in the genre you selected (see **Figure 13-6**).

8. Tap an album to see its songs (see **Figure 13-7**).

9. Tap the Add button (+) for each song you want to add to your playlist. The Add button changes to a check mark.

10. Tap Done to save the playlist. Your playlist appears on the Playlists screen.

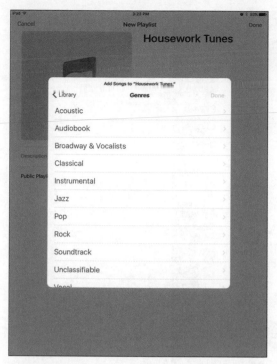

FIGURE 13-5

FIGURE 13-6

FIGURE 13-7

Edit a Playlist

1. With Music open, tap Playlists on the Library menu to open the Playlists screen.

2. Tap the playlist you want to edit.

3. On the playlist's screen, tap the Edit button in the top-right corner.

4. Add or delete songs by tapping the green + buttons or red – buttons, respectively (see **Figure 13-8**).

5. Change the order of songs in the playlist by dragging the three-bar icon at the right end of each song's name up or down in the list.

FIGURE 13-8

6. Add a photo or other image by tapping the camera icon on the playlist's cover image (refer to Figure 13-8) and then browsing to the image you want to use. By default, Music uses the cover image of the first song you added to the playlist.

7. Tap the Done button in the top-right corner to save your changes.

Search Your Music Library

1. With Music open, tap the Search tab on the bottom toolbar to open the Search screen, shown in **Figure 13-9**.

FIGURE 13-9

2. Enter a search term in the Search field, or tap the Dictation key on the onscreen keyboard and speak the search term. The results are displayed as you type. (See Chapter 2 for more on Dictation.)

3. Tap a result to play that song.

Play an Individual Song

1. With Music open, tap any category on the Library menu. You'll see the songs in that category.

2. Tap the song you want to hear.

   The song begins to play, and the playback controls slide up from the bottom of the screen (see **Figure 13-10**). You can also use the controls on the lock screen.

Timeline

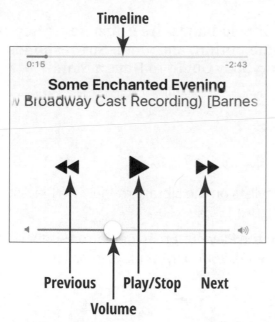

0:15   -2:43

Some Enchanted Evening
(New Broadway Cast Recording) [Barnes

Previous | **Play/Stop**   **Next**

Volume

FIGURE 13-10

3. Control playback by doing any of the following:

- Tap the Previous and Next buttons to navigate the song that's playing. The Previous button takes you back to the beginning of the item that's playing (or to the previous track if the current item is already at the beginning); the Next button takes you to the next item. These buttons also take you to the next or previous track if you're looking at tracks.

- Tap the Play button to start playback. It turns into a square Stop button.

- Tap the Stop button to pause playback.

- Adjust the volume with the volume control.

- Use the timeline to move forward and back within the song.

TIP

If the song you select in Step 2 is stored in iCloud, you may have to tap the iCloud icon next to it to download it to your iPad before it plays. See Chapter 3.

You can use Siri to play music hands–free. Just say "Hey Siri" or press and hold the Home button, and when Siri responds, say something like "Play 'Everybody Ought to Have a Maid'" or "Play 'Sondheim A Celebration.'"

Play a Playlist

1. With Music open, tap Playlists on the Library menu. The Playlists screen opens (refer to Figure 13-3).

2. Tap the playlist and then the Play button in the bottom-right corner of the screen (see **Figure 13-11**). Your playlist plays in order.

FIGURE 13-11

SHARING YOUR MUSIC

The Home Sharing feature of iTunes allows you to share music among devices that have Home Sharing turned on. Each device must use the same Apple ID on your network. After you set up the feature via iTunes, you can retrieve music and videos from your iTunes shared library to any of the devices. For more information about Home Sharing, visit https://support.apple.com.

With Family Sharing, up to six members of your family can share purchased content even if they don't use the same Apple ID. You can set up Family Sharing by tapping Settings ➪ iCloud ➪ Family. See Chapter 9 for more about Family Sharing.

Shuffle Music

If you want to play a random selection of the music that you've purchased or synced to your iPad (or the items in a playlist or album), you can use the Shuffle feature.

1. With Music open, tap Library at the top left of the screen.

2. Do one of the following:

- Tap Albums and then tap an album.
- Tap Playlists and then tap a playlist.

3. Tap a song to play it.

4. While a song is playing, tap the Shuffle button. Your content plays in random order.

TIP

The Shuffle button appears in various places in the Music app. You see it, for example, as the Shuffle All command in Figure 13-11.

Adjust the Volume

Music offers a volume control that you can adjust during playback. This volume is set relative to system volume, which you control by tapping Settings. If you set it to 50%, it plays at 50 percent of the system's volume setting.

1. With Music open, locate and tap a song to play it.

2. In the onscreen controls that appear (refer to Figure 13-10), tap and drag the button on the volume slider to the right (louder) or left (softer).

TIP

If the volume is set high but you're still having trouble hearing, consider getting a headset. It cuts out extraneous noises and may improve the quality of what you're listening to, as well as add stereo to the iPad's mono speaker. I recommend using a 3.5mm stereo headphone; insert its plug into the headphone jack at the top of your iPad.

Use AirPlay

AirPlay streaming technology is built into Apple TV, iOS devices, and the iTunes app. *Streaming* technology allows you to send media files from one device to play on another. You can send, say, a movie you've purchased on your iPad or a slide show of your photos to be played on your TV — and control the TV playback from your iPad. You can also send music to play over speakers.

You can take advantage of AirPlay in a few ways:

» You can purchase Apple TV and stream video, photos, and music to the TV.

» You can purchase AirPort Express and attach your speakers to it to play music.

» If you buy AirPort-enabled wireless speakers, you can stream audio directly to them.

One reason to stream to an Apple TV is that many people have powerful speakers attached to their TV. Even if your TV and high-quality speakers are in another room, as long as your neighbors (inside and outside the house) don't mind, you can stream from your iPad to have high-quality sound while you work or play.

Because this combination of equipment varies, my advice — if you're interested in using AirPlay — is to visit your nearest Apple Store or certified Apple Reseller and find out which hardware combination will work best for you.

iOS 10 supports peer-to-peer AirPlay support, which means that if you can make a direct connection to another device, you can share content such as music and photos without being on the same network.

If you get a bit antsy watching a long movie, one of the beauties of AirPlay is that you can still use your iPad to check email, browse photos or the Internet, or check your calendar while the media file is playing on the other device. Chapter 15 shows you how to use your iPad to add an extra window to your video playback.

APPLE MUSIC

Music (the app) works with Apple Music (a fee-based membership plan) to provide streaming versions of the songs you already own as well as unlimited access to millions more. Apple Music typically presents world premieres and exclusive releases. You can download songs for offline listening on any of your iOS or Android devices, and you can keep up to 100,000 songs in your own music library.

An Apple Music membership includes Beats 1, with on-demand and radio shows hosted by top DJs and artists. A three-month free trial is available.

For more information on memberships, see http://www.apple.com/music/.

Chapter 14

Playing with Photos

Photographers will people the world!

— JOSÉ MARTÍ, ARTICLE IN *LA OPINIÓN NACIONAL*
(CARACAS, VENEZUELA), 1831

Martí's prediction has come true. The combination of widely available and incredibly powerful cameras (did you realize how powerful your iPad's camera is?) and social media and photo-sharing services such as Facebook, Instagram, and Flickr has made that prediction come true. The possibilities of photography in communication, education, art, activism, advertising, and many other aspects of life seem to have been scarcely explored. Every day, it seems that there's something new, to the extent that we often don't notice just how incredible these advances are. (Perhaps Martí would just have smiled and nodded.)

You can take photos by using the iPad's built-in cameras in square and panorama modes, and you can edit your images with smart adjustment filters. You can also sync photos from your computer, iPhone, or digital camera. You can save images you find online or receive by email or Messages to your iPad. Then you can share photos with groups of people by using Photo Stream and your iCloud photo library, which make storing and sharing easier.

When you have photos to play with, the Photos app lets you organize photos and view photos in albums, individually, or in a slideshow. You can also view photos by the years they were taken, with images divided into collections based on where or when you took them. You can also AirDrop, email, message, or post photos to Facebook or Flickr; tweet photos to friends; print photos; or use your iPad as an electronic picture frame. Finally, you can create time-lapse videos with the Camera app, which allows you to record a sequence in time, such as a flower opening as the sun warms it. You can read about all these features in this chapter.

Understand the iPad's Cameras

The rear-facing camera on the 12.9-inch iPad Pro is an 8-megapixel iSight camera; on the 9.7-inch iPad Pro, it's a 12-megapixel iSight camera. The camera comes with an illumination sensor that adjusts to whatever lighting is available. Face detection balances focus across as many as ten faces in your pictures. The video camera offers 1080p high-definition (HD) video recording with video stabilization that makes up for some shaking as you hold the device to take videos. On the 9.7-inch iPad Pro 4K, video recording at 3840x2160 is provided. New video recording features on both models you'll want to check out are time-lapse and slo-mo. (For more about video on iPad, see Chapter 15.)

Review the Camera Controls

The Camera app's controls appear on the right of the screen, as shown in **Figure 14-1**. But some may not be visible, particularly when the iPad is in landscape mode. Figure 14-1 is a photo of a painted wall. That's not particularly interesting to most people, but I want you to focus on the camera controls that are sometimes hard to spot when you're looking at the trapeze artist or sunset in the photo.

Note that for several of these controls, one of the choices is "Auto." This lets your iPad and its Camera app just "do the right thing." I almost always use Auto for the flash setting.

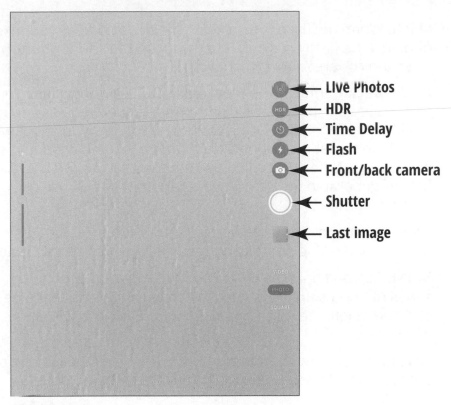

- ←— Live Photos
- ←— HDR
- ←— Time Delay
- ←— Flash
- ←— Front/back camera
- ←— Shutter
- ←— Last image

FIGURE 14-1

From top to bottom, here are the controls:

» **Live Photos:** Tap this control, and your photo will include the still image (JPEG) and a 3-second video that precedes the instant when you took the image. Your choices are LIVE OFF and LIVE.

» **HDR:** This control automatically takes three slightly different exposures and combines them into the best combination automatically. Your Choices are Auto, On, and Off.

» **Timer:** Frame your shot and focus (by tapping the center of the scene), then leave it somewhere sturdy (on a tripod if you want to be fancy), set the timer, and tap the Shutter button. At the end of the time interval, the photo will be taken. Your choices are Off, 3 seconds, and 10 seconds.

» **Flash:** When the flash is on, extra light is provided as you take photos. (The flash fires only when you tap the shutter button.) Your choices are Auto, On, and Off.

» **Front/Back Camera:** The Front/Back Camera control lets you switch between the front-facing camera (toward you as you hold the iPad) and the back-facing camera, which lets you shoot what you're looking at. The front-facing camera is often used for selfies and FaceTime. (When you use the front-facing camera, the flash is generated on the home screen that's facing you as you hold the camera.)

» **Shutter Button:** The large button is the shutter button. It's white when you're taking photos and red when you're recording video.

» **Burst:** Tap and hold the shutter button to take a continuing series of photos until you release it. You can then pick the best one and delete the rest. (This is great for kids, animals, and windy days.)

» **Last Image:** Below the shutter button is a thumbnail image of the last photo or video you took. Tap it to see it in Photos.

Beneath these settings, you'll find a vertically scrolling list of other settings. You'll have to scroll it to see all of them. From top to bottom, here's what you'll see:

» Time-Lapse

» Slo-Mo

» **Video:** This control (the shutter button, turned red for videos) has two options: Slo-Mo, which captures your video in slow motion, and Time Lapse, which captures video frames slowly so that when you play back the video, time seems to speed up.

» **Photo settings:** I describe the Photo, Square, and Pano options in "Take Pictures with the iPad" later in this chapter.

Take Pictures with the iPad

1. Tap the Camera icon to open the Camera app.

   You can also open the Camera app by swiping up from the bottom edge of the screen to open Control Center and then tapping the Camera icon.

   The orange highlighted word below the shutter button (see Figure 14-1) is the active setting.

2. Set an option by tapping it.

   - *Photo:* This is a standard photo.

   - *Square:* This setting lets you create square images like those you see on the popular Instagram site.

   - *Pano:* Tap Pano to take a panoramic view. You begin to capture an image, move the camera across the view keeping it on the horizontal line, as you see in **Figure 14-2**. When you complete the panorama, it is captured for you in a wide horizontal wrap-around image.

3. Move the camera around until you find a pleasing image on your iPad screen.

4. Make any adjustments you want to make. You can do a couple of things at this point to help your photo:

   - Use the slider to magnify the image.

   - Tap the area of the screen where you want the camera to autofocus. Tap the place in the image that you want to be in best focus; the rest of the image will be a bit less focused. Also, the lighting of the selected place in the image will be optimized.

   - You can also pinch in or out to include more or less of the image in your photo.

   - If you want a time delay before the camera snaps the picture, tap the Timer button near the top-right corner of the screen and then tap 3s or 10s for a 3- or 10-second delay. This setting can give you time to get into the shot.

   - Tap the icon with the camera and the two circular arrows to switch between the front camera and rear camera. Now you can take a selfie (picture of yourself), as the camera is now facing you.

FIGURE 14-2

5. Tap the large shutter button on the right-center side of the screen, and release it when you have the image in view. You've just taken a picture and that picture has been stored in the Photos app's gallery automatically.

6. You can see the last photo by tapping the Last Image button, as shown in Figure 14-2.

7. If you're done taking photos, press the Home button to close the Camera app.

TIP

You can also use the up switch or the volume buttons on the right side of your iPad to capture a picture or start or stop video camera recording.

PANORAMA TIPS

If you're planning to be at a place where you might want to take a panorama, practice beforehand. Take a panorama of your bedroom, the street you live on, or people gathered around a table (or unoccupied chairs). If you want a panorama of people at a feast, you really don't need the grief and aggravation of asking them to smile and not eat the delicious food that's in front of them while you fiddle with your iPad.

SETTING FOCUS

Before tapping the shutter button to take the following figure, I tapped a dark area of the chair to bring it into focus and adjusted the lighting to make that object clearer.

(continued)

(continued)

Compare the above photo with the next one in this sidebar for which I didn't tap anything to set the focus. The iPad's camera adjusted the focus and lens setting to make everything in the image more or less equally clear. Focusing your iPad's camera matters when you have differences in lighting between areas of your image as well as when parts of the image are at different distances from the camera.

TIP

If you want to capture a series of photos in rapid succession, use the Burst feature. Simply hold down the shutter button while aiming the camera at your subject; the iPad continuously snaps photos.

TIP

You can take photos of your iPad's screen by just pressing the Sleep/Wake button at the top of the iPad and the Home button at the same time. The screen image (called a *screenshot*) will be stored in your photo album inside the Camera app.

Import Photos

Your computer isn't the only photo source available to you. You can also import photos from a digital camera if you buy the iPad Camera Connection Kit from Apple. The kit contains two adapters (see **Figure 14-3**): a USB camera connector to import photos from a digital camera or another iOS device and an SD card reader to import image files from an SD card.

Import from a digital camera

To import photos from a digital camera, follow these steps:

1. Insert the USB camera connector into the Lightning connector slot of your iPad, as you see in Figure 14-3.

USB Camera Connector

SD Card Reader

FIGURE 14-3

2. Connect the USB end of the cord that came with your digital camera into the USB camera connector.

3. Connect the other end of the cord that came with your iPad into that device.

4. The Photos app opens and displays the photos on the digital camera.

5. Tap Import All on your iPad or — if you want to import only selected photos — tap those photos and then tap Import. A prompt asks whether you want to delete or keep the images on the media.

6. Make your choice at the prompt. The photos are saved to the Last Import album.

7. Disconnect the cord and the adapter. You're done!

Import from an SD card

To import photos stored on a secure digital (SD) memory card, simply insert the SD card reader into the iPad, insert the SD card containing the photos, and then follow Steps 5 through 7 of the preceding list.

Save Photos from the Web

1. Open Safari, and navigate to the web page containing the image you want.

2. Press and hold the image. A popover appears, as shown in **Figure 14-4**.

3. Tap Save Image. The image is saved to the Recently Added album in the Photos app.

For more about how to use Safari to navigate to or search for web content, see Chapter 6.

Many sites protect their photos from being copied by applying an invisible overlay. This blank overlay ensures that you don't actually get the image you're tapping. Even if a site doesn't take these precautions, be sure that you don't use images from the web in ways that violate the rights of the owner.

FIGURE 14-4

View an Album

The Photos app organizes your pictures into albums, using such criteria as the folder on your computer from which you synced the photos or photos captured with the iPad's camera. You may also have albums for images you synced from devices such as your iPhone or digital camera.

1. To view your albums, tap the Photos app's icon to open the app.

2. Tap the Albums tab at the bottom of the screen to display your albums, as shown in **Figure 14-5**.

3. Tap an album. The photos in it are displayed. **Figure 14-6** shows my Screenshots album. You may recognize some of the photos from this book.

FIGURE 14-5

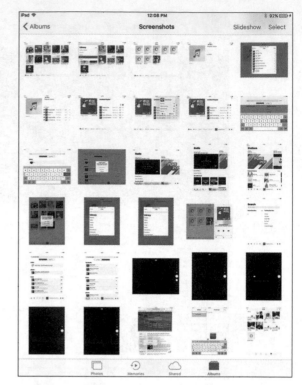

FIGURE 14-6

View Individual Photos

1. Tap the Photos app's icon to open the app.

2. Tap the Photos tab at the bottom of the screen. Your photos are displayed by criteria such as a time taken or location (see **Figure 14-7**).

3. Tap a photo to view it. You can place your fingers on the photo and then spread your fingers to expand it.

4. Flick your finger to the left or right to scroll through the album and look at the individual photos in it.

5. If you want to view the next-highest level of your photo collection, tap the arrow button in the top-left corner (which may display different words depending on where you are in a collection of photos).

FIGURE 14-7

TIP

You can place a photo from the Photos app on a person's information page in the Contacts app. For more about how to do it, see Chapter 20.

Edit Photos

The Photos app lets you edit photos with a variety of tools, including smart adjustment filters and smart composition tools.

1. Tap the Photos app's icon to open the app.

2. Locate and display a photo you want to edit.

3. Tap the Edit button.

The Edit Photo popover, shown in **Figure 14-8**, lets you duplicate a photo before editing it if you want. That way you don't have to worry about messing up your photos. (Also, as you'll see, as you go along you have the ability to experiment and not save your changes.)

FIGURE 14-8

4. Edit the photo. You have several controls on the left side of the screen to help you, as shown in **Figure 14-9**:

   • *Enhance:* Tap the Enhance button (it looks like a magic wand) to turn this feature on or off. Enhance improves the overall crispness of the figure. The enhancements are often less noticeable in large outdoor photos than in smaller photos of people, but experiment with them for yourself.

   • *Rotate and Crop:* This button lets you rotate the image, as you see in **Figure 14-10**. You can move the rotation dial up and down to control the angle of rotation. (This can fix those where a horizon line is not horizontal because you were holding the camera at an angle.) The four corners (highlighted as you see in Figure 14-10) are hot. Drag any corner to crop the photo.

- *Filters:* Apply any of nine filters (such as Fade, Mono, and Noir) to change the feel of your image, as shown in **Figure 14-11**. These effects adjust the brightness of your image or apply a black-and-white tone to your color photos. Tap the Filters button in the middle of the tools at the bottom of the screen and scroll to view available filters. Tap one and then tap Apply to apply the effect to your image.

Rotate and crop
Enhance
Done

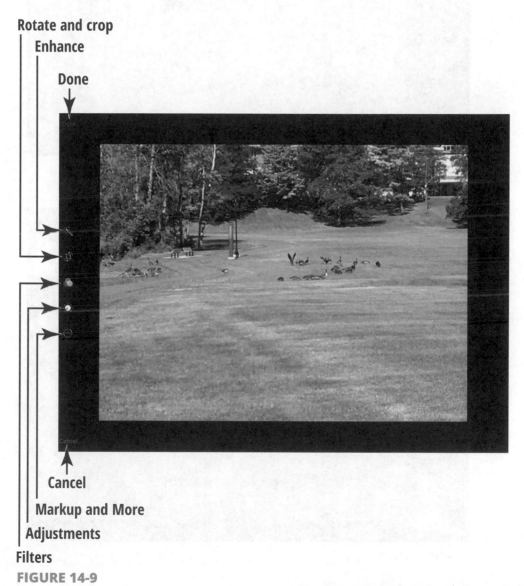

Cancel
Markup and More
Adjustments
Filters
FIGURE 14-9

FIGURE 14-10

FIGURE 14-11

- *Adjustments:* Tap Light, Color, or B&W to access a slew of tools that you can use to tweak contrast, color intensity, shadows, and more. (See Figure 14-12).

FIGURE 14-12

- *More:* You can annotate a photo with Markup in this option. If you have an Apple Pencil, you can provide clear instructions for someone to enhance the photo further using Markup.

5. When you're pleased with your edits, tap the Done button to save the edited photo. If you aren't pleased, tap Revert to Original to get rid of all your changes, as shown in **Figure 14-13.**

Each editing control has a Cancel and Done button. If you don't like the changes you made, tap these buttons to stop making changes or undo the changes you've already made. Cancel and Done are shown in Figure 14-9.

FIGURE 14-13

Create a New Album

The first step in organizing your photos into albums is to create an album into which to put the photos. Here's how you do that.

1. Tap the Albums tab in the bottom of the window.

2. Tap + at the top left to begin to create a new album.

3. You will be asked to name it, as you see in Figure 14-14.

Now you're ready to put photos into it.

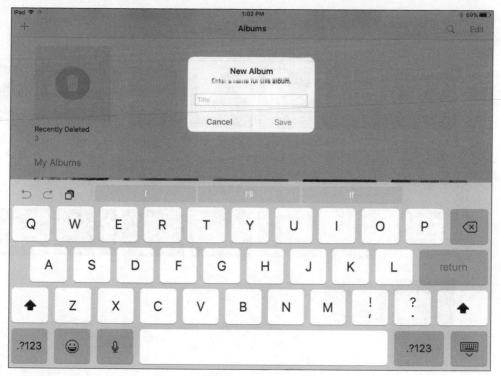

FIGURE 14-14

Organize Photos in an Existing Album

1. Tap the Albums tab at the bottom of the screen to display the albums you have now.

2. Tap the album you want to work with. You'll see its photos.

3. Tap the Select button in the top-right corner and then tap individual photos to select them. Small check marks appear on the selected photos (see **Figure 14-15**).

4. Tap the Add To button.

5. Then tap the album you want to use from the display of all albums.

You can combine creating an album and using it if you want. Just follow Steps 1 through 5. You'll see that the first album in the display of all albums is a gray square named New Album. . . .Tap it to create a new album and to use it immediately.

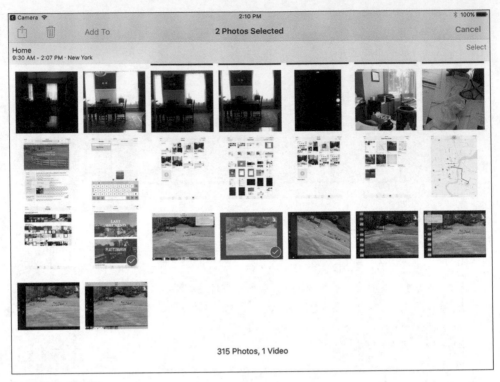

FIGURE 14-15

View Photos by Year and Location

You can view your photos in logical categories such as Years and Moments. These so-called smart groupings let you view all photos by criteria such as date taken or location where taken.

1. Tap the Photos app's icon to open the app.

2. Tap Photos at the bottom of the screen. The display of photos by date and location appears (refer to Figure 14-7 earlier in this chapter). (You may see another selection, but this is one of the basic settings.)

3. Tap Memories on the bottom toolbar to see photos organized by date and place, as shown in **Figure 14-16**.

   To go back to larger groupings, such as from a moment in a collection to the larger collection to the entire past year, just keep tapping the Back button in the top-left corner of the screen (which will be named after the next collection up in the hierarchy, such as Collections or Years).

FIGURE 14-16

Search for Photos

With all these photos available to you, you'll need to be able to search a library for the one you want.

1. Tap the Photos app's icon to open the app.

2. Tap Photos at the bottom of the screen.

3. Tap the Search button at the top of the screen. A list of so-called "smart" suggestions appears.

4. Tap one of these suggestions, or enter the date or time of the photo, a location, or an album name in the Search field to locate the photo.

Share Photos with Mail, Twitter, and Facebook

You can easily share photos stored on your iPad by sending them as email attachments, posting them to Facebook, sharing them via iCloud Photo Sharing or Flickr, or tweeting them via Twitter.

REMEMBER

You have to have the appropriate social media accounts and apps on your iPad before you use this feature.

1. Tap the Photos app's icon to open the app.

2. Tap the Photos or Albums button, and locate the photo you want to share.

3. Tap the photo you want to share and then tap the Share button (which looks like a box with an arrow jumping out of it).

4. Tap additional photos to share, if you want.

5. Tap Message, Mail, iCloud Photo Sharing, Twitter, Facebook, or Flickr.

6. In the message form that appears, make any modifications that apply in the To, Cc/Bcc, or Subject field; then type a message (for email) or enter your post or tweet text.

7. If you're using Mail, you can choose the size of the image you send (see **Figure 14-17**) by tapping the image-size information in the message.

8. Tap the Send or Post button, depending on which sharing method you chose. The message and photo are sent or posted.

TIP

Use the same process to add your photo to Notes or various other apps. Your choices depend on what's installed on your iPad.

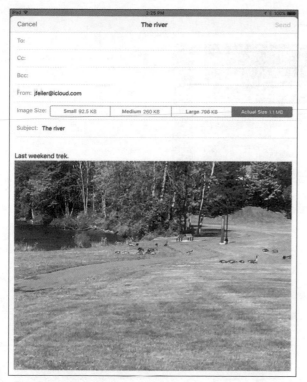

FIGURE 14-17

Share Photos with AirDrop

AirDrop allows you to share content such as photos with people who are nearby and who have AirDrop-enabled devices.

1. Tap the Photos app's icon to open the app.

2. Tap the Photos or Albums button, and locate the photo you want to share.

3. Tap the photo you want to share and then tap the Share button. If an AirDrop-enabled device is in your immediate vicinity (within 12 ft.), you see the device listed on the Share popover, as shown in Figure 14-18.

4. Tap the device name. Your photo is shared with the other device. The recipient has the option of accepting or declining the share.

FIGURE 14-18

TIP

The other iOS device has to have AirDrop enabled and has to be running iOS 7 or later. To enable a device, open Control Center by swiping up from the bottom of any screen and then tap the Air-Drop button in the bottom center of the screen. Tap the AirDrop button at the bottom of the screen, and choose Contacts Only or Everyone from the menu that appears to specify with whom you can use AirDrop.

Share Photos with iCloud Photo Sharing

iCloud Photo Sharing allows you to share photo streams with others when you're connected to a Wi-Fi network. You can also subscribe to another person's photo stream if she shares it with you.

1. To set up Photo Stream, tap Settings ⇨ Photos & Camera.

2. Tap the iCloud Photo Sharing on/off button to turn on this feature.

3. Tap My Photo Streaming to share with others who don't have iCloud accounts.

4. To share photos with somebody who has an iCloud account, return to the home screen, and tap Photos.

   Tap the Share button and then tap to select the photos you want to share just as you do to share photos with Twitter, Mail, and the other apps described previously. Tap iCloud Photo Sharing. An alert appears.

   Enter a comment and then tap Post. The selected photos are posted to your iCloud Photo Library. Tap Cancel if you decide not to share the photo.

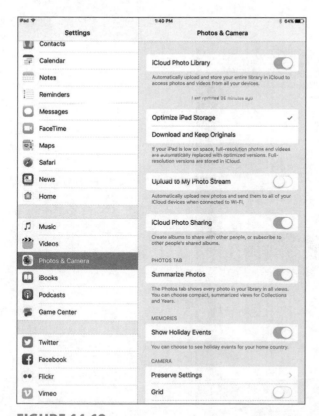

FIGURE 14-19

Print Photos

If you have a wireless printer that's compatible with Apple AirPrint technology or you use a device such as Lantronix xPrintServer plugged into your network, you can print photos from your iPad.

1. With the Photos app open, locate the photo you want to print, and tap it to maximize it.

2. Tap the Share button and then tap Print.

3. In the Printer Options dialog that appears, tap Select Printer. The iPad searches for any compatible printers on your local network (see **Figure 14-20**).

4. Tap to select the printer you want to use.

5. Tap the plus or minus symbol in the Copy field to set the number of copies to print.

FIGURE 14-20

6. If your printer supports double-sided or color printing, you'll see that option; set it as you want.

7. Tap the Print button. Your photo goes on its way to the printer.

Run a Slideshow

You can run a slideshow of your images in Photos and even play music and choose transition effects.

1. Tap the Photos app's icon to open the app.

2. Tap the Photos button.

3. Tap photos in a collection.

4. Tap the Share button.

5. Tap Slideshow in the bottom row to begin the slideshow.

6. To make changes, tap to pause the show and then tap the Options button in the bottom-right corner to display the Slideshow Options popover, shown in **Figure 14-21**.

7. If you don't want to play music along with the slideshow, tap the Music and then tap None.

8. To choose music to play along with the slideshow, tap Music, and in the list that appears, tap any selection in your Music library.

9. In the Slideshow Options dialog, tap Themes and then tap the transition effect you want to use for your slideshow.

10. Tap Music and select the music you want to play.

11. Adjust the volume slider if you wish.

12. Adjust the speed slider.

13. Tap outside the Options dialog to close it.

14. To stop the show, tap Done.

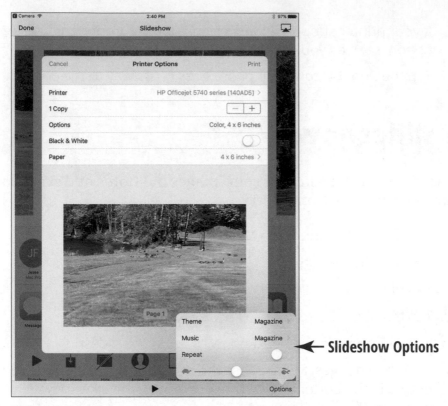

← Slideshow Options

FIGURE 14-21

TIP

To run a slideshow that includes only the photos contained in a particular album, tap the Albums button instead of the Photos button in Step 2, tap an album to open it, and then tap the Slideshow button in the top-right corner to run a slideshow.

Delete Photos

You may find that it's time to get rid of some old photos of the family reunion or the last community-center project. If the photos weren't transferred from your computer but were downloaded or captured as screenshots on the iPad, you can delete them.

1. Tap the Photos app's icon to open the app.

2. Tap the Albums or Photos button.

3. If you tapped Albums in Step 2, tap an album to open it.

4. Tap the Trash icon.

5. Tap Delete Photo (see **Figure 14-22**).

6. Tap the Delete Photo/Selected Photos button that appears to finish the deletion.

TIP

To delete more than one photo, with a collection or album displayed, tap Select; then tap all the photos you want to delete before tapping the Trash icon.

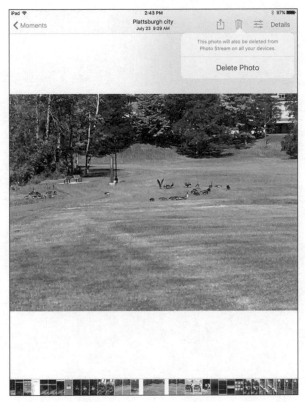

FIGURE 14-22

Chapter **15**

Getting the Most Out of Video Features

U sing the Videos app, you can watch downloaded movies or TV shows, as well as media you've synced from iCloud or your Mac or PC.

In addition, all iPads today have two cameras (one front and one back) that capture very clear video so that it looks terrific when you play it back on your iPad. (It also looks good when you use AirPlay to play it back on your high-definition TV.) By downloading the iMovie app (a more limited version of the longtime mainstay on Mac computers), you gain the capability to edit those videos.

In this chapter, I explain shooting and watching video content from a variety of sources.

Capture Your Own Videos with the Built-in Cameras

1. To capture a video, tap the Camera app on the home screen. The Camera app opens, as you see in **Figure 15-1**.

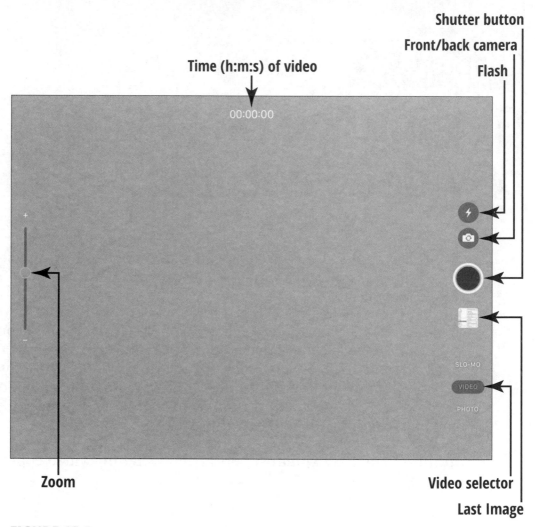

FIGURE 15-1

2. Tap Video in the list of options below the Shutter button on the right side below the Shutter button (see **Figure 15-1**). The shutter button turns red to show that it's now the Record button and the timer for your video appears at the top center of the display (it's not going to be captured in the video). Until you start recording, it's 0 hours, 0 minutes, and 0 seconds.

3. To switch between the front and back cameras, tap the camera with the two rotational arrows above the shutter button (refer to Figure 15-1).

4. Tap the Record button to begin recording the video. This button turns into a red square when the camera is recording, as shown in **Figure 15-2**. Also, the timer at the top of the screen starts to run, and a red flashing Record light appears to its left.

FIGURE 15-2

5. When you're finished, tap the Record button again. It changes back to the shutter button. Your new video is the topmost item in the list of photos and videos.

6. Open the list of photos and videos by tapping the square image just below the Record/shutter button. The photos and videos appear across the bottom of the screen, as shown in **Figure 15-3**. The newest one is shown full-size.

7. Tap the Play button to view your handiwork.

FIGURE 15-3

Play Movies or TV Shows

1. Tap the Videos icon on the home screen. The Videos app opens, showing tabs at the bottom of the screen for different types of content: Music, TV Shows, and Movies.

2. Tap one of the tabs at the bottom of the screen. Within each tab, you'll see a Genres button at the top left that you can use to navigate the genres within TV Shows, Music, Movies, and so forth. The Genres for TV Shows are shown in **Figure 15-4**.

FIGURE 15-4

3. Tap an item to open it. If you don't yet own it, you'll see information about it, as you see in **Figure 15-5**.

4. For movies, after you have purchased a movie, you can just tap it to play it from Step 3.

5. For TV Shows, you see a list of episodes, as shown in **Figure 15-6**.

6. Tap the episode you want to play as in Step 4 (see Figure 15-6).

7. Once you start playing a movie, you'll see the same playback tools you use on almost every device. With the playback tools displayed, take any of these actions:

   • Tap the Pause button to pause playback.

   • Tap Go to Previous Chapter or Go to Next Chapter to move to a different location in the video.

   • Tap the circular button on the Volume slider and drag it left or right to decrease or increase the volume, respectively.

If your controls disappear during playback, tap the screen to make them reappear.

8. To stop the video, tap the Done button to the left of the progress bar.

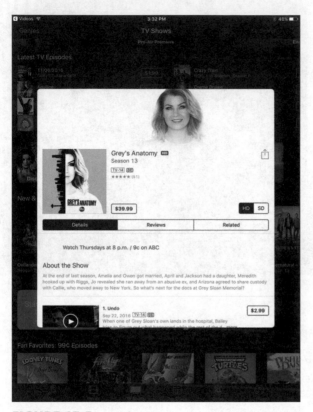

FIGURE 15-5

If you've watched a video and stopped it partway, it opens by default to the last location that you viewed. To start a video from the beginning, tap and drag the circular button on the progress bar all the way to the left.

If you like to view things on a bigger screen, you can use the iPad's AirPlay feature to send your iPad movies and photos to your Apple TV.

FIGURE 15-6

Turn on Closed Captioning

iTunes and the iPad offer support for closed captioning and subtitles. If a movie you purchased or rented has closed captioning or subtitles, you can turn on this feature in iPad. Look for the CC logo on media you download to use this feature. Video that you record won't have this capability.

1. Tap Settings ⇨ General ⇨ Accessibility.

2. On the Accessibility screen, tap Subtitles & Captioning.

3. On the menu that appears on the right side of the screen, tap the Closed Captions + SDH on/off button to turn on the feature.

When you play a movie that supports closed captioning, tap the Audio and Subtitles button to the right of the playback controls to manage this feature.

Go to a Movie Chapter or Episode

1. Tap the Videos app's icon on the home screen.

2. Tap the Movies or TV Shows tab.

3. Tap the title of the movie or TV show you want to watch. Information about the movie or TV show is displayed (see **Figure 15-6**).

4. Tap a chapter or episode to play it. You can use the playback tools to go back one chapter or forward one chapter. (See "Play Movies or TV Shows" earlier in this chapter for more information.)

TIP

If you buy a video using iTunes, sync to download it to your iPad, and then delete it from your iPad, it's still saved in your iTunes library. You can sync your computer and iPad again to download the video once more at no additional charge. Remember, however, that rented movies are gone with the wind when you delete them.

TIP

The iPad has much smaller storage capacity than your typical computer, so downloading lots of TV shows or movies can fill its storage area quickly. If you don't want to view an item you've downloaded again, delete it to free up space. With your TV Shows or Movies displayed, tap Edit. Tap the Delete button on an item and then tap Delete in the confirmation that appears.

Share a Video

You can share a video by using the iPad's Mail app, Twitter, or Facebook.

1. Tap the Videos app's icon to open it.

2. Tap the Store button.

3. Find and tap the video that you want to share.

4. In the information screen, tap the Share icon (a box with an arrow at the top of it at the top of the screen).

5. On the resulting menu, tap Mail, Twitter, or Facebook.

6. Enter the email settings you want to use or add a Facebook friend or your newsfeed. Add a comment if you want. And remember: In order to share copyrighted material (like TV shows, movies, and music), you must have permission to do so. Often, you can easily share a link to the item (your friend must have an account to play it or must purchase it before playing it). There are no restrictions on the content that you create.

7. Tap the Send button to send your recommendation by your preferred method.

Chapter 16

Playing Games

Digital games can be important parts of your life, enabling you to meet and interact with other people all over the world. The iPad is super for playing these games, with its bright screen (especially if you're using the Retina display on a third-generation or later iPad) and great sound system, as well as its capability to rotate the screen as you play and to track your motions. You can download games of all sorts from the App Store and play them on your device.

Scan the App Store, and you'll see games that involve such things as playing cards and other games with friends, learning new skills, joining volunteer groups and committees, and doing exercises at home or in a class. In some ways, your iPad can be a gateway to healthier living.

This chapter provides an overview of choosing and using games for your iPad. You can find familiar games that you may know from your own life — even from your youth. Even (gulp!) games from your parents' and grandparents' youths.

Your iPad and the Internet provide great opportunities. Need a fourth for bridge? There's an app for that. Are you into Mahjong? Search in the App Store (and make sure you swiping finger is limber. . . there are many, many Mahjong games to scroll through).

Do you like game shows on TV? Chances are your favorite game show has an app. Just search for it on the web or in the App Store.

There are endless new games and new kinds of games on your iPad. Every few months, a game seems to emerge and get the attention of people around the world. Who ever heard of Angry Birds before everyone seemed to be talking about it? What was that Pokémon thing (do a web search if you don't know or have forgotten)?

Some of the new games are incredibly complex, and others are maddeningly simple (maddeningly because they are simple and addicting). Many games on iPad (and other mobile devices) create entire imaginary worlds and characters. You can find games that let you enter one of these imaginary worlds or get to know amazing characters.

GAMES, GAMIFICATION, AND YOUR DIGNITY

Many people think they're too old, too sophisticated, or too dignified to play games — particularly computer and video games. For a long time, I passed up offers to play video, computer, and online games, saying that I spend my days sitting at a computer matching wits with Xcode (Apple's development environment) and the rules of that particular "game" (we call those rules application programming interfaces — APIs). You "play" that game by following the rules, and you win if your app is accepted into the App Store. So, I told people that I didn't need a game alongside my development work.

Like many other developers, I gradually saw that games themselves were even more complicated and challenging in many cases than writing code. As I taught classes in iOS and macOS development, I noticed that some of my students were interested in learning how to build games. Furthermore, I started to see that the students who were devotees of games were better students as a rule. Yes, there is a commonality between app development and playing a game: There are rules that you must obey; as you proceed, you win or lose (points, tokens, or apps in the App Store), depending on how well you follow the rules and how your strategy plays out.

Next step for me was discovering the word "gamification" — it refers to bringing techniques from games into non-game apps. We see it in many places. For example, on a social website, people who post frequently might earn a badge. People who offer advice that is accepted can earn different badges. The set of rules and the reward of badges are taken part and parcel from the world of games.

When people ask me today how to learn to build apps, I always ask them if they use apps. (It's amazing how many people want to build apps when they don't use them.) The next question I ask is if they play computers games. If the answer is "yes," I know they'll be the students in the front row of my class with their hands raised.

Don't get me wrong: My classes are basic coding and not specifically for game creators, but experience in playing games seems to stretch the mental "muscles" that matter in learning how to write code.

So, if you think you're too old, too dignified, or too sophisticated to be playing games on your iPad, just tell people you're honing your app development skills. Some people may roll their eyes, but if you attend a local developer MeetUp (meetup.com — a great local meeting site for people with common interests), people won't roll their eyes. They'll welcome you as a fellow developer.

Choose Games for Your iPad

Here are some things to look for in games:

>> **Number of players:** You can find single-player games and games for multiple players. Some multiplayer games allow you to play against yourself as both players. Sometimes, one of the

multiple players is the game itself, so you play against the house (to use casino jargon).

» **Type of game:** Common types of games include puzzles (such as crosswords and jigsaws); games involving chance, skill, or strategy (such as traditional card, dice, and board games); and role-playing games.

» **Team play:** Depending on the game, you may play as yourself or as a member of a team. In some cases, you can pass on your player role to someone else.

» **Leaderboard:** Many games have a *leaderboard*, which tracks scores along with information such as the players and the dates. Leaderboards are essential in multiplayer games but can be useful in single-player games as well. *The New York Times* Crossword Puzzle game, for example, keeps track of the time it takes you to solve a puzzle every day, with puzzles getting progressively harder each day of the week.

You can find games of all these types in the App Store, as described in the next section.

Explore Games in the App Store

1. Tap the App Store's icon to open that app.

2. Tap the Categories tab at the bottom of the screen.

3. Tap the Games category. You see the subcategories shown in **Figure 16-1**, which are curated (selected by the App Store).

4. Scroll down the screen to the Quick Links (see **Figure 16-2**). There are links for parents as well as links specifically to kids apps. Many games have in-app purchases where you can purchase game pieces or even clues to help you solve puzzles.

TIP

The About In-App Purchases Quick Link gives you advice on managing Family Sharing and parental controls so that you and your family members can spend your app budget wisely (and enjoyably).

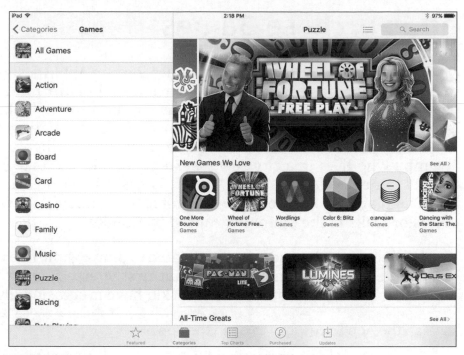

FIGURE 16-1

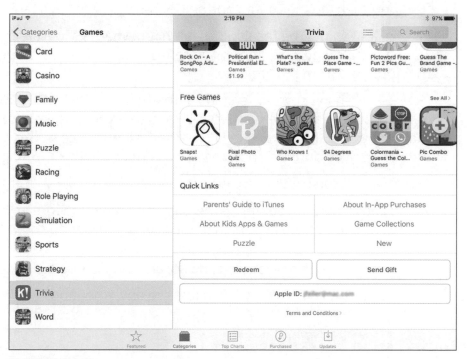

FIGURE 16-2

Find and Purchase Games

Disney's Where's My Water? game, which won an Apple design award in 2012, is one of the best-selling games for all platforms. As many people (including the developers) have remarked, it looks like a Disney cartoon in the great tradition of cartoons dating back to "Steamboat Willie" (1928). The game is about an alligator named Swampy who lives in a city sewer system and likes to take showers. Cranky, an evil alligator in the sewer, keeps disrupting the plumbing. The player's job is to route the water to Swampy's shower from ponds or leaks in the plumbing caused by Cranky.

TIP

If you think you're too old or sophisticated to play a game like this, you can get it for a grandkid. Try it out first yourself, and then, remember that you must let the grandkid have it occasionally.

1. Tap the App Store's icon to open the app.

2. Tap the magnifying-glass icon at the upper right corner of the screen to display the search page; type the name of the game in the search field and then tap the Search button on the onscreen keyboard.

   Figure 16-3 shows the result of a search for Where's My Water? (Your search results may look different because titles and prices change in the App Store from time to time.)

   Figure 16-3 shows several versions of this game: paid versions (which list their prices), a puzzle-pack bundle, and free versions (denoted by the Get button). The text *In-App Purchases* below a price or Get button means that you purchase new features from within the app.

3. Tap an app's icon to get more info about it.

4. When you're ready to get the game, sign in to the App Store (if you haven't already signed in) and then tap the Buy or Get button.

5. If you're asked to verify your age, do so, and tap Continue.

   The game downloads to your iPad just like any other app.

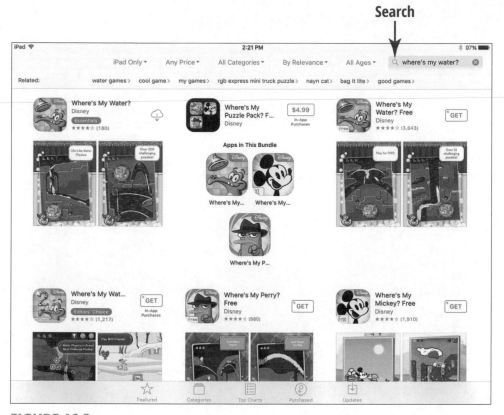

FIGURE 16-3

Chapter 17

Finding Your Way with Maps

The latest version of Maps in iOS 10 can give you directions for walking, driving, and (in some locations) using mass transit or ride sharing. Maps also branches out in two new directions:

» **Proactive maps:** Now Maps can not only give you directions, but also point out places of interest en route. Proactive maps provide *you* with more information as you search and travel.

» **Integrated maps:** Because of the integration of Maps with Open Table (the service for online bookings at restaurants), you can find a restaurant and make a reservation. You can also make requests for rides from transportation networks such as Uber and Lyft. More and more apps and databases are being integrated with Maps every day by developers.

The buzzwords in real estate are "location, location, location," but today, location isn't enough. People want to know more than just the directions to a place: They want to know what they can do there, what their friends have done there, and what friends of friends (and even strangers) think. This chapter helps you explore Maps and get the most out of it — think of it as sort of "beyond location."

View Your Current Location

The iPad can figure out where you are and display your location if you have an Internet connection and have turned Location Services on in Privacy Settings.

To view your current location, follow these steps:

1. Tap the Maps app's icon to open the app.

2. Tap the Current Location icon (the small arrow in the top-right corner; see **Figure 17-1**). Your approximate location is displayed with a pulsating blue circle around it. Your actual location can be anywhere within the circle.

3. Double-tap the screen to zoom in on your location. (Additional methods of zooming in and out are covered in "Zoom In and Out" later in this chapter.)

TECHNICAL STUFF

Maps can identify streets and places of interest. Places of business (orange in Figure 17-1) are generally drawn from Yelp! The geographic data is drawn from a variety of sources. Other items are derived from your Contacts app and other sources of data.

TIP

Mapping requires Internet connectivity via a Wi-Fi network or a cellphone network. It doesn't work if Airplane Mode is turned on.

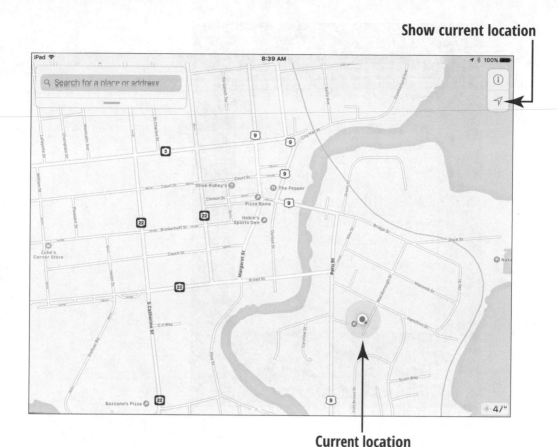

Show current location

Current location

FIGURE 17-1

Set Your Map Options and Preferences

You can set options for Maps using Settings as well as using in-app preferences. The two mechanisms provide different options.

The Info button above the location button in the top-right of Figure 17-1 lets you set options for Maps. Tap the Info button to open the basic preferences, as shown in **Figure 17-2**.

The three types of views (Map, Transit, and Satellite) are discussed in the following section. You can turn the traffic display on and off, but note that it is dependent on local data so it tends to be more effective in fairly large cities.

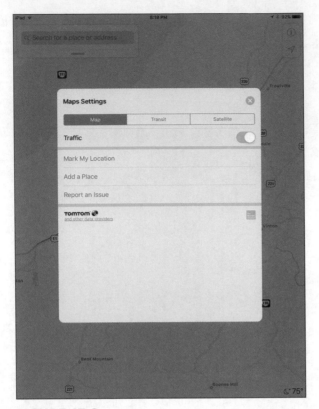

FIGURE 17-2

Change Views

The Maps app offers three views: Map, Satellite, and Transit. By default, you see Map view (refer to Figure 17-1) the first time you open Maps. To change views, follow these steps:

1. With Map view open, tap the Info button in the top-right corner of the screen. The window shown in Figure 17-2 appears.

2. Tap the Satellite tab. Satellite view opens (see **Figure 17-3**).

3. Tap Transit to open Transit view (see **Figure 17-4**).

Transit view is available only in locations where mass transit exists. Thus, while Figures 17-1 and 17-3 show the city of Plattsburgh, New York, Figure 17-4 shows a nearby but somewhat larger city: Montreal.

FIGURE 17-3

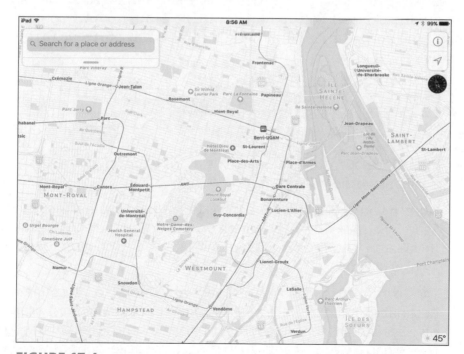

FIGURE 17-4

Zoom In and Out

The Zoom feature lets you see more- or less-detailed views and move around a map. With a map displayed, do any of the following:

» With a map displayed, double-tap with a single finger to zoom in.

» Double-tap with two fingers to zoom out, revealing less detail.

» Place two fingers together on the screen and then move them apart to zoom in.

» Place two fingers apart on the screen and then pinch them together to zoom out.

» Press your finger to the screen and then drag the map in any direction to move to an adjacent area.

TIP

It can take a few moments for the map to redraw itself when you enlarge, reduce, or move around it, so have a little patience. Areas that are being redrawn look like blank grids that fill in eventually. Also, if you're in Satellite or Transit view, zooming in may take some time; be patient, because the blurred image will resolve itself.

Find a Location

1. With Maps open, tap the Search field in the top-left corner. The onscreen keyboard appears.

   Note: If you've displayed directions for a route, you won't see the Search field; tap the Clear button on a directions screen to get back to the Search field. See "Get Directions" later in this chapter for how you display directions.

2. Type a location, such as a street address, a stored contact name, or a destination (such as *Empire State Building* or *Detroit airport*). Maps first displays buttons for categories such as Food and Health that you can use to narrow your search; then it displays suggestions as you type. To expand the search results, drag down (see **Figure 17-5**).

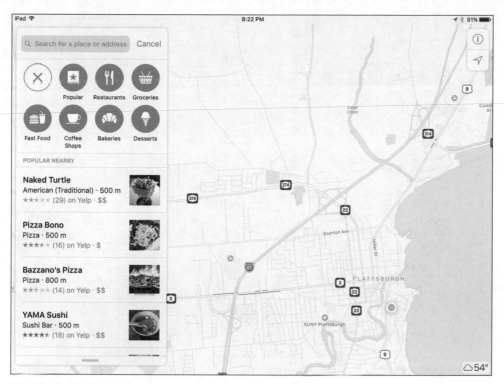

FIGURE 17-5

3. Tap a suggestion or tap the Search key on the keyboard. A map of the location appears, with a pin inserted into it, a label identifying the location, and an Information icon. If several locations match your search term, several pins may appear in a suggestions list.

4. Tap an item in the suggestion list or a site on the map to see more information about it (see **Figure 17-6**). The information varies depending on what you tap, but typically, you get directions, a phone number, a website, the address, and hours of operation. (The iPad is smart enough to briefly note whether the location is open or closed at the moment.)

5. Tap the screen and drag in any direction to move to a nearby location.

FIGURE 17-6

Get into the habit of adding places and people to Contacts. Maps relies on many data sources, but perhaps the most valuable data source is the information you've entered in Contacts. Siri also uses this data, so try to get in the habit of entering names and addresses (and email addresses and other information) in Contacts as soon as you get it.

TIP

If you enter a destination such as *zoo*, you may want to enter a city and state as well. There are lots of zoos in the world, and Maps may find quite a few near you.

TIP

Get Directions

You have a few ways to get directions from Maps in iOS 10:

>> **Ask Siri.** Perhaps the simplest method is to ask Siri. If you say (for example) "Hey Siri, directions to Albany New York," you get

a map of Albany and directions to it. Alternatively, you can say "Hey Siri, directions to Albany Institute of History and Art." Maps looks up the street address and finds the location for you. (See Chapter 5.)

» **Use Dictation.** You can tap the Dictation key on the onscreen keyboard and speak a location to the iPad. Tap the Search button on the keyboard, and Maps displays the location. (See Chapter 2.)

» **Search inside a map.** You can also use the search field in a displayed map, as described in "Find a Location" earlier in this chapter. Type an address or location, and Maps finds it for you, as you see in **Figure 17-7**.

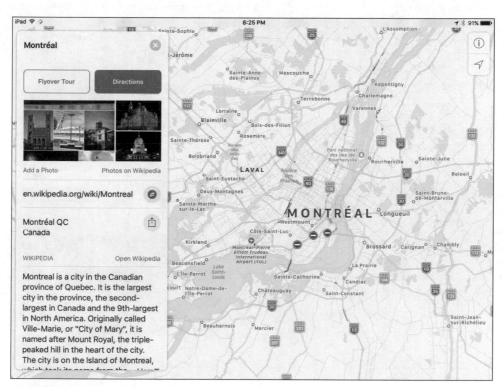

FIGURE 17-7

When your general location is found, follow these steps to get directions:

1. If you want, choose a view (refer to "Change Views" earlier in this chapter).

2. Tap directions in Figure 17-6. You see a map like the one shown in **Figure 17-8**.

3. Tap the Details link to see more details on any route shown. You can change the starting location (by default, My Location) or your mode of transport, and you can see alternate routes by tapping the green Go button for the one you want to use to see the route shown in **Figure 17-9**.

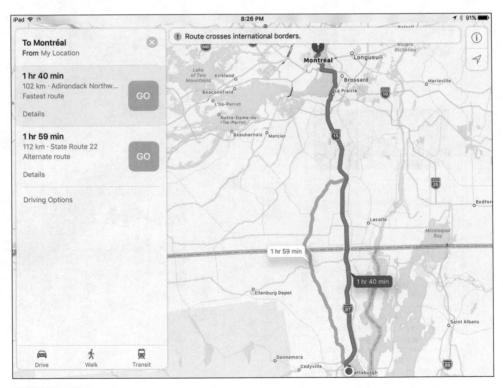

FIGURE 17-8

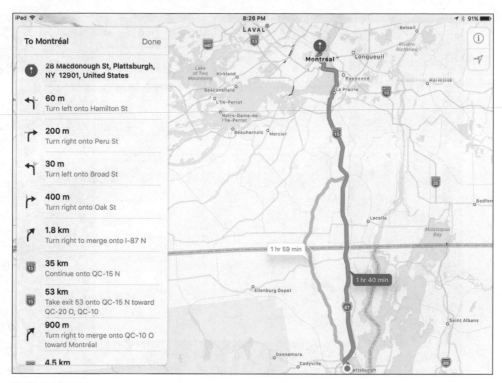

FIGURE 17-9

Share Location Information

You can share your route information with others (or yourself).

1. Display a route (refer to Figure 17-9), following the steps in "Get Directions" earlier in this chapter.

2. Scroll down to the bottom of the route map, and tap the Share link in the bottom-left corner. A Send Route window opens (see **Figure 17-10**).

3. You can print the route out, or you can search for routing apps in the App Store that can give you alternate directions. As always, the options you see in the Share window vary depending on the apps you have installed and the specific version of iOS you have. The options change all the time as Apple and developers provide more functionality.

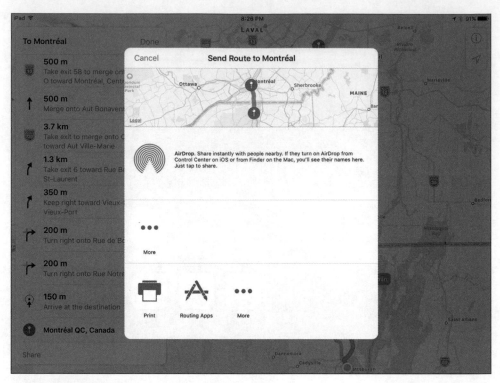

FIGURE 17-10

5

Managing Your Life and Your iPad

IN THIS PART. . .

Keep track of time and your calendar.

Let your iPad remind and notify you of appointments and what's happening.

Remember names and addresses with your iPad.

Use your iPad to take notes . . . everywhere you go.

Read news from all over with the News app.

Chapter **18**

Keeping On Schedule with Calendar and Clock

Whether you're retired or still working, you have a busy life full of activities (even busier if you're retired, for some unfathomable reason). You may need a way to keep on top of all those activities and appointments. The Calendar app on your iPad is a simple, elegant, electronic daybook that helps you do just that.

Another preinstalled app that helps you stay on time is Clock. Though simple to use, Clock helps you view the time in multiple locations, set alarms, and use a timer.

In this chapter, you master the simple procedures for getting around your calendar, creating a family calendar, entering and editing events, setting up alerts, syncing, and searching. You also learn the simple ins and outs of using Clock.

View Calendars

Calendar offers several ways to view your schedule.

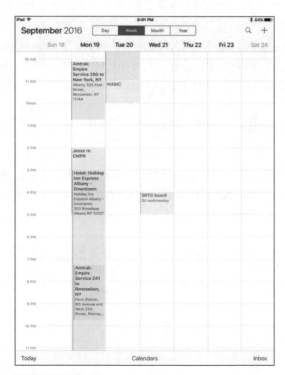

1. Tap the Calendar app's icon to open the app.

2. If you're using Calendar for the first time, you may be asked whether Calendar can use your location. Tap Allow or Don't Allow. (If you don't allow Calendar to use your location, its functionality will be limited — for example, it won't compute travel time to your next appointment so it can alert you when you need to leave.)

If you've used Calendar before, depending on what you had open last, you may see a daily, weekly, monthly, or yearly calendar with today's date highlighted. You may also see an open event.

3. If today's calendar page isn't already displayed, tap the Today button at the bottom left of the screen. You'll see today's appointments, as shown in **Figure 18-1**.

FIGURE 18-1

4. Tap the Search button to see your saved appointments in a popover. (see **Figure 18-2**).

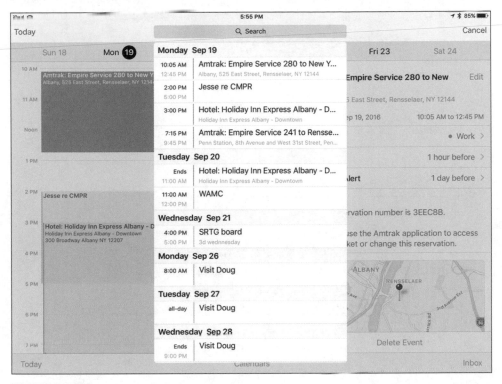

FIGURE 18-2

5. Tap an event in the list to view more details about it, as you see in **Figure 18-3**.

6. Tap Week at the top of a calendar view such as Figure 18-1 to view all events for that week. A calendar page appears, listing your weekly events (as in **Figure 18-2**).

7. Tap the Month tab at the top of Figure 18-1 to get an overview of your busy month (see **Figure 18-4**).

8. Tap the Year tab to see all months of the year (see **Figure 18-5**). And if that's enough for you, swipe up or down to go other years.

FIGURE 18-3

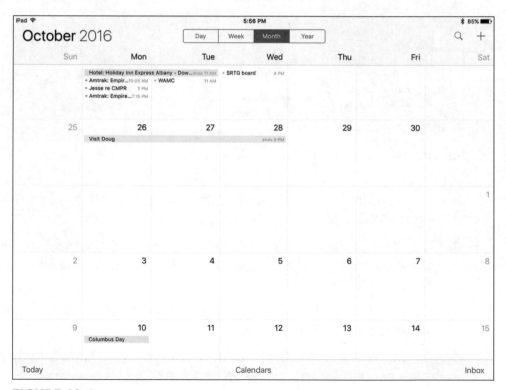

FIGURE 18-4

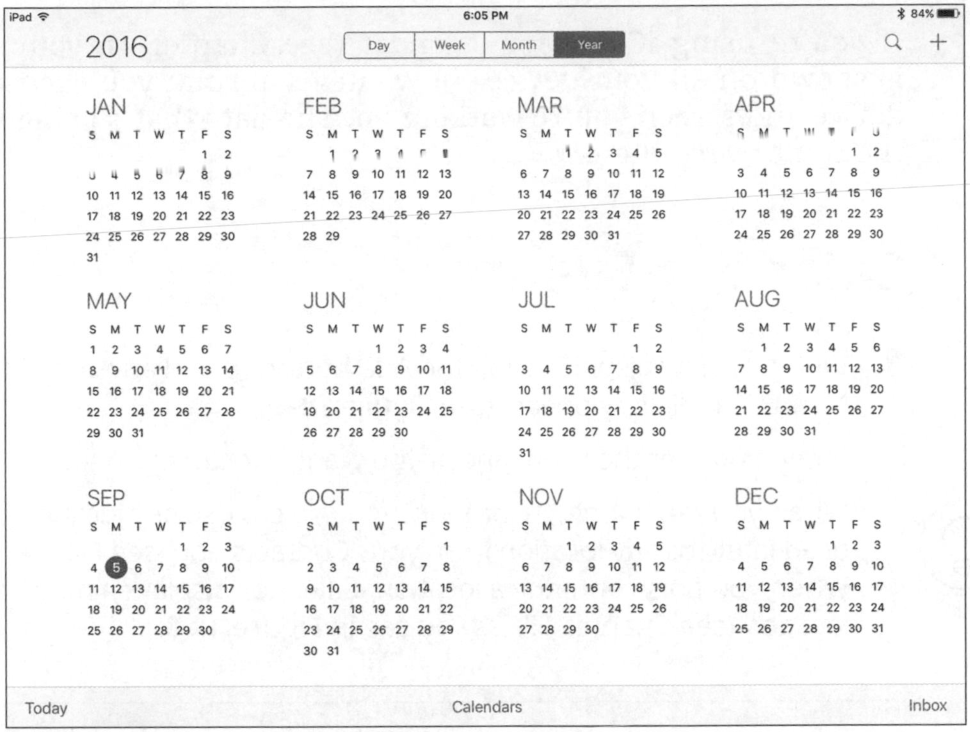

![Screenshot of iPad Calendar in Year view showing the year 2016 with all twelve months (JAN through DEC). The top bar shows "iPad", "6:05 PM", and "84%" battery. View options Day, Week, Month, Year appear at top, with Year selected. Bottom bar shows Today, Calendars, and Inbox. September 5 is circled.](image showing iPad calendar year view)

FIGURE 18-5

TIP

Calendar looks slightly different when you hold your iPad in portrait and landscape orientations. Turn your iPad in both directions to see which orientation you prefer to work in.

Navigate Calendars

To move around a calendar, do any of the following:

» In any calendar view, tap the Search button to display List view, which lists all your commitments (refer to Figure 18-1).

» To move from one month or year to another, use your finger to scroll up or down the list and then tap an item.

» To jump back to today, tap the Today button in the bottom-left corner.

If you're using iCloud for Calendar (see Chapter 3), your calendar is shown on all your devices in whatever format you choose for the device and screen you're working on. The data that's being shown is the same everywhere.

Add Calendar Events

1. With any view displayed, tap the Add button to add an event. The New Event dialog appears (see **Figure 18-6**).

2. Enter a title for the event and, if you want, a location.

TIP

When you tap to enter a location, you can choose any location you've used lately or any location from your Contacts app (see **Figure 18-7**). When you finish entering a location, Calendar displays a map of that location (see Chapter 17), as you see in **Figure 18-8**.

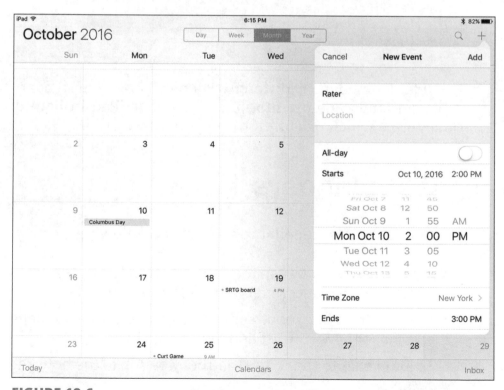

FIGURE 18-6

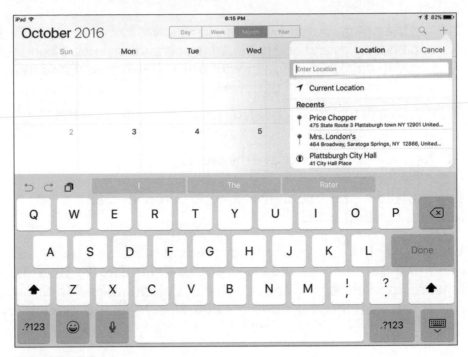

FIGURE 18-7

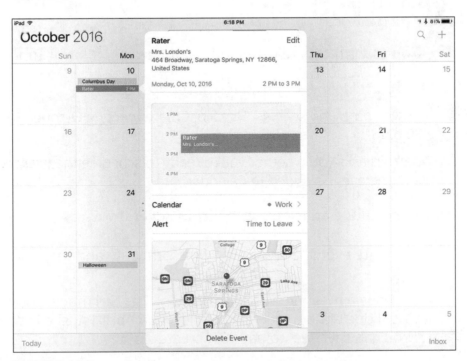

FIGURE 18-8

3. Tap the All-Day on/off switch for an all-day event, or tap the Starts and Ends fields and add the starting and ending times. Place your fingertip on the date, hour, minute, or AM/PM column, and move your finger to scroll up or down.

4. If you want to add a note, scroll down in the dialog to the Notes field, and type your note.

5. Tap the Add button to save the event.

You can edit any event by tapping it on a calendar and then tapping the Edit link.

You can use information within an email (such as a flight number or phone number) to add an event to Calendar. To turn on this feature, tap Settings ⇨ Mail, Contacts, Calendars and then turn on the on/off switches for Contacts Found in Mail and Events Found in Mail.

Add Events with Siri

Play around with this feature and Calendar; it's a lot of fun!

1. Press and hold the Home button or say "Hey Siri."

2. Speak a command such as "Hey Siri. Create meeting October 3rd at 2:30 p.m."

3. When Siri asks you whether you're ready to schedule the event, say "Yes." The event is added to Calendar.

You can schedule an event with Siri in several ways:

» Say "Create event." Siri asks you first for a date and then for a time.

» Say "I have a meeting with John on April 1st." Siri may respond by saying "I don't find a meeting with John on April 1st; shall I create it?" You can say "Yes" to have Siri create it.

Create a Repeating Event

If you want an event to repeat, such as a weekly or monthly appointment, you can set a repeating event.

1. With any view displayed, tap the Add button to add an event. The New Event dialog appears (refer to Figure 18-6).

2. Enter a title and location for the event, and set the start and end dates and times (refer to "Add Calendar Events" earlier in this chapter).

3. Tap Edit in the top right.

4. Scroll down the page, if necessary, and tap the Repeat field. The Repeat dialog appears (see **Figure 18-9**).

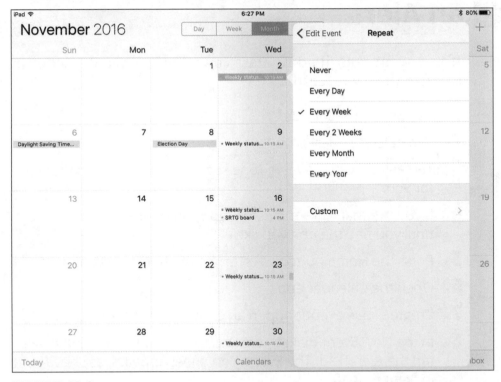

FIGURE 18-9

5. Tap a preset time interval (Every Day, Week, 2 Weeks, Month, or Year), or tap Custom and enter a frequency and day. You could create an event to happen once every three months or every three days, for example.

6. Tap New Event to close the Repeat dialog.

7. Tap the Add button. You return to the calendar.

View an Event

Remember, tap an event anywhere — on a day view, week view, month view, or list view to see its details.

Add an Alert

If you want your iPad to alert you when an event is coming up, you can use the Alert feature.

1. Tap Settings ➪ Sounds.

2. Tap Calendar Alerts.

3. Tap any tone in the Alert Tone section. The iPad plays that tone for you.

4. If you like that tone, move to Step 5; otherwise, continue to tap tones until you find the one you like.

5. Press the Home button to return to the home screen.

6. Open the Calendar app.

7. Create a new event or open an existing event for editing.

8. In the New Event dialog (refer to Figure 18-8) or the Edit dialog, tap the Alert field. The Event Alert sheet appears, as shown in **Figure 18-10**.

FIGURE 18-10

9. Tap any preset interval, from 5 Minutes to 2 Days Before or at the time of the event.

10. Tap New Event or Edit Event to return to the New Event or Edit Event dialog.

11. Tap Add (for a new event) or Done (if you're editing an existing event) to save the alert.

TECHNICAL
STUFF

If you've entered a location with an address, Calendar can include travel time in your alert. Tap Travel Time in the main event display, and the sheet shown in **Figure 18-11** appears.

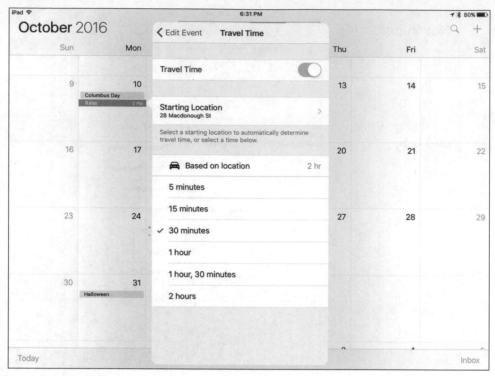

FIGURE 18-11

Search for an Event

1. With Calendar open in any view, tap the Search button in the top-right corner.

2. Tap the Search field to display the onscreen keyboard.

3. Type a word or words to search by and then tap the Search key. While you type, the Results dialog appears, as shown in **Figure 18-12**.

4. Tap any result to display the event details.

FIGURE 18-12

Subscribe to Calendars

If you use a calendar from an online service such as Apple, Yahoo!, or Google, you can subscribe to that calendar to read events saved there on your iPad. You can read but not edit these events.

Working with Apple accounts

Here are the basic steps to subscribe to Apple calendars (other services are shown in the following sections).

1. Tap Settings ⇨ Calendar ⇨ Accounts. The Accounts screen appears (see **Figure 18-13**).

2. Tap Fetch New Data to see the screen shown in **Figure 18-14**.

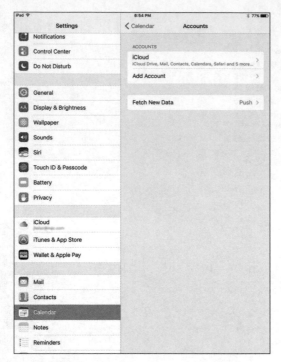

FIGURE 18-13

3. On the screen that appears (see **Figure 18-14**), set the Push option's on/off switch to on and then, at the bottom, set how frequently data should be pushed to your iPad: every 15 or 30 minutes, hourly, or manually.

4. You can set these options for each account and calendar you have. In Figure 18-14, you'll see a holiday calendar from Apple, iCloud (for all your iCloud accounts), and two outside accounts for mail (my ChamplainArts and North Country Consulting accounts). Tap the option at the right for each one to choose whether data is pushed to your iPad or fetched. The difference is that with fetch, your iPad checks periodically for new data (see the fetch options at the bottom of the view). With push, the mail or calendar server pushes the data to your iPad and it responds. Push is generally faster and more efficient, but not all servers support it.

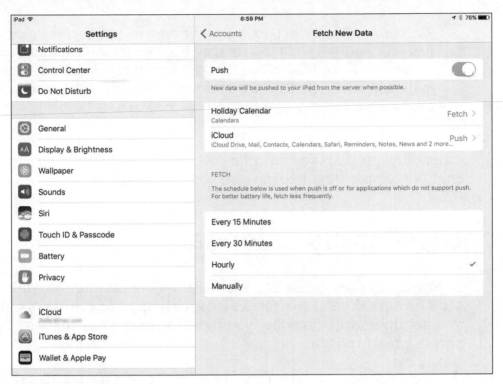

FIGURE 18-14

Working with other acccounts

You can choose to use another account like Gmail or Yahoo! for your calendar or email.

1. To use another email or calendar server, tap the relevant service or Other in the previous list of steps.

Tap an email choice such as Outlook.com, Gmail, or Yahoo! to subscribe to another service's calendar.

2. In the settings that appear enter any requested information for the external service, such as name, email address, and email account password. Each one is different: If you need help, contact the Help Desk at the external service.

3. Tap Next or Sign In, depending on the type of account. The iPad verifies your address and retrieves data from your calendar at the interval you set to fetch data. To review these settings, tap the Back arrow in the top-left corner, and then tap the Fetch New Data option in the Calendars pane of Settings as you see in Figure 18-14.

If you store your contacts' birthdays in the Contacts app, the Calendar app displays each one when the day comes around so that you won't forget to pass on your congratulations.

Create a Family Calendar

If you set up the Family Sharing feature (see Chapter 9), you can create a group calendar to share events with up to five other people. After you set up Family Sharing, you have to make sure that the Calendar sharing feature is on.

1. Tap Settings ⇨ iCloud to open the iCloud screen. If Family Sharing is set up, you see Family; proceed to Step 2. If not, you see Set Up Family Sharing; see Chapter 9 for directions.

2. Tap the Calendars on/off switch to turn that setting on if it's not already on (see **Figure 18-15**).

3. Press the Home button to return to the home screen.

4. Open the Calendar app.

5. Tap the Calendars link at the bottom of the screen.

6. On the resulting screen, scroll down to make sure that Family is selected.

7. Tap Done. Now when you create a new event in the New Event dialog, tap Calendar and choose Family or Show All Calendars. The event details will note that the event is from the Family calendar.

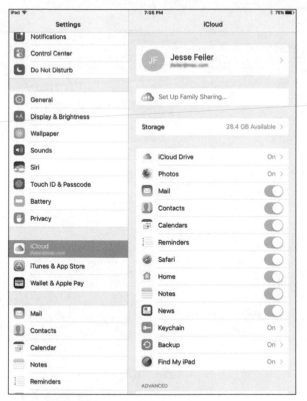

FIGURE 18-15

Delete an Event

When an upcoming luncheon or meeting is canceled, you may want to delete the appointment.

1. In the Calendar app, tap an event.

2. Tap Delete Event at the bottom of the screen (see **Figure 18-16**).

If this event is a repeating event (see "Create a Repeating Event" earlier in this chapter), you see two buttons that offer you the option to delete this instance of the event or this instance and all future instances of the event (see **Figure 18-17**). Tap the button for the option you prefer. The event is deleted, and you return to Calendar view.

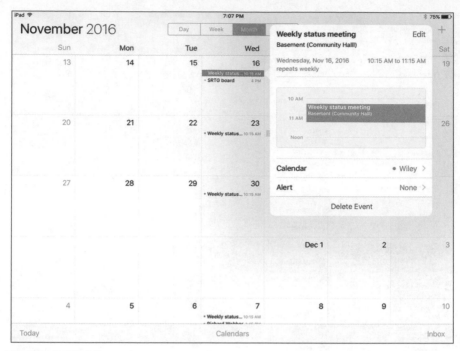

FIGURE 18-16

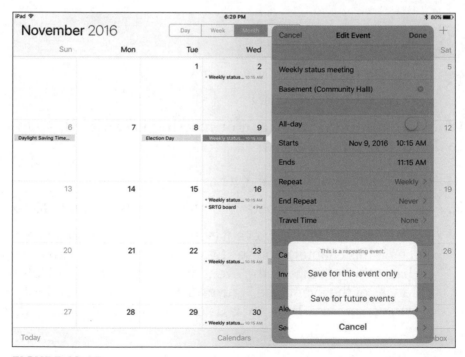

FIGURE 18-17

TIP

If an event is moved but not canceled, you don't have to delete the old one and create a new one: Simply edit the existing event to change the day and time in the Edit dialog

Display Clock

Tap the Clock app's icon to open the app. In World Clock view, preset location clocks are displayed along the top of the screen, and the locations of these clocks are displayed on a world map (see **Figure 18–18**).

TIP

Clocks for cities that are currently in night time are displayed in black. Clocks for cities that are currently in daytime are displayed in white.

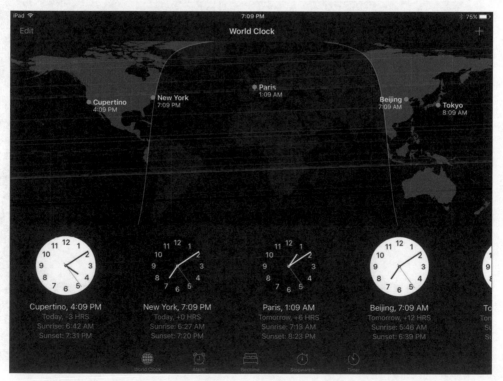

FIGURE 18-18

Add or Delete a Clock

You can add a clock for many (but not all) locations around the world.

1. With Clock open, tap the plus sign (+) in the top-right corner of the screen.

2. Tap a city in the resulting list, or tap a letter on the right side of the screen to display locations that begin with that letter and then select one. The appropriate clock appears in the last spot on the right side of the screen, and the location is displayed on the world map.

3. To delete a clock, tap the Edit button in the top-left corner of the World Clock screen; tap the minus sign (-) next to a location and then tap the Delete button (see **Figure 18-19**).

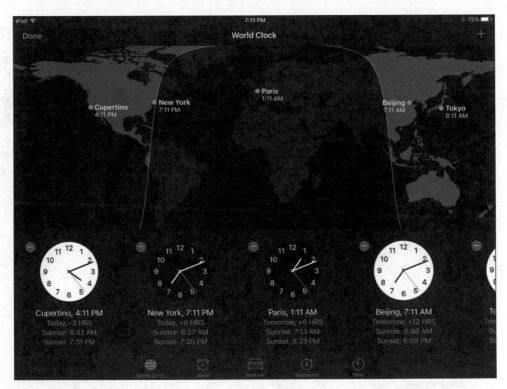

FIGURE 18-19

Set an Alarm

1. With the Clock app open, tap the Alarm tab at the bottom of the screen.

2. Tap the + in the top-right corner. The Add Alarm dialog opens (see **Figure 18-20**).

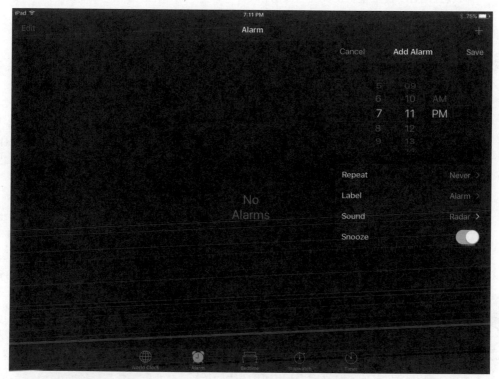

FIGURE 18-20

3. Take any of the following actions, tapping the Back button after you make each setting to return to the Add Alarm dialog:

   - Tap Repeat if you want the alarm to repeat at a regular interval, such as every Monday or every Sunday.

   - Tap Label and enter a name such as "Take Pill" or "Call Mom."

   - Tap Sound to choose the tone the alarm will play.

   - Tap the Snooze on/off switch if you want to use the Snooze feature.

4. Place your finger on the three wheels at the top of the dialog, scroll to set the time when you want the alarm to occur, and tap Save. The alarm appears on the calendar's Alarm tab.

TIP

To delete an alarm, tap the Alarm tab and then tap Edit. All alarms appear. Tap the red circle with a minus in it next to the alarm and then tap the Delete button.

Use Stopwatch and Timer

Sometimes, life seems like a countdown or a ticking clock counting the minutes you've spent on a certain activity. You can use the Stopwatch and Timer tabs of the Clock app to count down to a specific time, such as the moment when your chocolate chip cookies are done, or to time a walk.

TIP

» To use Stopwatch, tap the Stopwatch or Timer tab and tap the Start button (see **Figure 18-21**). When you set the Timer app, the iPad uses a sound to notify you when time's up. When you start the Stopwatch app, you have to tap the Stop button when the activity is done.

» If you want to time incremental events, such as a series of laps you swim in a pool, with the Stopwatch running, tap the Lap button at the end of each segment and each segment is displayed in a list beneath the main timing field.

» The Bedtime tab at the bottom of Clock lets you set your bedtime and wake time. You can choose the music to wake up to as well. Experiment with it to see how you can improve your health by getting enough sleep.

1. Tap Bedtime in the Clock app.

2. Tap Options in the top left of the screen to show the options in **Figure 18-22**. Set the options you want.

3. Tap Done.

FIGURE 18-21

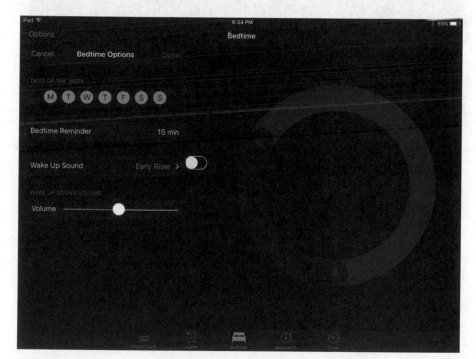

FIGURE 18-22

4. Once you have set the options, you can see the summary by just tapping the Bedtime tab in the Clock app, as you see in **Figure 18-23**.

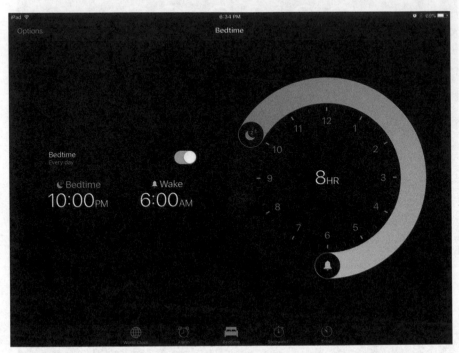

FIGURE 18-23

Chapter 19

Working with Reminders and Notifications

The Reminders app and Notification Center features warm the hearts of those of us who occasionally have a "senior" moment. Reminders is a to-do list that lets you create tasks and set reminders so you don't forget important commitments. Notifications allows you to review all the things you should be aware of, in one place, such as new mail messages, text messages, calendar appointments, reminders, and alerts. You can also display weather and stock reports in Notification Center.

If you occasionally need to escape all your obligations, try the Do Not Disturb feature. Turn this feature on, and you won't be bothered by alerts until you turn it off again.

In this chapter, you discover how to set up and view tasks in Reminders, and you see how Notification Center can centralize all your alerts.

Create a Task in Reminders

1. Tap the Reminders icon to open the app.

2. On the screen that appears, tap any list on the left to add a task to it (see **Figure 19-1**). I used the Reminders list in Figure 19-1.

3. Tap + to add a reminder.

4. The onscreen keyboard appears.

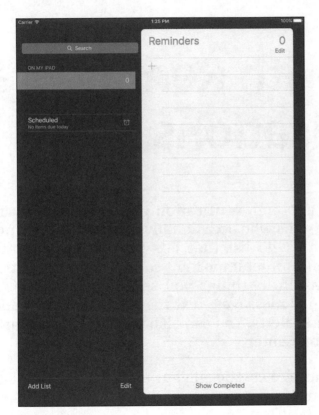

FIGURE 19-1

5. Enter a task name or description and tap the Done button. The new task is added to the Reminders list, as you see in Figure 19-2. You're able to tap in the circle to mark the task as completed.

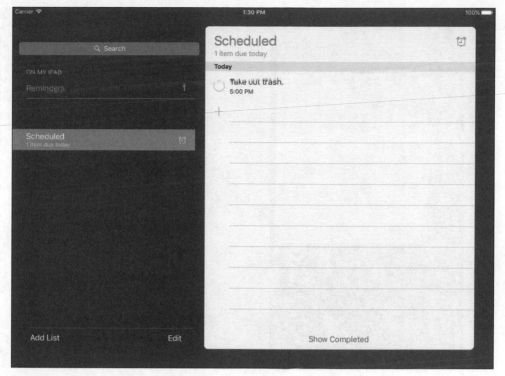

FIGURE 19-2

TIP

You can create your own list categories. See "Create a List" later in this chapter to find out how.

Edit Task Details

1. With the Reminders app open, tap a task to edit its name. The onscreen keyboard appears.

2. Tap a task and then tap the Details button that appears to the right of it. The Details popover opens (see **Figure 19-3**).

3. Tap a priority. From left to right in Figure 19-3, the options are None, Low, Medium, and High.

4. Tap Done to save the task details.

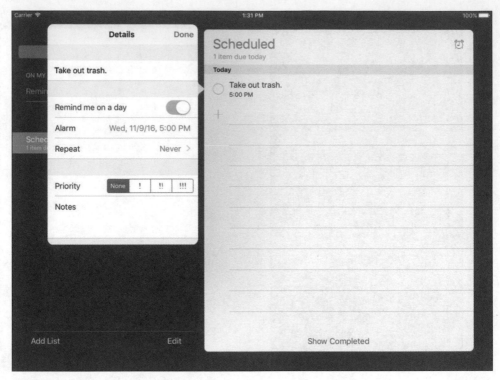

FIGURE 19-3

Schedule a Reminder

One of the major purposes of Reminders is to remind you of upcoming tasks. To set a reminder, follow these steps:

1. With the Reminders app open, tap a task and then tap the Details button that appears to the right of it. The Details popover opens (refer to Figure 19-3).

2. Tap the Remind Me on a Day on/off button to turn the feature on.

3. Tap the Alarm field that appears below Remind Me on a Day. The settings shown in **Figure 19-4** appear.

4. Tap and flick the day, hour, and minutes fields to scroll to the date and time for the reminder.

5. Tap Done on the popover to save the settings for the reminder.

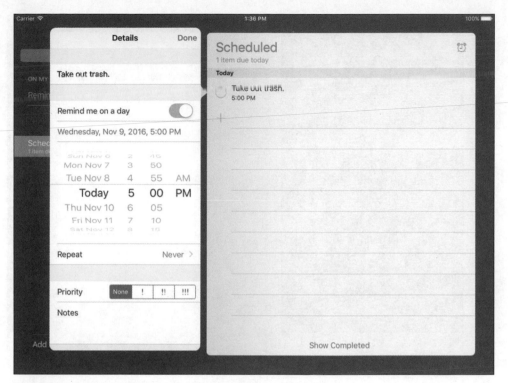

FIGURE 19-4

TIP

If you want a task to repeat with associated reminders, tap the Repeat field in the Details popover, and in the dialog that appears, tap Every Day, Week, 2 Weeks, Month, or Year. To stop the task from repeating, tap End Repeat in the Details dialog, tap End Repeat Date, and select a stop date from the scrolling calendar.

Create a List

You can create your own lists of tasks to help yourself keep different parts of your life organized.

1. With the Reminders app open, tap Add List to display the New List form, shown in **Figure 19-5**.

2. Enter a name for the list.

3. Tap a color.

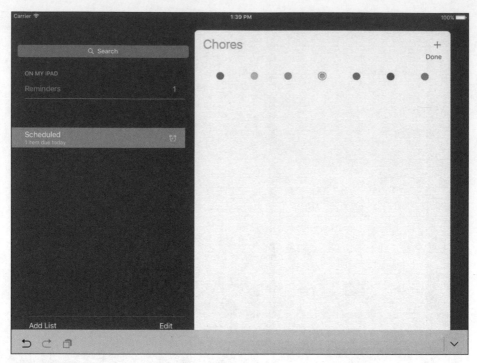

FIGURE 19-5

4. Tap Done. The list appears in List view with the name and color you chose.

5. Tap a blank line to create a task, and enter the desired text.

Sync with Other Devices and Calendars

You can determine which tasks are synchronized with other devices or calendars, such as Outlook.

1. Tap Settings ⇨ iCloud.

2. In the iCloud screen, make sure that the Reminders on/off button is set to on (see **Figure 19-6**).

3. Tap Calendar in the list on the left side of the screen.

4. Tap the Sync field.

5. Set how far back to sync reminders (see **Figure 19-7**).

FIGURE 19-6

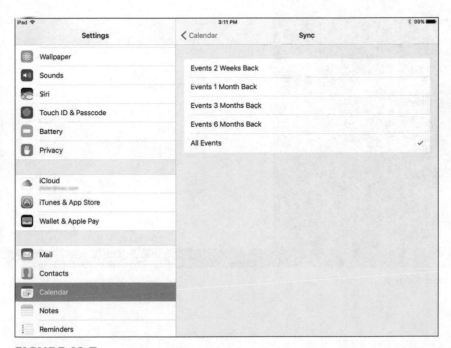

FIGURE 19-7

Mark as Complete or Delete a Reminder

You may want to mark a task as complete or delete it so that you don't continue to get notifications about it.

» With Reminders open and a list of tasks displayed, tap the button to the left of a task to mark it as complete.

» To delete one or more tasks, display a list and then tap Edit in the top-right corner. Red circles appear to the left of the tasks, as shown in **Figure 19-8**. Tap the red circle to the left of the task and then tap the Delete button that appears. The task is deleted. To delete all tasks, simply tap Delete List at the bottom of the screen.

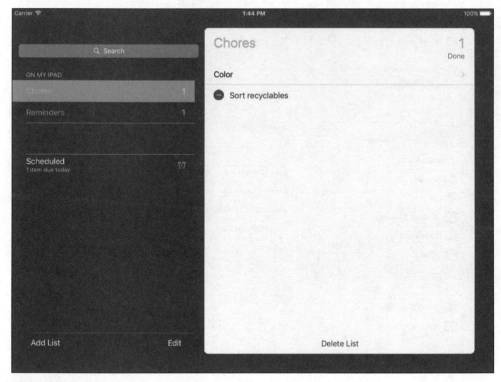

FIGURE 19-8

Set Notifications

Notification Center is a list of alerts, appointments, and useful information (such as stock quotes and weather) that you can display by swiping down from the top of any iPad screen. Notification Center is on by default. You can configure settings to control what types of notifications are displayed. Follow these steps:

1. Tap Settings ⇨ Notifications. The Notifications screen (see **Figure 19-9**) lists the items you can set to be included in Notification Center.

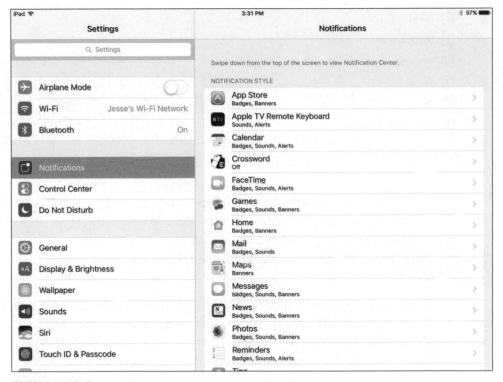

FIGURE 19-9

2. Tap any item.

3. On the resulting screen (see **Figure 19-10**), tap the Show in Notification Center on/off button to include that item in or exclude that item from Notification Center.

FIGURE 19-10

4. If you turn an item on in Step 3, tap an option in the Alert Style When Unlocked section. You can have no alert, a banner across the top of the screen, or a boxed alert. If you choose Banner, the banner appears and then disappears automatically. If you choose Alerts, you must take an action to dismiss the alert when it appears.

5. (Optional) Tap the Badge App Icon on/off button to turn that feature on, if you want. Badge App Icon places a red circle and number on icons on your home screens to represent alerts associated with those apps, such as the number of new unread email messages waiting.

6. (Optional) If you want to be able to view notifications when the screen is locked, tap the Show on Lock Screen on/off button to turn that feature on.

7. Tap the Notifications button to go back to the Notifications screen, or press the Home button to return to the home screen.

View Notification Center

After you've made settings to specify what should appear in Notification Center, you'll want to look at those alerts and reminders regularly. On any screen, tap at the top and drag down to display Notification Center (see **Figure 19-11**). Note that items are divided into lists by type, depending on what notifications you have now, such as Reminders, Mail, and Calendar.

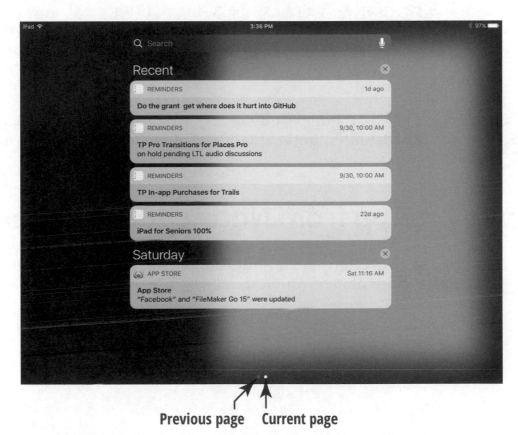

Previous page   Current page

FIGURE 19-11

To close Notification Center, tap the bold arrow at the bottom center of the notification area.

To determine what's displayed in Notification Center, see the preceding section.

TIP

You can also view Notification Center from the lock screen. Just swipe down from the top of the screen to reveal it, and swipe up to hide it again.

Check Out Notification Pages

The two dots at the bottom of the Notification Center indicate that it has two pages. You can swipe to the right to see the next page or to the left to see the previous page. The page shown in **Figure 19-11** is organized by date. The other page is organized by Reminders, Calendar, Music, Notes, and other apps that may be populating the list.

To change what's shown on the Today tab, with it displayed, tap Edit. Tap the minus button to the left of any item you don't want displayed.

Go to an App from Notification Center

You can easily jump from Notification Center to any app that caused an alert or reminder to appear.

1. Tap the top of the screen, and drag down to display Notification Center.

2. Tap any item in a category, such as Reminders or Stocks. The originating app opens.

Get Some Rest with Do Not Disturb

Do Not Disturb is a simple but useful setting you can use to stop any notifications alerts and FaceTime calls from appearing or making a sound when your iPad is locked. You can make settings to allow calls from certain people through or to allow several repeat calls from the same person in a short period to come through. (Apple assumes that such repeat calls may signal an emergency or an urgent need to get through to you.)

1. Tap Settings and then tap Do Not Disturb.

2. Tap the Manual switch to turn the feature on (or off).

3. In the other settings shown in **Figure 19-12**, do any of the following:

   - Tap the Scheduled switch to allow alerts during a specified time period to appear. You can tap From/To to set the hours you want.

   - Tap Allow Calls From, and in the next screen, select Everyone, No One, or All Contacts.

   - Tap the Repeated Calls switch to allow a second call from the same person in a three-minute period to come through.

4. Press the Home button to return to the home screen.

TIP

Normally, when your iPad is locked (either manually or because you've set its auto-lock time in Settings⇨Display & Brightness⇨Auto-Lock, your are notified of alerts, notifications, and FaceTime calls. That's the behavior people expect. When you use Do Not Disturb, those items don't get through. Certain sounds such as alarms do get through: The assumption is that if you've set an alarm you want to hear it. When it comes to alerts, notifications, and FaceTime calls, you can't control when they may come in, so using Do Not Disturb prevents you from being surprised.

If you're planning to use Do Not Disturb at a concert or church service, you might want to ask in advance what the best way to silence your iPad is. Chances are, the manager will be glad you asked and may even be glad to experiment with you so that other people can find out how to set their iPads.

For what it's worth, when I do my monthly radio gig on WAMC Public Radio for the Northeast, I put my electronics in my bag and put it just outside the studio door, and I don't worry about setting Mute or Do Not Disturb. Simple is often best.

Chapter **20**
Managing Contacts

C ontacts is the iPad equivalent of the dog-eared address book that used to sit by your home phone. The Contacts app is simple to set up and use, and it has some powerful features beyond simply storing names, addresses, and phone numbers.

You can pinpoint a contact's address in the iPad's Maps application, for example. You can use your contacts to address emails, Facebook messages, and tweets quickly. If you store a contact record that includes a website, you can use a link in Contacts to view that website instantly. And, of course, you can easily search for a contact by a variety of criteria, including people related to you by family ties and mutual friends or by groups that you create.

In this chapter, you discover the various features of Contacts, including how you can save yourself time by syncing many email contacts lists to your iPad instantly.

Add a Contact

1. Tap the Contacts app's icon to open the app. If you haven't entered any contacts yet, you see a blank address book (except for your own contact information, which may have been added when you set up your iPad), like the one shown in **Figure 20-1**. Note that Figure 20-1 has two sections: On the left is a list of contacts, and on the right is the detailed information for a selected contact in the list.

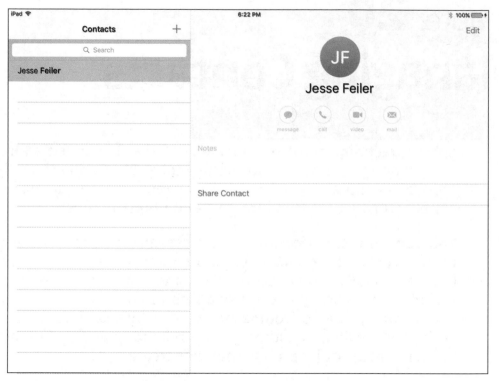

FIGURE 20-1

2. Tap the Add button at the top of the contacts list (it has a plus sign — + on it). A blank New Contact page opens (see **Figure 20-2**), and the onscreen keyboard displays.

FIGURE 20-2

3. Enter any contact information you want. (You have to enter only first name, last name, or company to create a contact.)

   To scroll down the contact page and see more fields, flick up the page with your finger.

4. If you want to add even more information, such as a mailing or street address, tap the Add Field link at the bottom of the New Contact page. The Add Field page appears (see **Figure 20-3**).

5. Tap a field to add.

6. Tap the Done button when you finish making entries. The new contact appears in your address book.

Cancel	**Add Field**
Prefix	
Phonetic first name	
Pronunciation first name	
Middle name	
Phonetic middle name	
Phonetic last name	
Pronunciation last name	
Maiden name	
Suffix	
Nickname	
Job title	
Department	
Phonetic company name	

FIGURE 20-3

TIP

If your contact has a name that's difficult for you to pronounce, consider adding the Phonetic First Name or Phonetic Last Name field, or both, to that person's record (refer to Step 6).

Assign a Photo to a Contact

1. With Contacts open, tap a contact to whose record you want to add a photo.

2. Tap the Edit button in the top-right corner of the screen.

3. On the screen that appears, tap Add Photo (at the top left of Figure 20-2). The popover shown in **Figure 20-4** opens.

FIGURE 20-4

4. Do one of the following:

- Tap Choose Photo to select an existing photo from the Photos app's Gallery. Tap a photo to select it, and move the photo around to center the most important part in the selection circle (see **Figure 20-5**). Then tap the Use button. The photo is added to the contact's details page.

  Tap the Use button to use the photo for this contact. The photo appears on the contact's details (see **Figure 20-6**).

- Tap Take Photo to take that contact's photo on the spot with the iPad's camera (see Chapter 14).

5. Tap Done to save your changes.

FIGURE 20-5

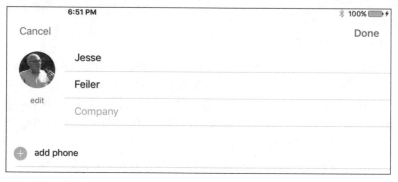

FIGURE 20-6

Set Ringtones for Contacts

If you want to hear a unique tone when you receive a text or a Face-Time call from a particular contact, you can set up this feature in Contacts. If you want to be sure that you know instantly when your spouse, sick friend, or boss is calling, set a unique tone for that person.

1. With the Contacts app open, tap an existing contact or add a new one (see "Add a Contact" earlier in this chapter).

2. Tap the Edit button in the top-right corner of the screen.

3. On the next screen, tap the Ringtone field to display the Ringtones page (see **Figure 20-7**). From here, you can set tones that help you distinguish between notifications from FaceTime, Messages, and Alerts (see Chapter 19). You see those notifications and alerts in the relevant apps, but you set the ringtones here in Contacts.

   To buy additional ringtones from Apple, scroll to the top of the list of tones and tap Buy More Tones.

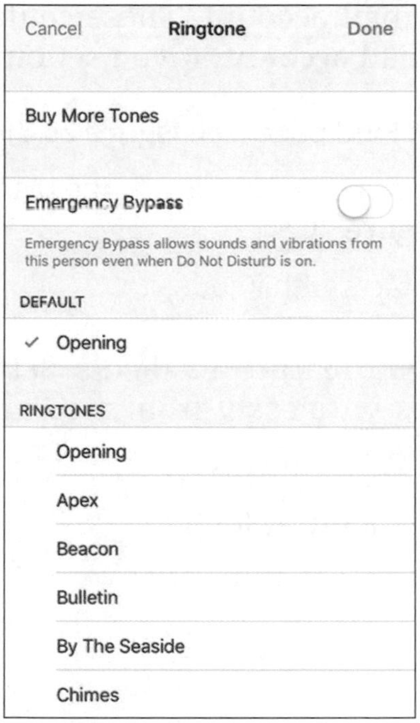

Cancel	**Ringtone**	Done

Buy More Tones

Emergency Bypass ⬜

Emergency Bypass allows sounds and vibrations from this person even when Do Not Disturb is on.

DEFAULT

✓ Opening

RINGTONES

Opening

Apex

Beacon

Bulletin

By The Seaside

Chimes

FIGURE 20-7

4. Tap a tone to preview it.

5. When you hear a tone that you like, tap Done.

6. Tap Done again to close the Contacts form.

You can set a custom tone by tapping Settings ⇨ Sounds.

If your Apple devices are synced via iCloud, setting a unique ring-tone for an iPad contact also sets it for your other iOS devices, as well as for FaceTime.

Sync Contacts with iCloud

You can use your iCloud account to sync contacts from your iPad and various services, such as an email account. These contacts also become available to your iCloud email account, if you set one up.

1. Tap Settings ⇨ iCloud to open the iCloud page (see **Figure 20-8**).

2. Tap the Contacts on/off button to turn that feature on. The Merge with iCloud? dialog appears (see **Figure 20-9**).

3. Tap Merge to merge your iPad contacts with iCloud.

You can use the iTunes Wi-Fi sync feature in iPad's Settings under General to sync with iTunes wirelessly from a computer connected to the same Wi-Fi network.

See Chapter 3 for more information about iCloud.

FIGURE 20-8

FIGURE 20-9

Search for a Contact

1. With Contacts open, tap the Search field at the top of the left pane. The onscreen keyboard opens.

2. Type the first letter of the contact's first or last name or the contact's company. All matching results appear as you type.

3. If more than one result appears while you're typing or when you've typed as much as you know of the name, tap a result to display that person's contact information.

TIP

You can search Contacts by phone number, website, or address as well as by name.

TIP

If you've entered many contacts, you can use the alphabetical listing along the right side of All Contacts to locate a record. Tap and drag to scroll down the list of contacts.

Address Email with Contacts

If you've entered an email address for a contact, the address automatically becomes a link in the contact's record, and you can address an email from the Contacts app.

1. With the Contacts app open, tap a contact's name to display the person's contact information.

2. Tap the email address link at the right in Figure 20-1.

3. A new email message enters that is addressed to the contact. Enter the subject and message itself.

4. Tap Send.

As you see in Figure 20-1, other buttons on the contact card let you initiate a phone call, a message, or a video Facetime chat in addition to email.

Share a Contact

After you've entered contact information, you can share it with others via an email message.

1. With Contacts open, tap a contact name to display its information.

2. Tap Share Contact (it's at the bottom of Figure 20-1 and most views of contacts).

3. In the sharing popover that appears, tap Mail. The New Message form appears, as shown in **Figure 20-10**.

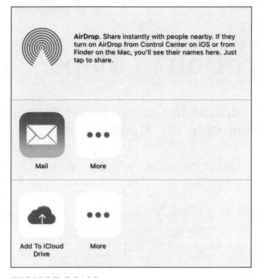

FIGURE 20-10

4. Use the onscreen keyboard to enter the recipient's email address.

5. Modify the information in the Subject field, if you like.

6. Enter a message.

7. Tap the Send button. The message goes to your recipient, with the contact information attached as a .vcf file. (This format, called vCard, is commonly used to transmit contact information.)

When a person receives a vCard containing contact information, all she must do is click or tap the attached file to open it. At this point, depending on the recipient's email or contact management program, she can perform various actions to save the content. Mac and iOS device users can easily import `.vcf` records into their own Contacts apps. Even PC and Android users can do this if their contact management programs support `.vcf` records, as most do.

In Step 3, you can select AirDrop and then tap the name of a device near you to send the contact information to that device wirelessly. This feature works with recent iOS devices and Macs that run OS X Yosemite or later.

View a Contact's Location in Maps

If you've entered a person's address in Contacts, you have a shortcut for viewing that person's location in the Maps application.

1. With the Contacts app open, tap the contact whose location you want to view.

2. Tap the address. Maps opens and displays a map of the address.

For more about using the Maps app, see Chapter 17.

Delete a Contact

1. With the Contacts app open, tap the contact you want to delete.

2. Tap the Edit button in the top-right corner of the screen.

3. Scroll down the screen that appears and then tap the Delete Contact button at the bottom, as shown in **Figure 20-11**.

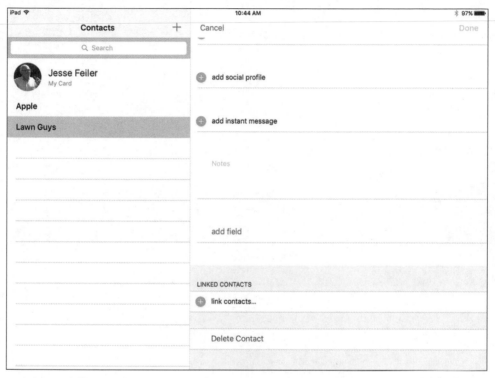

FIGURE 20-11

4. Tap Delete Contact from the popover that appears to confirm the deletion.

WARNING

If you change your mind before you tap Delete Contact, tap anywhere outside the popover or tap Cancel at the top of the screen. Anything except an affirmative answer ends the process.

Chapter **21**
Making Notes

Notes is the preinstalled app that you can use to do everything from jotting down notes at meetings to keeping to-do lists. Notes is a place where you can put those clippings, memos, and (yes) notes. You have a range of options for saving what used to be clippings and scraps of paper.

When you pair Notes with Apple Pencil, you have a terrific combination for work, or play and even those strange things that are taking shape and you can't figure out what they're going to become. Everything you do without a pencil still works — you just tap with your Apple Pencil instead of with your finger. And instead of relying on the keyboard, you use the pencil. Notes can be typed text or drawings done with your Apple Pencil or your finger. Try it.

This chapter shows you how to create notes, add text or images to notes, and how to share them with others. Basically, everything you do with those clippings and scraps of paper.

Open a Note

1. Tap the Notes app's icon to open the app. If you've never used Notes, a blank Notes list appears. If you've used Notes before, it opens to the last note you were working on.

2. Tap a note to open it in the main section of the window (see **Figure 21-1**).

TIP

If you're holding the iPad in landscape orientation, a list of notes appears by default on the left side of the screen. If you're holding the iPad in portrait orientation, you can display this list by tapping the Notes button in the top-left corner of the screen. Tap any note in the list to open it.

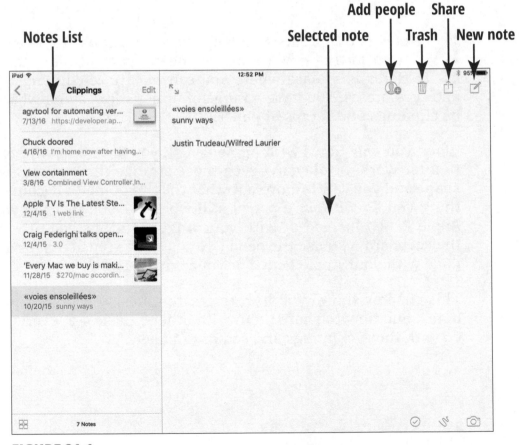

FIGURE 21-1

Create a Note

1. With Notes open, tap the New Note icon in the top-right corner. A new blank note appears.

2. Start typing your note with the onscreen keyboard, shown in **Figure 21-2**; it appears as soon as you start typing.

3. You don't have to save your note: Just move on to create another note or do something else. If you don't want your note to be saved or want to delete it, tap the Delete button.

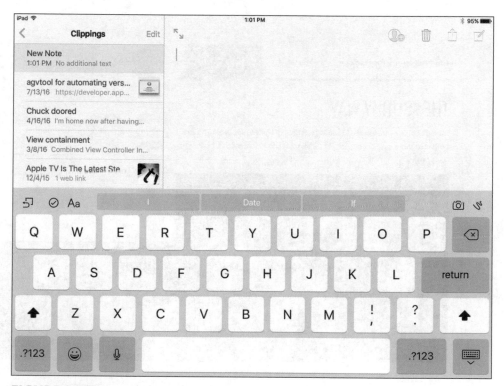

FIGURE 21-2

TIP
If your iPad is in portrait orientation and you want to display the list of saved notes beside the current note, tap the Notes button to see a drop-down list of notes.

Create a Note from a Document

You can create a new note from a clipping, article, or another document.

1. Navigate to the document, web page, or another item you want to share.

2. Tap the Share button (the box with the up arrow).

3. In the popover that appears (see **Figure 21-3**), tap Add to Notes.

FIGURE 21-3

4. Add your own text to the note, if you want.

5. Tap Save to save the note (see **Figure 21-4**).

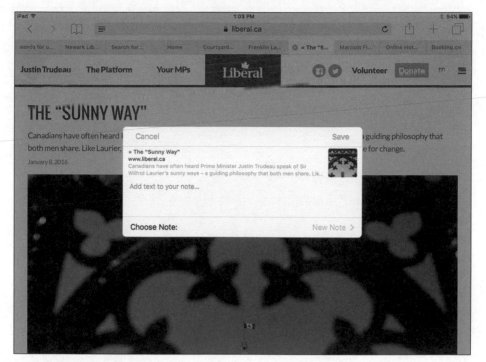

FIGURE 21-4

Copy and Paste Text from a Note

The Notes app includes two essential editing tools that you're probably familiar with from using word processors: Copy and Paste.

1. With a note displayed, press and hold a word. A pop-up menu
appears (see **Figure 21-5**).

2. Tap Select to select part of the note text or Select All to select all of it.

3. Tap Copy in the pop-up menu.

4. Press and hold the spot in the document where you want to place the
copied text. A pop-up menu appears.

5. Tap Paste. The copied text appears in the document.

To extend a selection to adjacent words, drag one of the handles
that extend from the edge of a selection.

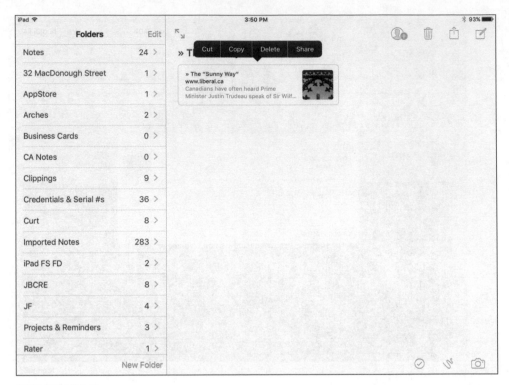

FIGURE 21-5

TIP

You can tap the Edit button in the top-left corner of the onscreen keyboard and then tap the Copy button to copy text with the keyboard. Then continue with Step 4 to paste the content into your note.

Insert a Photo or Video into a Note

1. With Notes open, tap to create a new note or tap to edit an existing note.

2. Tap the center of the note to display the keyboard, as shown in **Figure 21-6**.

FIGURE 21-6

3. Tap the Picture icon (shaped like a camera) above the keyboard. This will show your options, as shown in **Figure 21-7**.

4. Do one of the following:

   - Tap Photo Library (see Figure **21-7**) to insert a picture you've already taken and choose the photo you want to insert.

   - Tap Take Photo or Video, and take a new photo or video on your iPad.

5. Tap Use. The photo or video you selected in Step 4 is inserted into your note.

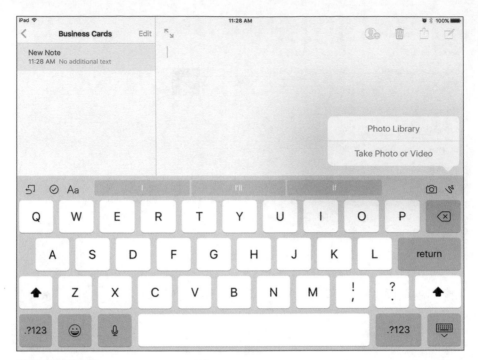

FIGURE 21-7

Add a Drawing or Sketch

1. With your Apple Pencil, you can create a drawing to add to your note. With a note open, tap in the note to display the keyboard.

2. Click the Drawing tool (a squiggle near the right side of the top of the keyboard). The drawing tools appear.

3. Tap a drawing tool (Pen, Marker, or Pencil).

4. Tap a color in the color palette that appears.

5. When you've finished drawing, click Done.

TIP

Tapping the Ruler tool places a ruler-shaped item onscreen that you can use to help you to draw straight lines.

Apply a Text Style to a Note

Text styles — including Title, Heading, Body, Bulleted List, Dashed List, and Numbered List — are available on the new shortcut toolbar above the onscreen keyboard.

1. With a note open, tap and hold some text until the shortcut toolbar is displayed, as you see in **Figure 21-8**.

Cut, copy, paste

Checklist

Styles

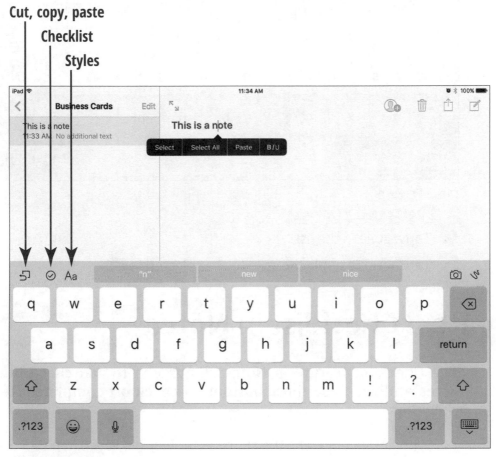

FIGURE 21-8

2. Choose Select to select text or Select All to select all of it.

3. Tap the Text Style tool above the keyboard (labeled Aa) to display a list of styles (see **Figure 21-9**).

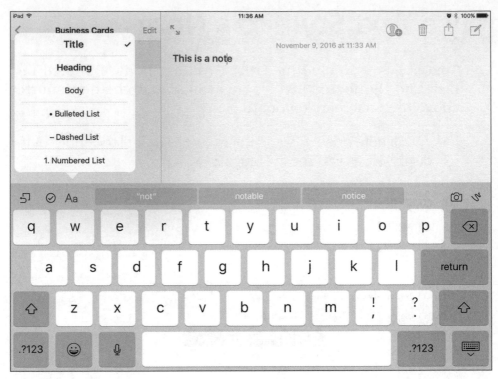

FIGURE 21-9

4. Tap a style in the list.

5. Tap Done to apply the style to the selected text.

Create a Checklist in Notes

The Checklist feature in Notes allows you to add check buttons to notes and then use those buttons to check off completed items in a checklist.

1. With a note open and the shortcut toolbar displayed, tap the Checklist button.

2. Enter the first item of your checklist, and tap Return on the keyboard. A second checklist item appears.

3. When you're done entering checklist items, tap the Checklist button again to turn the feature off.

TIP

You can apply checklist formatting to existing text by pressing and holding the text, choosing Select or Select All from the pop-up menu, and then tapping the Checklist button.

Search for a Note

1. With Notes open, tap the Notes button to display the notes list. You'll see the Search field at the top of the list, as in **Figure 21-10**.

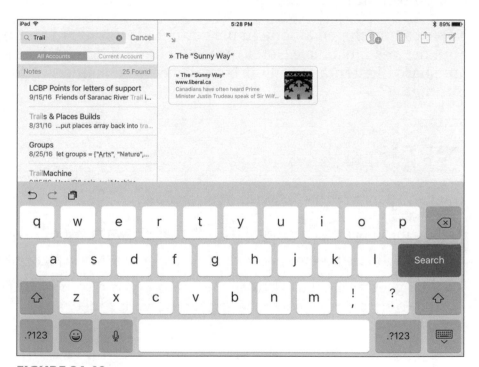

FIGURE 21-10

2. Tap the Search field at the top of the notes list. (You may have to drag down to reveal it.) The onscreen keyboard appears.

3. Begin to enter the search term. All notes that contain matching words appear in a list of search results (see Figure 21-10).

4. Tap a result to open the pertinent note.

Share a Note

Figure 21-3 showed you how to create a note using the Share button. You can do the same thing to share a note with any of the available tools shown in Figure 21-3.

TIP

Notes can be shared among Apple devices via iCloud. In Settings, both devices must have Notes turned on under iCloud. New notes are shared instantaneously if both devices are connected to the Internet.

Add People

You can share your notes with other people.

1. Tap the image of a person with a + sign, as shown in Figure 21-3.

2. Tap to choose how to send your invitation, as you see in **Figure 21-11**.

   Your guests will get a link to your note and everyone can share it — they can view it and make changes for everyone to see.

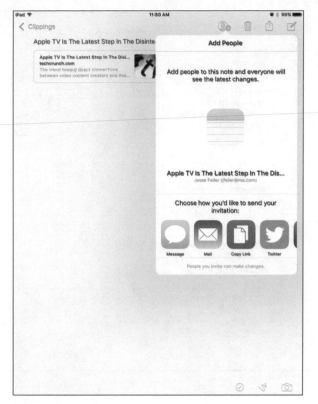

FIGURE 21-11

Adjust Notes Settings

1. Tap Settings ⇨ Notes to display the Notes screen (see **Figure 21-12**).

2. Tap an option to select and set it.

Your Sort Notes By options, for example, are Date Edited, Date Created, and Title.

TIP

If you'll be adding media to your notes, tap the Save Media to Notes on/off button to turn this feature on.

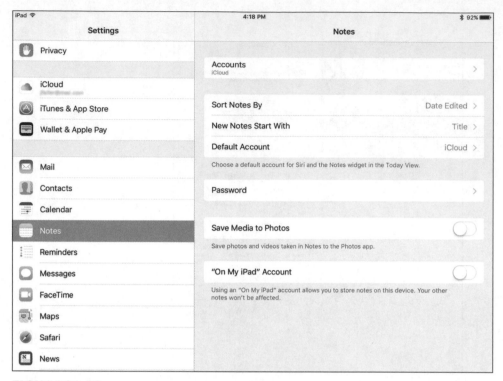

FIGURE 21-12

TIP

If you'll be using iCloud with notes, you may want to turn off the "On My iPad" Account setting so that everything goes to iCloud. (Don't worry: If iCloud is temporarily unavailable, your data will be uploaded when it returns.)

Delete a Note

There's no sense in letting your notes list become cluttered, making it harder to find the ones you need. When you're done with a note, it's time to delete it.

1. With Notes open and the iPad in landscape orientation, tap a note in the notes list to open it.

2. Tap the Trash icon.

3. There's no confirmation — the note is just deleted. But before you panic, notice that at the bottom of the Notes list is a Recently Deleted folder. That's where it is.

Moving a Note

Here's how to move a note from one folder to another (like rescuing from Recently Deleted notes).

1. Open the Notes List.
2. Tap Edit and the top right of the list.
3. You'll see a selection circle next to each note.
4. Tap to select the note(s) you want to move.
5. Tap Move To at the bottom left of the Notes list.
6. You'll see a list of folders: Tap the one to which you want to move the note(s).

Notice that you can also use these steps to select one or more notes and delete them all at once rather than deleting them individually.

Chapter 22

Getting the News You Need

The News app gathers news stories that match your news reading habits or the channels and topics you've selected. You can choose which news sites are your favorites, search for news on a particular topic, and save news stories to read later. News combines the interests and favorites you select with your reading behavior to customize the articles you see. (Technically, this app is a *smart news aggregator*.) In this chapter, you get an overview of all these features.

Explore News

Figure 22-1 shows the basic News layout. Each article has its own headline and summary (and often an image or a video). For more information, you can tap the article to go to its original source. You can see where each article came from, and in small print, you also can see how long ago it was posted.

FIGURE 22-1

The familiar Share button (the box with the arrow pointing up) is also available for each option. As always, the Share options depend on what you're looking at. **Figure 22-2** shows some News Share options that you may not have seen before. The heart button — sometimes called a Favorites button — is now Love. And in response to many, many comments on social media sites, there's now a Dislike button.

Specific to News is the Mute Channel button, which mutes the channel the article came from so that if the topic interests you but you don't particularly like the channel (or publication), you can continue to express your interest in the topic while not seeing more from that channel.

The more you use buttons such as Love, Dislike, and Mute Channel, the smarter News will be.

TIP

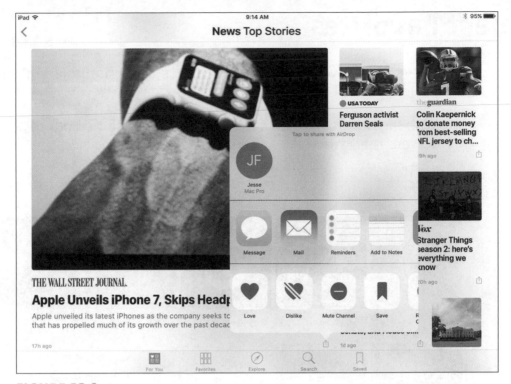

News Top Stories

USA TODAY
Ferguson activist Darren Seals

the **guardian**
Colin Kaepernick to donate money from best-selling NFL jersey to ch...

9h ago

Tap to share with AirDrop

JF

Jesse
Mac Pro

Message   Mail   Reminders   Add to Notes

*V*ox
Stranger Things season 2: here's everything we know

20h ago

THE WALL STREET JOURNAL.

Apple Unveils iPhone 7, Skips Head

Apple unveiled its latest iPhones as the company seeks to
that has propelled much of its growth over the past decac

Love   Dislike   Mute Channel   Save

17h ago

1d ago

For You   Favorites   Explore   Search   Saved

FIGURE 22-2

TIP

The order of the buttons in the bottom row may be different on your iPad. You can drag the buttons around so that the ones you use most often are together. You can't, however, drag items from the top row (colored buttons) to the bottom row (black-and-white buttons), or vice versa.

Read Your News

1. Tap the News app's icon to open the app. The For You tab of news stories (refer to Figure 22-1) appears by default, though whichever tab you last chose will appear next time you open the app.

2. Scroll down the page to see the news stories of the day.

Select Favorites

Favorites allows you to select the topics and channels you prefer to include in your news.

1. With the News app open, tap the Favorites tab at the bottom of the screen. The screen shown in **Figure 22-3** appears.

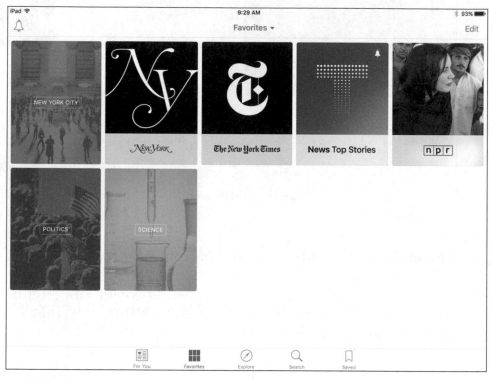

FIGURE 22-3

2. Tap the Edit button in the top-right corner.

3. Tap the X button on an item (see **Figure 22-4**) to delete it from Favorites.

4. Tap Done.

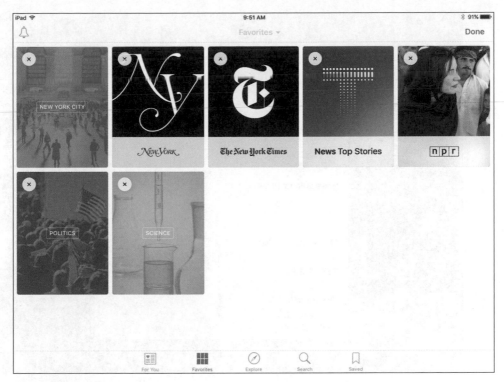

FIGURE 22-4

Set Notifications

1. With the News app open, tap the Favorites tab at the bottom of the screen to open the Favorites screen (refer to Figure 22-3).

2. Tap the Notification button (the bell) in the top-left corner to open the Notifications dialog (see **Figure 22-5**).

3. Tap the on/off buttons of the topics you want notifications for.

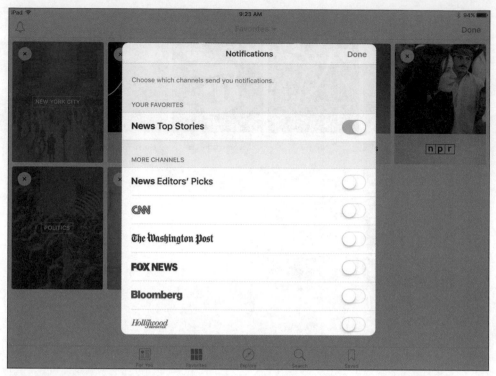

FIGURE 22-5

Explore Channels and Topics

Using the Explore feature, you can select channels to add to Favorites.

1. With the News app open, tap the Explore tab at the bottom of the screen. The Explore screen opens (see **Figure 22-6**).

2. Tap a topic to see articles within that category in the standard News display, like Figure 22-1.

3. Tap the Back button to return to the screen shown in Figure 22-6, and if you like what you saw, tap the + to turn it into a check mark.

4. Swipe right or down to explore more items.

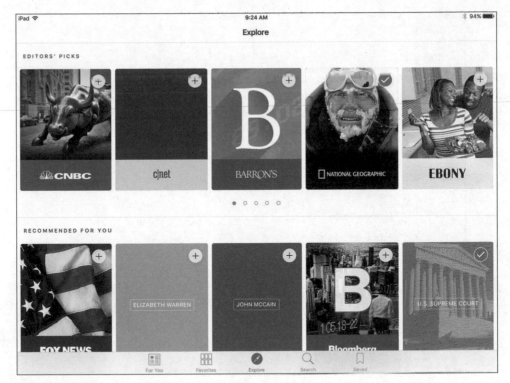

FIGURE 22-6

Search for News

If you'd like to follow a news story, you can search for it in News.

1. With the News app open, tap the Search tab at the bottom of the screen. You see a Search field as well as some suggestions (see **Figure 22-7**).

2. Enter a search term or phrase, and tap Done.

3. Tap the plus sign (+) for more search results.

TIP

If you don't find what you want in the results, tap the Show More Topics or Show More Channels link in the results list.

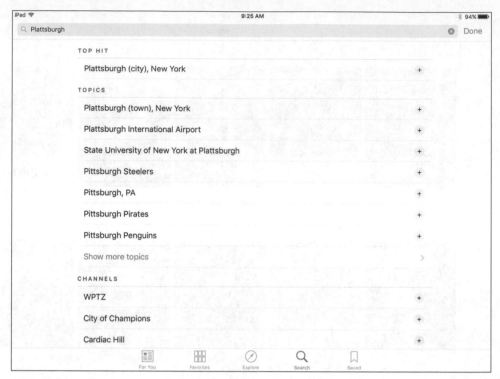

FIGURE 22-7

FOLLOWING FAVORITE TOPICS

The stories that you see in News depend on your favorites, your browsing history, and (most important) the stories that are available. If you're interested in following the latest news about archeological discoveries in Foggy Bottom, for example, you can mark all the favorites you want, but you won't see any stories unless someone makes a discovery. Make your choices, and wait a few days.

Index

Numerics

3.5mm headphone jack, 26
3D Touch, 11
3G/4G LTE technology, 18–20, 61
4G/4G LTE, 61
10/12W USB power adapter, 23–24

A

A8/8X/9 chips, 10
About In-App Purchases Quick Link
  (App Store), 316
Abram, Carolyn (author)
  Facebook For Dummies, 6th Edition, 164
accessibility settings
  access restrictions, 99–101
  brightness, 84–85, 249–250
  dexterity, 98
  features, 81–82
  hearing, 93–96
  iBooks app, 249–251
  label settings, 92
  reduce motion, 92
  subtitles and captions, 309
  text appearance, 91–92
  VoiceOver, 87–91
  wallpaper, 85–87
  zoom setting, 91
accessories
  adding in HomeKit, 218–222
  adjusting in HomeKit, 223–225

Camera Connection Kit, 281
cases, 21
combining with Scenes in HomeKit,
  228
Digital AV Adapters (Apple), 22
HomeKit, 217–225
Lightning Connector, 25
Lightning-to-USB cable, 23–24
power adapter, 23–24
printers, 21
stands, 22
activating Do Not Disturb feature,
  182
Activity icon, 61
address book
  adding contacts, 374–376
  birthdays, 350
  deleting contacts, 384–385
  features, 64, 373
  iCloud syncing, 380–381
  Mail app integration, 382
  Maps app integration, 384
  phonetic name fields, 376
  photos, for contacts, 376–378
  ringtones, 378–380
  search feature, 382
  vCards, 384
AirDrop
  sharing contact information, 384
  sharing photos, 295–296

AirPlay, 259, 270–272

AirPrint
  photos, 298–299
  web pages, 135–136

alarm clock, 355–356

alerts
  calendar, 344–346
  Do Not Disturb setting, 370–371
  Notification Center, 367–368

Anker PowerPort, 5, 31

AOL email, 144–147

App Store, 66, 202–207, 316–317

appearance
  brightness, 84–85, 249–250
  iBooks app display, 249–251
  label settings, 92
  reduce motion, 92
  text appearance, 91–92
  VoiceOver, 87–91
  wallpaper, 85–87
  zoom setting, 91

Apple (website), 28, 182

Apple Digital AV Adapters, 22

Apple ID, 69–73

Apple iPad (website), 3

Apple Music, 271

Apple Pencil, 9, 11, 22, 41

Apple Store, 20

Apple TV, 270

appointments. *See* Calendar app

apps
  about, 215–216
  App Store features, 66

Calendar. *See* Calendar app

Camera, 63, 274–280

Clock, 64, 335, 353–358

Contacts. *See* Contacts app

deleting, 211–212

Dock, 62

FaceTime, 183–185

features, 201

going to from Notification Center, 370

home screen, 62–66

HomeKit, 216–235

iBooks. *See* iBooks app

iTunes Store. *See* iTunes Store

jiggling, 209

Mail. *See* Mail app

Maps. *See* Maps app

Music. *See* Music app

News, 65

Notes, 65, 387–402

organizing, 207–211

passcodes, 98–100

Photos. *See* Photos app

Podcasts, 66

preinstalled, 61–66

Reminders, 65, 359–366

searching App Store, 202–204

Settings, 66

third-party, 112–113

types, 201–202

updating, 212–214

Videos. *See* Videos app

AssistiveTouch, 96–98

AT&T (website), 19

audio. *See also* Music app
  hearing settings, 93–94
  muting FaceTime, 184
  ringtones, 378–380
  sending and receiving with messages, 179–180
  3.5mm headphone jack, 26
  volume controls, 26, 270
Autofill, 122
automation. *See* HomeKit
AV Adapters (Apple), 22

B

Back button, 124
background image, changing, 85–87
backups, 76–77
barometer sensor, 11
batteries, charging, 30–32
Battery Life icon, 61
birthdays, 350
Block Cookies, 140–141
blue circle, 150
blue marker, Maps app, 322
Bluetooth, 61
body, 10
bold text formatting, applying, 154–156
bookmarks
  saving to home screen, 133–134
  web, 128–130
books
  adding PDFs, 257–258
  bookmarks and highlights, 253–256
  dictionary, 257

display settings, 249–251
features, 239–240
iPad, compared to others, 243
reading, 246–249
searching within books, 252
shopping for content, 241–243
Braille, 90
brightness setting, 84–85, 249–250
browsing, web
  bookmarks, 128–130
  features, 115–116
  gestures, 119
  history, 123–124
  link sharing, 134–135
  navigating, 120–122
  photos, saving and posting, 137–139, 282–283
  printing, 135–136
  privacy settings, 139–141
  Reader feature, 132–133
  Reading List, 130–131
  saving photos, 282–283
  Share button, 125–127
  tabbed browsing, 122–123
  Web Clips, 133–134
  web searches, 124–125
Burst feature, 276, 280

C

Calendar app
  adding events, 340–342
  alerts, 344–346
  birthdays, 350

Calendar app *(continued)*
  deleting events, 351–353
  Family Sharing, 350–351
  features, 63, 335
  Mail app integration, 148
  navigation and views, 336–340
  Reminders app integration, 364–365
  repeating events, 343–344
  sharing, 347–350
Camera app, 63, 274–280
Camera Connection Kit, 281
cameras
  basic operation, 66–68
  Camera Connection Kit, 281
  importing photos from, 281–282
  iSight, 274
  location, 25, 26
  taking photos, 277–280
  volume rocker controls, 278
captioning, 94–95
CarPlay feature, 7, 20
cases, 21
cellphone hotspot feature, 19
channels (News app), 408–409
charging battery, 30–32
Cheat Sheet (website), 3
checklists, creating in Notes app,
  397–398
chips, A8/8X/9, 10
Clear button, 124
clearing iMessages, 178–179
Clock app, 64, 335, 353–358
closed captioning, 309

commands, issuing to Siri, 110–111
configuration
  AirDrop, 295–296
  dexterity, 98
  e-readers, 249–251
  Guided Access, 99–101
  hearing, 93–96, 309
  iCloud, 75–78
  Notification Center, 367–368
  privacy, 139–141
  vision, 82–87
connections, data
  compared, 17–20
  Wi-Fi, 17–20, 116–118
Contacts app
  adding contacts, 374–376
  assigning photos, 376–378
  birthdays, 350
  deleting, 384–385
  features, 64, 373
  iCloud syncing, 380–381
  Mail app integration, 382
  Maps app integration, 384
  phonetic name fields, 376
  photos, for contacts, 376–378
  ringtones, 378–380
  search feature, 382
  vCards, 384
Control Center, 56–58, 296
copy text, 392–393
copyright, 138
cost, 13

D

data connections
  compared, 17–20
  Wi-Fi, 17–20, 116–118
deleting
  apps, 211–212
  Calendar events, 351–353
  contacts, 384–385
  email messages, 160–161
  notes, 401
  photos, 300–301
design features, 8
dexterity settings, 98
Dictation feature
  Mail app, 153
  Maps app, 329
Dictation key, 96
dictionary, 257
Digital AV Adapters (Apple), 22
display settings
  brightness, 84–85, 249–250
  iBooks app, 249–251
  label settings, 92
  Magnifier, 82–83
  Night Shift, 85
  reduce motion, 92
  text appearance, 91–92
  VoiceOver, 87–91
  wallpaper, 85–87
  zoom setting, 91
Do Not Disturb feature, 182, 370–371
Do Not Track, 140
Dock, 62

Dock Connector-to-USB cable, 23
documentation, 23
double tap gesture, 38, 90, 119
drawings, adding in Notes app, 395
driving directions, 328–331

E

e-books. *See* e-readers; News app
effects, photos, 287
elllipsis button (. . .), 127
email
  adding accounts, 144–147
  Contacts app integration, 382
  creating events, 159–160
  deleting messages, 160–161
  features, 143
  flagging, 157–159
  formatting text, 154–156
  marking as unread, 157–159
  organizing messages, 161–162
  reading messages, 148–150
  replying and forwarding messages,
    151–153
  searching messages, 156–157
  sending links, 134–135
  sending messages, 153–154
  sharing photo streams, 296–297
  sharing photos, 294–295
e-readers. *See also* News app
  about, 85
  adding PDFs, 257–258
  bookmarks and highlights, 253–256
  dictionary, 257

e-readers. *(continued)*
 display settings, 249–251
 features, 239–240
 iBooks. *See* iBooks app
 iPad, compared to others, 243
 reading, 246–249
 searching within books, 252
 shopping for content, 241–243
events, creating, 159–160

F

Facebook app, 164–166, 294–295
Facebook For Dummies, 6th Edition
  (Abram), 164
FaceTime app
 camera views, 185
 custom ringtones, 380
 features, 63, 183
 making calls, 183–184
 muting sound, 184
 requirements, 183
 taking and ending calls, 184–185
Family Sharing
 about, 269
 calendars, 350–351
 setting up, 197–200
favorites (News app), 406–407
filter effects, photos, 287
Find My iPad, 78–80
Fitton, Laura (author)
 Twitter For Dummies, 3rd Edition, 164
five-finger swipe gesture, 51

flagging email, 157–159
Flash, 276
flash drives, 14
flick gesture, 39, 90, 119
Flickr app, 167–168
focus, setting, 279–280
folders, organizing apps in,
  209–211
4G/4G LTE, 61

G

games
 about, 313–315
 App Store, 316–317
 choosing, 315–316
 purchasing, 318–319
 searching for, 318–319
GB (gigabytes), 15
Genius playlist feature, 192
gestures
 double tap, 38, 90, 119
 flick, 39, 90, 119
 four- or five-finger swipe, 51
 one-finger swipe, 39, 119
 pinch, 38, 51, 63, 98, 326
 press and hold, 39
 Status bar tap, 39
 swipe, 150
 tap, 38
 two-finger swipe, 119
gigabytes (GB), 15
Gmail, 144–147

GPS (Global Positioning System)
   navigation, 20, 61
group messaging, 182
Guided Access settings, 99–101

H

HDR, 275
headphone jack, 3.5mm, 26
hearing settings
   captioning, 94–95
   closed captioning, 309
   mono audio, 95–96
   subtitles, 94–95
   volume, 93–94
home automation. *See* HomeKit
Home button
   click speed, 98
   features, 24–25
   multitasking operation, 49
   triple press, 100
   waking iPad from sleep mode, 60
Home screen
   apps, 62–66
   features, 33–34
   organizing, 207–211
   web bookmarks, 133–134
Home Sharing, iTunes (website), 269
HomeKit
   about, 215–217
   Scenes, 225–231
   setting up accessories, 217–225
   setting up rooms, 231
   using automations, 231–235
hotspots, 19, 116–118

I

iBooks app
   about, 85
   adding PDFs, 257–258
   bookmarks and highlights, 253–256
   dictionary, 257
   display settings, 249–251
   reading, 246–249
   searching within books, 252
   shopping for content, 241–245
iCloud
   about, 30
   account setup, 75–76
   adding email to Mail app, 144–147
   Backup, 76–77
   features, 75–76
   sync Contacts, 380–381
   sync Reminders, 364–365
   sync settings, 77–78
   Tabs, Safari, 122–123
iCloud Photo Library feature, 273
iCloud Photo Sharing, 296–297
iCloud Tabs feature, about, 115
icons
   in book, explained, 2
   Home screen, 207–211
   status bar, 60–61
iDevices Switch, 218
images

images *(continued)*
add to Contacts, 376–378
albums, 283–285
basic camera operation, 66–68
deleting, 300–301
editing photos, 285–290
effects, 287
features, 63, 273–274
importing from other devices, 281–282
inserting in Notes app, 393–394
iSight camera, 274
organizing photos, 291–292
printing photos, 298–299
saving from Safari, 137–138, 282–283
sending and receiving with messages, 180–181
sharing photo streams, 296–297
sharing photos, 294–295
shooting videos, 304–306
slideshows, 299–300
taking pictures, 277–280
viewing photos, 283–285, 292–293
IMAP email accounts, 147–148
iMessage app. *See* Messages app
integrated maps, 321
Internet browsing
bookmarks, 128–130
connecting, 116–118
features, 115–116
gestures, 119
history, 123–124
link sharing, 134–135
navigating, 120–122

photos, saving and posting, 137–139, 282–283
printing, 135–136
privacy settings, 139–141
Reader feature, 132–133
Reading List, 130–131
saving photos, 282–283
Share button, 125–127
tabbed browsing, 122–123
Web Clips, 133–134
web searches, 124–125
Internet resources
Apple, 28, 182
Apple ID, 73
Apple iPad, 3
Apple Music, 271
AT&T, 19
Cheat Sheet, 3
Facebook app, 164
Home Sharing, iTunes, 269
iCloud, 75
iDevices Switch, 218
iPad For Seniors For Dummies Cheat Sheet, 3
iWork, 75
Project Gutenberg, 245
Sprint, 19
T-Mobile, 19
Verizon, 19
Invert Colors, 91
iOS (iPhone Operating System)
definition, 8
iOS 10 version, 8–9, 48–49

iPad. *See also specific topics*
  accessibility settings, 81–101
  accessories, 21–22
  email, 143–162. *See also* Mail app
  FaceTime, 183–185
  hardware features, 24–26
  Internet browsing with Safari, 115–141.
    See also Safari
  iTunes Store, 66, 189–200
  models, compared, 13–14
  new features, 8–9
  package contents, 22–24
  settings, basic. *See* settings
  syncing, 73–75
  used, 28
iPad For Seniors For Dummies Cheat
    Sheet (website), 3
iPad mini, 8
iPad Pro, 8
iPad User Guide (Apple), 91
iPhone, hotspot feature, 19
iPhone Operating System (iOS)
  definition, 8
  iOS 10 version, 8–9, 48–49
iSight camera, 274
italic text formatting, applying, 154–156
iTunes
  Genius playlist feature, 192
  syncing iPad to computer, 73–75
  versions, in book, 3
  video purchases, 310
  website, 73

iTunes Match, 76, 192
iTunes Store
  buying content, 196
  features, 66, 189
  navigating, 189–193
  previewing content, 195–196
  renting movies, 196–197
  restrictions, 196
  searching and browsing, 193–194
iTunes U, 66
iWork (website), 75

J
jiggling apps, 209

K
keyboards
  basic operation, 41–46
  options for, 11
  Smart Keyboard, 22
  split feature, 45–46
  undocking, 44

L
label settings, 92
language options
  Braille, 90
  VoiceOver, 90
Language Rotor, 90
Lightning Connector, 25
Lightning-to-USB cable, 23–24

live photos, 11
Live Photos, 275
location data. *See also* Maps app
  Find My iPad feature, 77–80
  photos, 292–293
Location Services, 322
lock screen, 32–33

M

M8/9 Motion Coprocessor, 10
Magnifier, 82–83
Mail app
  adding accounts, 144–147
  creating events, 159–160
  deleting messages, 160–161
  features, 62, 143
  flagging email, 157–159
  formatting text, 154–156
  marking email as unread, 157–159
  organizing messages, 161–162
  reading messages, 148–150
  replying and forwarding messages, 151–153
  searching messages, 156–157
  sending messages, 153–154
  sharing photos, 294–295
Maps app
  about, 12
  Contacts app integration, 384
  directions, 328–331
  displaying current location, 322–323
  features, 64–65, 321–322
  location information, 331–332

options and preferences, 323–324
searching for locations, 326–328
view modes, 324–325
zoom feature, 326
marking email as unread, 157–159
memory, 14–16
Messages app
  clearing conversations, 178–179
  features, 62
  group messaging, 182
  reading messages, 173–178
  sending and receiving audio, 179–180
  sending and receiving photos and video, 180–181
  sending messages, 171–178
  settings, 169–170
Microsoft Outlook email, 144–147
models, compared, 13–14
movies
  playing, 306–309
  previewing, 195–196
  purchasing, 196, 310
  renting, 196–197
  searching and browsing, 193–194
  sharing, 310–311
multitasking
  basics, 49
  definition, 49
  four- or five-finger swipe, 51
multi-touch screens
  double tap gesture, 38, 90, 119
  features, 32–36
  flick gesture, 39, 90, 119

four- or five-finger swipe, 51
one-finger swipe, 39, 119
pinch gesture, 38, 51, 63, 98, 326
press and hold gesture, 39
single tap gesture, 38
Status bar tap, 39
two-finger swipe, 119
Music app
  AirPlay, 270–271
  features, 62
  iTunes Match, 192
  playing, 266–268
  playlists, 261–265, 268
  searching, 265–266
  shuffle, 269
  viewing library, 259–260
  volume controls, 270
mute
  AssistiveTouch controls, 98
  FaceTime calls, 184

N

navigation
  Contacts app integration, 384
  directions, 328–331
  displaying current location, 322–323
  features, 65, 321–322
  location information, 331–332
  options and preferences, 323–324
  searching for locations, 326–328
  view modes, 324–325
  zoom feature, 322, 326

network connections
  compared, 17–20
  Wi-Fi, 17–20, 116–118
networking, social
  FaceTime, 183–185
  features, 163–164
  Messages app, 169–181
  sharing links, 134–135
  sharing photos, 294–295
  Twitter features, 166–167
News app
  about, 12
  channels, 408–409
  exploring, 403–405
  features, 65, 403
  notifications, 407–408
  reading, 405
  searching, 409–410
  selecting Favorites, 406–407
Night Shift, 85
Notes app
  about, 12
  adding drawings, 395
  adding shared items, 399–400
  creating checklists, 397–398
  creating notes, 389–391
  deleting notes, 401
  features, 65
  inserting pictures, 393–394
  moving notes, 402
  opening, 388
  search feature, 398–399

Notes app *(continued)*
  selecting and editing text, 392–393
  settings, 400–401
  sharing notes, 399–400
Notification Center
  about, 35–36
  Do Not Disturb setting, 370–371
  features, 359
  going to apps from, 370
  Notifications tab, 369–370
  settings, 367–368
  Today tab, 370
  viewing, 369–370
notifications
  calendar, 344–346
  Do Not Disturb setting, 370–371
  News app, 407–408
  Notification Center, 367–368
Notifications tab (Notifications Center), 369–370

O

one-finger swipe gesture, 39, 119
online calendars, 347–350
Operating System, iPhone (iOS)
  definition, 8
  iOS 10 version, 8–9, 48–49
Outlook (Microsoft), 144–147

P

panorama, 279
parallax effect, 39
passwords

network, 118
  set passcodes, 99–100
paste text, 392–393
PDFs, adding, 257–258
Philips Hue Bridge, 217
Philips Hue bulbs, 217
phone hotspot feature, 19
Phonetic Name fields, 376
Photo app, 63
Photo Stream, 63, 296–297
photos
  about, 10
  add to Contacts, 376–378
  albums, 283–284, 290–291
  basic camera operation, 66–68
  deleting, 300–301
  editing photos, 285–290
  effects, 287
  features, 63, 273–274
  importing from other devices, 281–282
  inserting in Notes app, 393–394
  iSight camera, 274
  organizing photos, 291–292
  printing photos, 298–299
  saving from Safari, 137–138, 282–283
  searching, 293
  sending and receiving with messages, 180–181
  sharing photo streams, 296–297
  sharing photos, 294–297
  shooting videos, 304–306
  slideshows, 299–300

taking pictures, 277–280
viewing photos, 283–285, 292–293
Photos app
  add to Contacts, 376–378
  albums, 283–284, 290–291
  basic camera operation, 66–68
  deleting, 300–301
  editing photos, 285–290
  effects, 287
  features, 273–274
  importing from other devices, 281–282
  iSight camera, 274
  organizing photos, 291–292
  printing photos, 298–299
  saving from Safari, 137–138, 282–283
  sending and receiving with messages, 180–181
  sharing photo streams, 296–297
  shooting videos, 304–306
  slideshows, 299–300
  taking pictures, 277–280
  viewing photos, 283–285, 292–293
Picture in Picture, 150
pictures
  add to Contacts, 376–378
  albums, 283–284, 290–291
  basic camera operation, 66–68
  deleting, 300–301
  editing photos, 285–290
  effects, 287
  features, 63, 273–274
  importing from other devices, 281–282
  inserting in Notes app, 393–394

iSight camera, 274
organizing photos, 291–292
printing photos, 298–299
saving from Safari, 137–138, 282–283
searching, 293
sending and receiving with messages, 180–181
sharing photo streams, 296–297
sharing photos, 294–297
shooting videos, 304–306
slideshows, 299–300
taking pictures, 277–280
viewing photos, 283–285, 292–293
pinch gesture, 38, 51, 63, 98, 326
playlists, 261–265, 268
Podcasts app, 66
POP3 email accounts, 147–148
power adapter, 23–24
preinstalled apps, 61–66
press and hold gesture, 39
printers, 21
printing
  photos, 298–299
  web pages, 135–136
privacy
  Find My iPad, 78–80
  iTunes Store restrictions, 196
  passcodes, 99–100
  passwords, 99–100, 118
  Safari privacy settings, 139–141
  Safari settings, 139–141
  unsecured Wi-Fi networks, 118

Private Browsing, 139–140
proactive maps, 321
Project Gutenberg (website), 245

Q

questions, asking to Siri, 109–110

R

Reader feature, 132–133
reading iMessages, 173–178
Reading List, 130–131
reduce motion effects, 92
registration process, 17
Remember icon, 2
Reminders app
  completed tasks, 366
  creating and editing tasks, 360–362
  features, 65, 359
  scheduling reminders, 362–363
  syncing, 364–365
  task lists, 363–364
removing
  apps, 211–212
  Calendar events, 351–353
  contacts, 384–385
  email messages, 160–161
  notes, 401
  photos, 300–301
resolution, screen, 8–9
Retina display, 8–9
ringtones, 378–380
rooms, setting up with HomeKit, 231

S

Safari
  bookmarks, 128–130
  features, 62, 115–116
  gestures, 119
  history, 123–124
  link sharing, 134–135
  navigating, 120–122
  photos, saving and posting, 137–139,
    282–283
  printing, 135–136
  privacy settings, 139–141
  Reader feature, 132–133
  Reading List, 130–131
  tabbed browsing, 122–123
  Web Clips, 133–134
safety
  Find My iPad, 78–80
  iTunes Store restrictions, 196
  passcodes, 99–100
  passwords, 99–100, 118
  Safari privacy settings, 139–141
  unsecured Wi-Fi networks, 118
Scenes (HomeKit)
  about, 225
  adding, 225–227
  adjusting, 228–231
  combining accessories and, 228
Screen Orientation Lock icon, 61
screen resolution, 8–9
screens
  double tap gesture, 38, 90, 119
  features, 32–36

flick gesture, 39, 90, 119
four- or five-finger swipe, 51
one-finger swipe, 39, 119
pinch gesture, 38, 51, 63, 98
press and hold gesture, 39
single tap gesture, 38
Status bar tap, 39
screenshot, 280
SD (secure digital) memory cards, 281
search engines, setting default, 124
search feature
App Store, 202–204
Calendar, 346–347
Contacts app, 382
e-books, 252
features, 47–48
iTunes Store, 193–194
movies, 193–194
Music app, 265–266
News app, 409–410
Notes app, 398–399
web, 124–125
secure digital (SD) memory cards, 281
security
Find My iPad, 78–80
iTunes Store restrictions, 196
passcodes, 99–100
passwords, 99–100, 118
Safari privacy settings, 139–141
unsecured Wi-Fi networks, 118
settings
AirDrop, 296
dexterity, 98

e-readers, 249–251
Guided Access, 99–101
iCloud, 77–78
Notes app, 400–401
Notification Center, 367–368
privacy, 139–141
syncing, 75
text messaging, 169–170
vision, 82–87
settings, accessibility
access restrictions, 94–101
brightness, 84–85, 249–250
dexterity, 98
features, 81–82
hearing, 93–96
iBooks app, 249–251
label settings, 92
Magnifier, 82–83
Night Shift, 85
reduce motion, 92
subtitles and captions, 309
text appearance, 91–92
VoiceOver, 87–91
wallpaper, 85–87
zoom setting, 91
settings, display
brightness, 84–85, 249–250
iBooks app, 249–251
label settings, 92
Magnifier, 82–83
Night Shift, 85
reduce motion, 92
text appearance, 91–92

settings, display *(continued)*
  VoiceOver, 87–91
  wallpaper, 85–87
  zoom setting, 91
settings, hearing
  captioning, 94–95
  closed captioning, 309
  mono audio, 95–96
  subtitles, 94–95
  volume, 93–94
settings, vision
  brightness, 84–85, 249–250
  iBooks app display settings, 249–251
  label settings, 92
  Magnifier, 82–83
  Night Shift, 85
  reduce motion, 92
  text appearance, 91–92
  VoiceOver, 87–91
  wallpaper, 85–87
  zoom setting, 91
Settings app, 66
Share button, 125–127, 168–169
sharing
  calendars, 347–350
  contact information, 383–384
  Home Sharing, iTunes, 269
  links, 134–135
  movies, 310–311
  notes, 399–400
  photo streams, 296–297
  photos, 294–297

  videos, 310–311
Shutter button, 276
Siri
  about, 12, 105
  adding Calendar events, 342
  asking questions to, 109–110
  AssistiveTouch control, 98
  issuing commands to, 110–111
  Maps app, 328–329
  playing music, 268
  tips, 111–112, 113–114
  turning on, 105–108
  using with third-party apps, 112–113
size, 8
sleep mode, 60
Sleep/Wake button, 25, 60
Slide Over, 150
Slide Over feature, 52–54
slideshows, photo, 299–300
Smart Case/Cover, 21, 60
Smart Connector, 11
smart groupings, photos, 292
Smart Keyboard, 22, 45
smartphone hotspot feature, 19
social networking
  Facebook, 164–166
  FaceTime, 183–185
  features, 163–164
  Flickr, 167–168
  Messages app, 169–181
  Share button, 168–169
  sharing links, 134–135

sharing photos, 294–295
  Twitter features, 166–167
  Vimeo, 167–168
software updates, 48–49, 212–214
software versions, in book, 3
sound
  AssistiveTouch controls, 98
  hearing settings, 93–94
  muting FaceTime, 184
  ringtones, 378–380
  3.5mm headphone jack, 26
  volume controls, 26, 270
speakers, 26
Split View, 55, 150
Sprint (website), 19
stands, 22
Status bar features, 60–61
Status bar tap gesture, 39
stopwatch, 356–358
storage capacity, 14–16, 310. *See also*
    iCloud
streaming, 14, 19, 270
subtitles, 94–95
surfing, Internet
  bookmarks, 128–130
  features, 115–116
  gestures, 119
  history, 123–124
  link sharing, 134–135
  navigating, 120–122
  photos, saving and posting, 137–139,
    282–283

printing, 135–136
  privacy settings, 139–141
  Reader feature, 132–133
  Reading List, 130–131
  saving photos, 282–283
  Share button, 125–127
  tabbed browsing, 122–123
  Web Clips, 133–134
  web searches, 124–125
swipe gestures
  about, 150
  four- or five-finger, 51
  one-finger, 39, 119
  two-finger, 119
syncing
  Contacts, 380–381
  iCloud, 75–78
  iTunes, 73–75
  Reminders, 364–365

T

tabbed browsing, 122–123
tap gestures, 38
Technical Stuff icon, 2
television
  AirPlay, 259, 270–271
  Apple Digital AV Adapters, 22
  Apple TV, 270
  playing purchased content, 306–309
  previewing shows, 195–196
10/12W USB power adapter, 23–24

text, applying styles to in Notes app, 395–397

text appearance settings, 91–92

text messaging
  features, 163–164
  sending messages, 171–178
  settings, 169–170

third-party apps, using Siri with, 112–113

third-party email, 144–147

3D Touch, 11

3G/4G LTE technology, 18–20, 61

Time icon, 61

timer, 356–358

Timer, 275

Tip icon, explained, 2

T-Mobile (website), 19

Today tab (Notification Center), 370

Today view, 34–35

Touch ID, 11, 24–25, 59

touchscreens
  double tap gesture, 38, 90, 119
  features, 32–36
  flick gesture, 39, 90, 119
  four- or five-finger swipe, 51
  one-finger swipe, 39, 119
  pinch gesture, 38, 51, 63, 98, 326
  press and hold gesture, 39
  single tap gesture, 3
  Status bar tap, 39
  turning on, 29–30

TV
  AirPlay, 259, 270–271
  Apple Digital AV Adapters, 22
  Apple TV, 270
  playing purchased content, 306–309
  previewing shows, 195–196

Twitter
  features, 166–167
  sharing links, 134
  sharing photos, 294–295

Twitter For Dummies, 3rd Edition (Fitton), 164

two-finger swipe gesture, 119

U

underlined text formatting, applying, 154–156

undocking keyboard, 44

updates, 3, 48–49, 212–214

USB sticks, 14

User Guide, 91

V

vCards (.vcf files), 384

Verizon (website), 19

videos
  controls, 306–309
  features, 65
  iTunes purchases, 310
  navigating, 310
  playing, 306–309

recording, 10

sending and receiving with messages, 180–181

sharing, 310–311

shooting videos, 304–306

Videos app

controls, 306–309

features, 65

navigating, 310

playing, 306–309

recording, 10

sending and receiving with messages, 180–181

sharing, 310–311

shooting videos, 304–306

Vimeo app, 167–168

vision settings

brightness, 84–85, 249–250

iBooks app display settings, 249–251

label settings, 92

Magnifier, 82–83

Night Shift, 85

reduce motion, 92

text appearance, 91–92

VoiceOver, 87–91

wallpaper, 85–87

zoom setting, 91

VoiceOver

enabling, 87–89

gestures, 90

language options, 89

settings, 87–91

usage, 89–90

volume

AssistiveTouch controls, 98

controls, 26, 270

hearing settings, 93–94

muting FaceTime, 184

volume rocker, as camera control, 278

W

wallpaper, changing, 38, 85–87

Warning icon, 2

web browsing

bookmarks, 128–130

features, 115–116

gestures, 119

history, 123–124

link sharing, 134–135

navigating, 120–122

photos, saving and posting, 137–139, 282–283

printing, 135–136

privacy settings, 139–141

Reader feature, 132–133

Reading List, 130–131

saving photos, 280–283

tabbed browsing, 122–123

Web Clips, 133–134

web searches, 124–125

websites

Apple, 28, 182

Apple ID, 73

Apple iPad, 3

Apple Music, 271

AT&T, 19

websites *(continued)*

Cheat Sheet, 3

Facebook app, 164

Home Sharing, iTunes, 269

iCloud, 75

iDevices Switch, 218

iPad For Seniors For Dummies Cheat
Sheet, 3

iWork, 75

Project Gutenberg, 245

Sprint, 19

T-Mobile, 19

Verizon, 19

Wi-Fi

features, 10

hotspots, 19, 116–118

options, 17–20

Wi-Fi icon, 61

Wi-Fi-only iPad, 17–20

Wikipedia, 252

wireless networking. *See* Wi-Fi

World Clock, 353

Y

Yahoo! Mail, 144–147

Z

zoom

accessibility settings, 91

double-tap gesture, 38

Maps app, 322, 326

About the Author

Jesse Feiler is a developer, consultant, teacher, and author specializing in Apple technologies. He is the creator of Minutes Machine for iPad, Saranac River Trail app, and the forthcoming PathMachine app. As a consultant, Jesse has worked with small businesses and nonprofits on such projects as production control, publishing, and project management, usually involving FileMaker and iOS Core Data. His books include *Introduction to SQLite for Mobile Developers, Swift For Dummies, iOS App Development For Dummies,* and many more.

Jesse speaks regularly on The Roundtable on WAMC Northeast Public Radio. He also writes frequently for Cutter Consortium (https://www.cutter.com/experts/jesse-feiler).

He is past president of the Plattsburgh Public Library Board (New York), and founder of Friends of Saranac River Trail, Inc. Previous nonprofit experiences include the board of HB Studio, Library Trustees Association of New York, and Village of Philmont Main Street Committee and Philmont Public Library.

Recent projects for Jesse combine his experiences with nonprofits and apps as he has developed apps to visualize risk in nonprofit organizations as well as apps to support community involvement in environmental action.

He can be reached at jfeiler@northcountryconsulting.com.

Author's Acknowledgments

Many people have helped make this book possible. At Wiley, Colleen Diamond, Project Manager and editor has been a wonderful collaborator, as has Amy Fandrei, Acquisitions Editor. These people and many more behind the scenes make books like this possible.

I'm also grateful to two long-time associates. Caole Jelen, at Waterside Productions, has represented me (and many of the most important tech authors) for many years. I rely on her excellent judgment with every book.

Aaron Crabtree, the technical editor, is a thorough and great person to work with: His questions and suggestions are, as always, invaluable.